TRAVIS JARED

A Life Away

Mandy,
Thank you for all your love and support when I went to Afghanistan in 2006. The author Travis was one of my peers in Mazar Sharkiff. I will always remember the letters, cards, and gifts. It was a great memory seeing you at the airport! I love you!

FOR FRANK

love
mom

a workshopolis publication.

First Edition. Copyright © 2014 Travis Jared Marmarellis Bunt

All rights reserved.

ISBN: 1502790238   ISBN-13: 978-1502790231

A Life Away

FOREWORD BY DR. JESSE KEENAN — vii

BOOK I : BLUE TO GREEN — 23

BOOK II: LETTERS FROM AFGHANISTAN — 71

BOOK III: REQUIEM — 348

FOREWORD

Americans have long thought of themselves as builders of nations, as our own nation was an outcome of a process of 'Nation Building' under military enforcement culminating in the Southern Reconstruction following the Civil War.[1] However, a theory of Nation Building as contemplated by policy makers and executed by the U.S. Armed Forces as an extra-juridical act began at the end of the 19th century as a consequence of the territorial prizes from the Spanish-American War.

From the Philippines to Cuba, Nation Building was little more than the preservation of law and order in the perpetuation of U.S. commercial interests. This same logic extended following the reconstruction of the Japanese and West Germany economies. At least this was the rhetorical appeal to the American public, with the larger perceived threat and ulterior motive being the thwarting of Soviet world domination. With the heating up of the Cold War—from South Korea to El Salvador—the geopolitical landscape defined somewhere between security and soft influence dictated a slight distinction between the notion of 'State Building' and Nation Building.

The concept behind State Building was to build an autonomous state apparatus based on existing social and political hierarchies and institutions who were beholden—or at least sympathetic—to U.S. interests.[2] As Nathan Hodge so artfully described in The Armed Humanitarian: The Rise of the Nation Builders (2010), this can be accomplished with nothing more than some measured diplomacy under the veiled threat of military action and "cash as a weapon."

This is somewhat different from Nation Building, which can be thought of to be working in a geography which has no natural political borders, socioeconomic cohesiveness, or even physical or human infrastructure in order to otherwise give form and operation to a nation. From Haiti to Afghanistan, periodic moments of internal dysfunction have resulted in significant humanitarian crises when the delicate balancing act of the status quo is interrupted by external events. The responsive ordering by the international community has been security, first. As a consequence, military forces from across the globe have been asked to expand their role along a spectrum from combatants to peace keepers to civil servants—or, in the most unconventional sense, social workers. Between war zones, a regular series of mega-disasters ranging from hurricanes to earthquakes has provided a testing ground for developing competencies in the development of a type of permeant and durable infrastructure which far surpassed the requirements of a war zone.

The durability, quality and cost of these activities has been subject to significant domestic critiques in the wake of increasing military budget cuts. However, the counterpoint has been the regular news reports of waste and graft by private contractors who have served similar functions for the State Department, USAID, and other federal agencies. Likewise, many social critics have questioned the extent to which one nation has the objective capacity to create another—regardless of the cost. This ontological critique has itself been challenged by the practical desire to maintain a moral high ground in favor of susceptible and vulnerable populations whose vulnerability has in part been derived from violence outside of their control. In this regard, nation building is less about winning the 'hearts and minds' of people as it is about empowering people to build their own nation, as the true cost of building a nation is well beyond the capacity of even the U.S.. This is a hard reality learned by the operations in Iraq.

To accommodate ongoing downsizing of the military and to minimize unbounded contractor expenditures, the military returned to the leadership of the U.S. Naval Mobile Construction Battalion (the "Seabees") who have 73 years of distinguished service around the globe in designing, engineering and constructing virtually anything and everything from ports to schools. Through a joint service model, the Seabees in recent years have found themselves paired with other blue water Navy and land-locked

Army personnel in hybrid units which are tasked with building coalitions, technical training, and physical construction. What has been asked of these units is not only building physical infrastructure but the development of the soft infrastructure necessary for improving the predicate conditions for civil society, including but not limited to aspects of security, education and public health. This has been a tall order for the engineers, technicians, architects, and constructors whose training and larger mission has largely been oriented towards construction over communication.

This book is the story of a young architect and a blended unit of sailors and soldiers who struggle with the tension between building hard and soft infrastructure within the context of an unforgiving environmental landscape and infinitely foreign cultural divide. Yet, it is a story about the common human elements which bridge these divides through the language of the built environment under the conditions of mere survival. In a world with endless amounts of cash and very little to spend it on, it is a story about innovation and making do with what you have.

While the economics seem to make little sense in a conventional setting, the true product of these efforts is chronicled to be the building of a domestic capacity built upon technical skills and personal relationships which will bear fruit well beyond the last deployment. The equal demonstration of these successes and failures come at a tremendous personal cost and sacrifice by men and women who are often working within the confines of an indeterminate larger policy which at times vacillates between being rhetorical and practical.

Working in a country which has resisted change for many thousands of years, this book highlights the tone deaf nature of a higher command who is entirely reliant on sailors and soldiers who must find meaning in their work in order to succeed. Yet, this reality check is deferential to a long military tradition which honors the independent intellectual and moral drive of leadership within the ranks of junior officers and enlisted men and woman.

History has taught us that wars are won by generals, but this book teaches us that nations are built by carpenters, doctors, masons, teachers and maybe even a junior grade Lieutenant or two. While only time will tell as to the nature and definition of success of building a nation in Afghanistan, this journey leaves little doubt that one camp, one unit and one person can actually make a difference in bridging two peoples caught up in the course of a circumstantial history which will redefine the values of the U.S. as much as it will those of the Afghani people.

DR. JESSE M. KEENAN [3]
CENTER FOR URBAN REAL ESTATE, COLUMBIA UNIVERSITY

NEW YORK, 10 DECEMBER 2014

....

1. See generally, Suri, J. (2011). *Liberty's Surest Guardian: American Nation-building from the Founders to Obama.* Simon and Schuster.

2. Connor, W. (1972). Nation-building or nation-destroying?. *World politics,* 24(03), 319-355; Smith, G. (Ed.). (1998). *Nation-building in the post-Soviet borderlands: The politics of national identities.* Cambridge University Press.

3. Editor's note: Dr. Keenan is a proud descendent of Admiral George Dewey, who is the highest ranking naval officer in U.S. History at the rank of Admiral of the Navy and is remembered as the hero of the Spanish-American War following his decisive victory at the Battle of Manila Bay.

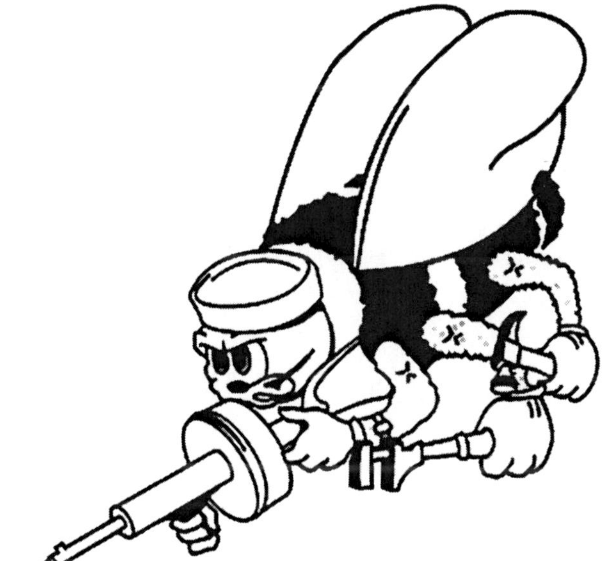

PREFACE

I enlisted in the Navy a few days shy of my 21st birthday, roughly halfway through the Bachelor's of Architecture program at the University of Arizona. Part of a specialized recruitment drive for the Civil Engineer Corps, it was a so-called delayed-entry commitment, allowing candidates to finish school before beginning active service.

Unbeknownst to me at the time, the CEC's renewed focus on the professional ranks of engineers and architects to staff its own ranks was no post-modern peacetime aberration. Rather, the blurring of civilian qualifications with military ones has been integral to the idiosyncratic Corps' unique slotting within the larger US armed forces apparatus.[1]

Though various accounts cite professional engineering support embedded in Navy operations as far back as the War of 1812, the CEC officially traces its history to the 1842 establishment of the Bureau of Navy Yards and Docks (colloquially remembered in most accounts as the BuDocks), with a wholly civilian staff led by a chief civil engineer. It would be another 25 years before a Congressional act began the transition of the formerly civil service to a military staff corps.[2] In 1881, the ten-member officer corps would gain official recognition from President Garfield as well as authorization to wear the regulation Navy officer's uniform and hold "relative rank," though their largely advisory role (as engineering experts within the service) would continue mostly unchanged for the next two decades, until the outbreak of the Spanish-American War in 1898.

In the half dozen years to follow, the Corps would expand four-fold and its professional engineers would gain actual military rank and custom. BuDocks itself was formally and permanently placed under the command of the senior-most CEC officer. This latter stipulation was perhaps most important, as the first decades of the 20th century saw the rapid expansion of the US military footprint around the world, from the Panama Canal to new naval stations as far afield as Tunisia, Ireland, and the Philippines. In most simple terms, the CEC was now responsible for all shore and land-based infrastructure across the globe, essentially, every non-floating (or flying) component of the Navy.

As mobilization for World War I accelerated, a hundred new civilian engineers were recruited into the CEC ranks, swelling the Corps to nearly two-hundred active duty officers, planning and executing the massive construction program. Despite the urgency of staffing, nearly all held professional certifications or degrees from technical colleges and universities, at a time when the majority of Americans did not complete high school.[3]

World War II brought about another major recruiting drive, however, in a now-celebrated innovation,[4] the CEC targeted neither young men nor degreed professionals, but experienced construction workers from jobsites around the country. Under the command of CEC officers, the enlisted ranks of the Naval Mobile Construction Battalions built the infrastructure underlying the Allied war effort, above and below the water, and deep into active war zones. Already technically-savvy, the three-hundred-some-thousand tradesmen were taught the basics of armed defense, such that their teams could operate independently and not require dedicated protection from the Marine and Army units they served.[5] This core concept, as well as the continued straddle of nominally civilian and military duties, is reflected in the motto of the SeaBees, "We build, we fight."

Lessons learned from the second Great War brought further integration with the broader military apparatus, with an emphasis on combat training and fluency in general Navy doctrine. The numbers of the officer and enlisted ranks would wax and wane over the remainder of the 20th century, following the cycle of peace and conflict.

In 1966, BuDocks was superseded by the Naval Facilities Engineering Command (NAVFAC). The 1980's saw further integration of the training pipeline, where the CEC belatedly joined the Supply Corps as the only two staff corps whose members were required to complete the same rigorous indoctrination training as sea-going line officers.[6] Unlike their blue-water brethren, however, CEC officer eligibility was limited to those holding architecture and (certain) engineering degrees. Promotions past the junior ranks were contingent on receiving professional certification (as a Registered Architect or Engineer) in addition to military achievements. At the dawn of the 21st century, only 1500 hybridized military-professionals made up the modern Civil Engineer Corps, less than 3% of all officers and a tiny fraction of the more than 300,000 active duty Navy personnel.

~

It was the spring of 2001 when I signed the papers that forfeited eight years of self-determination, five months before the collapse of the twin towers signified the changing of America's world. While I was at my drafting desk contemplating line weights and wall thicknesses, the Seabees were off doing humanitarian missions, building schools, hospitals, and infrastructure around the developing world.

Or so the personally-addressed recruiting letter told me. Given the apparent choice between spending the next few years as an underpaid architectural intern slaving over CAD drawings on one hand, and changing the world on the other, I was certainly swayed.

My physician father was a conscientious objector in the 60's; my mother would have been a hippie if her immigrant parents had allowed such a thing. Academic, intellectual professionals, my parents were less than enthralled with the idea of military servitude. They saw no room in the armed forces for a creative — particularly one so head-strong as their artist son.

Outside the red-brick campus in downtown Tucson, the recession of the early aughts saw many talented designers among the unemployed, flavoring my analysis of post-graduation opportunities. The blessing of my mentor (and eventual thesis-advisor), who saw the incomparable value of such experience, helped seal the decision.

Two and a half years later, steaming under the Pensacola sun and verbally dismembered by Marine Corps drill sergeants, I had the first of many opportunities to wonder just what it was I'd gotten myself into.

What, indeed.

TRAVIS JARED

NEW YORK, 1 OCTOBER 2014

....

1. The perhaps better-known Army Corps of Engineers is almost exclusively a civilian service. An Army officer on a Combat Engineering or similar career path might do two short stints in an ACE outfit in a 20 or 30 year career, first as a junior officer (for exposure) and later as the commanding officer. More often than not, the officer will have no other engineering training or expertise, and is not required to.

2. As originally intended, staff corps officers were distinct from line officers in that only the latter were eligible for command. Navy staff corps represent fields that are professions unto themselves, and also include the Supply corps, Medical corps, Chaplain corps, and the Judge Advocate General Corps.

3. This section draws heavily on the exhaustive History of the Civil Engineer Corps text, part of the training materials at CECOS (Civil Engineer Corps Officer School) and available for public download from https://www.netc.navy.mil/centers/csfe/cecos/_documents/bc4.pdf

4. The blue-collar influx was immortalized in the 1944 John Wayne film, "The Fighting Seabees." An extensive history of the Seabees is available on the Navy's official history site online, at http://www.history.navy.mil/faqs/faq67-1.htm

5. As distinct from other engineering support outfits, including the Air Force's heavy-construction unit RED HORSE, which necessarily require drawing away resources from the fighting forces to the protection of the supporting outfit.

6. This is intended to prepare CEC officers for Operational Command (i.e., of warfighting units), the only staff corps to be eligible. I say "belatedly" because, as outlined, CEC officers had assumed such responsibilities (sans training) four decades prior.

Build for your NAVY!
R. MUCHLEY
ENLIST!
PENNA ART WPA
CARPENTERS, MACHINISTS, ELECTRICIANS ETC.
FOR INFORMATION APPLY TO YOUR NEAREST RECRUITING STATION
U.S. NAVY- BUREAU OF YARDS & DOCKS

EDITOR'S NOTE

The following pages follow the course of one young officer's deployment as part of the now 13 year-long War on Terror.

Trained as an architect, he had been recruited into the US Navy's Civil Engineer Corps while still a student, a half year before the attacks of September 11th. Fresh off the completion of his first tour in New Orleans and only months into his second posting, at Pearl Harbor, the still quite green Lieutenant was abruptly called up for emergency deployment to Afghanistan, as one of the Navy's first "Individual Augmentees" sent to support the Army overseas.

These missives were sent back to the States on a weekly basis to a continually growing list of readers — some eagerly awaiting peeks inside the opaque military apparatus, others searching to find out "just what the hell we're doing over there," and still others (probably the majority) merely trying to keep tabs on the young man's whereabouts.

The original letters have been lightly edited for clarity, and annotated sparingly.

The *Requiem* is a collection of newly written essays, reflecting on the entirety of the experience, including its aftermath, from a safe distance.

TRAVIS GOES TO AFHGANISTAN

4 March

Family, friends, compatriots, and everyone
in-between, both, or all three...

As most of you now know, the Good Navy has decided
to send my skinny ass off to war. Well, not really
off-to-war, so much as off-to-rebuild because of the war.

Short version: I'm about to leave Hawaii for training — literally,
two hours from now — in lovely, lovely Hattiesburg, Mississippi.
After a few months there, I will be shipping off to the Afghan
desert for a year. We will be working with the local government
in Herat to build and rebuild infrastructure and teach them
proper "Facilities Management." Could be exciting like cliff-
diving, could be exciting like unbuttered toast. We will see.

I fully intend to send regular updates of my various antics in the
desert. If you aren't interested in receiving them... well, that's
what the delete key is for. Pretend to like it. And when I get back,
tell me how exciting it was to read along with my adventures
of sitting out in the cold in a little tent surrounded by the Silly
Haircut Brigade. And for god's sake, offer to buy me a beer.

Be safe, all of you, and I will try and do the same.

/ t

BOOK 1

Blue to Green

TRAVIS GOES TO AFHGAN...ERR..NORFOLK

12 March

It is Sunday the 12th. I've been in Norfolk, Virginia a week for "processing"—a term which, in my experience, generally refers to things like making olive loaf and other plastic wrapped ungodliness (and thus seems completely a'propos). There has been nothing resembling organization. Had there been, I would have been through here in two days. The word is that when we finally do get to Mississippi, the Army will redo everything that's been done here. Ah, Bureaucracy.

Nothing really to update at this point, no new information has been given, nothing has been gained. There are some good people here that I've met—similarly pulled from their daily lives and tossed in this preparatory bucket. A few of them I will be working with in Herat, but most will be spread across the country.

The one thing I have picked up is how experimental this whole thing is; we are part of the first attempts to supplement Army units with Navy folks... as you've probably read in the papers, seen in the news, or overheard from your resident minstrel, the Army's tired. Real tired. And they don't have the manpower to support the mission in Afghan-land. So the Navy is offering up its cadre of ship drivers, pilots, sonar operators, and paint chippers to assist in training the Afghani Army how to be a proper Army. Its an interesting concept.

Out of the 80 or so active-duty folks here and 200 reservists, less than 10% are Civil Engineer Corps or SeaBees—the small part of the Navy intended to be on the ground. Everyone else: blue water people.

Far as I know, Afghanistan is land-locked.

Hmmm...

IN THE ARMY NOW

16 March

CAMP SHELBY, MISSISSIPPI, USA — I can't say I expected to see this part of the country again so soon, having only just traded the Gulf Coast for Pearl Harbor some six or eight weeks ago. Then again, it's not like I am seeing all that much of it. We are more or less stranded on this Army island, and will be for the better part of the next two months. Eventually, we will begin some sort of "training," but for now, more processing.

I've overheard talk that Camp Shelby's main purpose is to make us thankful for the accommodations we will receive over in Afghanistan... and as I think of my 20 new roommates in the open-bay barracks and the 100 some-odd gentlemen I now share a bathroom with, I can't say I disagree. And the weather hasn't even started to turn bad yet.

Yesterday they began gear issue—web belts, canteens, body armor, camo-this and camo-that—a couple duffel bags worth of shit. Most of the guys were rather excitedly sorting through their loot trying on the various paraphernalia like it was some apocalyptic Christmas morning.

Sitting on the edge of my bunk surveying the holiday scene before me, I thought to myself, "you know, this really isn't my thing."

I doubt it will be the last time that thought crosses my mind.

DAMN TOURISTS

29 March

Growing up, we travelled a lot (moved a fair bit too, as I recall). My parents have the dust of a thousand lands under their feet — which is not an indictment of their hygiene, but a mostly unnecessary illustration of the kind of family unit I was born into. By my tenth birthday I had seen more of this country than nine-tenths of Americans do in their whole lives. "Itchy feet" we like to say. We are gypsies... consumed and experienced travellers, if you will.

My father, from whom I inherited much of my authority to make absolute proclamations about the state of things, has seldom visited a somewhat popular destination without grumbling about its unfortunate infestation: "DAMN TOURISTS."

The difference between a traveller and a tourist is obvious to most observers...and mainly because a tourist makes himself so obvious. Tourists cluster, clog, and gawk; they follow the Reader's Digest tours and announce their presence loudly in voice and dress. They annoy and insult the locals (or strenuously avoid them) and then they leave with no greater understanding of a place than can be gleaned from a postcard stand. Travellers adjust, adapt, and integrate. They engage the locals and attempt to learn their customs. Travellers move on with an intimate connection to each place they have passed through.

And naturally, the traveller despises the tourist

~

I will be the first to admit that I am far from being a military-minded individual. I find myself in this Navy way-station for no other reason than that, in a moment of weakness some years ago, my pragmatic side overcame the dreamer and signed away nearly a decade of independence for the sake of experience. I didn't watch Top Gun and fantasize about being a Naval Officer, I didn't play Soldier as a kid. While other kids pretended to have mock wars, I was building the forts.

This is a gratuitously anecdotal way of saying that it's quite an accident that I am here. I didn't seek out the military, as many of my compatriots did. In staffing its Civil Engineer Corps, the military sought me because of my architectural skill set and promised to develop it.

While it is no secret that my current occupation I do not consider ideal, I have taken it seriously. Whether this is a result of a quality upbringing or the lack of some necessary brain cells is up for debate, but the point of the matter is this: regardless of the circumstances that brought me into this military machine, I am here to do a job and project an image and I will do so to the best of my ability.

A scant quarter of these 150 some-odd people the Navy has volunteered here are Active Duty. We were snatched from various ships, planes, and bases with little ceremony and even less warning. As for the other portion, the bulbous mob that makes up the remainder of our number are your neighborhood Reservists. While there are many readily apparent differences between the two groups, the main division is that where the military is our job, the military is their HOBBY. This is a very important distinction.

They came en masse from all corners of our country. Their eyes are wide and their necks swivel like tabletop fans, trying to take it all in. Like unruly Disneyland crowds, they are constantly snapping pictures, even of the most mundane things. They mill about in their soldier costumes and gush with excitement. A smallish and overly talkative round-shaped individual remarks to me that he came here because he wanted to do something that would make him *feel like A Man*.

Someday soon I will be standing in Afghanistan, doing the job that I have been told to do. The success of the mission — and the success of my personal mission to return home with all important parts still attached — are dependent on the performance of this unit. To my

left is a schoolteacher from Kansas who can't figure out how to wear
his uniform correctly and to my right the financial analyst from
Jersey has his M-16 slung upside down, his camouflage cap hung off
the barrel above his shoulder like he's Johnny-fucking-Appleseed.

I'm flipping through anxiety, depression, fear,
apprehension, detachment, and any number of other
psychological responses shrinks throw pills at —

— and they're just happy to be here.

DAMN TOURISTS.

THIS IS MY RIFLE

4 April

THERE ARE MANY LIKE IT, BUT THIS ONE IS MINE.

We have now endured just over three weeks of training.

"Endured" being the operative word.

Up until just few days ago, all of our instruction was classroom based and powerpoint dependent. There are few experiences quite as mind numbing as sitting for 10 hours watching a miscellaneous drone read Powerpoint slides to you. Retention is minimal, as is interest. And yet, this is the standard of excellence for government education. Whether it be a 2-week Contracting course in San Diego, a Navy Indoctrination Brief in Pensacola, or "How To Organize and Run Your Very Own Convoy" in Camp Shelby, MS, it will be dry, the instructor will have less interest in the material than you, and it will consist of approximately 67 slides — copies of which will be printed out and placed at your seat. 62 of these slides will be read verbatim to you, the other five will cause the instructor to pause and stare blankly for a beat before they are skipped over without explanation. There will be a 10-minute break, and then the cycle begins again. When it's all over, a check goes by your name and Social, and the government forevermore considers you trained in that subject. This particular checked box is of monumental importance, exalted well above competence.

Trapped within this endless reincarnation cycle of education, practical training is a temporary Nirvana. The past three days have been spent on the range, familiarizing ourselves with and qualifying on our M-16 rifles and 9mm sidearms. They have been long and sometimes frustrating days; we return dirty and exhausted, but they have been the most satisfying days here. To a man, we finally feel as though we are doing something valuable and relevant — an important thing if one has any concern about morale (they don't, however, but that's fodder for another epistle).

Those with some firearm experience might now be somewhat quizzical of the need for basic introductions to the standard weaponry of the US military, but the suprising amateurism of many members of our "armed" services is real: for many among our number, their first shots ever taken with these weapons were shots with which to qualify their expertise. Some had never shot any weapon before. Yet, beyond Powerpoint instruction, the only practical training received before our first trigger squeeze was: "Pick up the ten-round magazine to your left. Lock and load. Rotate your selector switch from Safety to Semi and Scan Your Lane."

Boom.

From what I understand, regularly-deploying military units take months to progress from familiarization through qualification on a particular firearm, with plenty of practice in between. We took a day with each weapon. But, we all have checkmarks by our names, so we are good to go.

Those of us who could manage to qualify on a weapon the same day we received it were lucky, the others will be forced to repeat the qualifying test over and over until they can pass it. Its somewhat like attending a class on European history where on the first day the instructor drops a comprehensive exam on your desk then leaves the room. At the end of class he returns, reads off the scores, and tells everyone with a 70% and above to go home. To everyone who has not passed, he brings a fresh set of tests exactly the same as the first and passes them out. The process repeats indefinitely until the last student has guessed enough answers to garner a passing score. The instructor declares everyone European History qualified and the evolution is completed.

This is not to say that all of our young men and women serving overseas receive this level of instruction, it is merely to point out the incredulity inherent in this blue to green experiment (i.e., using Navy personnel with no prior ground combat training to supplement and replace career Army individuals). It is not practical to train us to be their equivalent, nor do they have the understanding of our respective backgrounds to properly utilize our inherent skills and training. So we exist in some netherworld where we are taught just enough to learn how little we understand.

And thus our survey course on the Army continues.

CARNIVAL RIDE, PART 1

10 April

There's a razor's edge between anticipation and apprehension.

I find myself vacillating between excitement, at this opportunity to experience something utterly new and unique, and fear, of that very same unknown.

~

Saturday was my birthday. With such an anniversary, one is almost compelled to be retrospective, but I don't have to back up an entire year to fill an album of emphatic memories. The past six months have been the most tumultuous period of my entire life — this is not to say that dramatic and emotional things had escaped me in the 25 1/2 years prior, but that the magnitude and number of life altering events have been staggering.

One half year ago I watched helplessly as a swirling mass covered the Gulf of Mexico and headed directly for my New Orleans home. I evacuated and returned a week later to a crippled city and a devastated coast. I saw destruction like I had never seen. I walked alone down desolate urban streets that hadn't seen emptiness in a century.

I lost all semblance of my prior life there... and rather emerged into some land of parallel existence with different characters, different roles, different rules — but just enough eerie similarity to make it all incredibly, unnervingly surreal.

Through an amazing combination of dumb luck, coincidence, and alignment of various stars with nothing else to do that evening, I met the woman who would become my wife (the impossibility of which can be discussed at a later date).

Originally due to leave New Orleans for Pearl Harbor at summer's end, Katrina's aftermath saw my orders changed at the last possible minute and my stay extended, though all my possessions were already sent off and my lease cut. I moved twice. I lived for a time in the empty house evacuated by my neighbors, then with a pair of strippers, and finally with the aforementioned woman of destiny.

I watched a city's rebirth. I watched a people's rebirth.

I moved again. 6000 miles away. New job, new home, new roommates, new life, new routine. I moved said woman of destiny said 6000 miles and prepared to settle in. I proposed. And I was made to leave again. First to Virginia, and then to Mississippi, in preparation to give away a year-plus of my life — our lives — on the other side of the world, in service of the newest Great War.

In brief: hurricane. change of plans. surreal everything.
move. meet. move. move far. new everything. move
her. engaged. move. move. move really far.

And a thousand smaller dramatics in between.

Perhaps you've seen those semi-popular "stress tests" which assign point values to various seminal events in one's life (it's one of those rare items at home in either a general psych textbook or a random issue of *Cosmopolitan*). Though I do not have an exact copy in front of me at this particular moment, doubtless I could put a check in nearly every box (with multiple marks in some). Quite surely my point total exceeds the limits of any given chart.

~

Though none quite like this, many portions of my life have resembled the tosses and turns of so many carnival rides. Just before me is a new plunge, and having now begun its drop, the shock of its existence has mostly left me and I am resigned to its course.

Some days, particularly the ones focused on learning culture or language, I find myself genuinely excited by the prospects of a new and different land. Others, I can't help but worry about the possible dangers and about those close to me left behind.

But all days I regret another year without a home.

CARNIVAL RIDE, PART II

16 April

"This is Ahrrrrrmy Training"

I must admit ignorance to the origin of the above quote. I'm sure it is a classic reference lifted from some seminal boot camp related flick in the vein of "Full Metal Jacket" or even "Stripes." But, by virtue of my relatively recent birth in relation to their respective releases, their numerous quotable lines never became lodged in my brain in the manner they seem to be in others. In any event, this is a phrase that perfectly sums up the mood of the previous week (and presumably the remaining 4 or 5) and has thus been repeated over and over by my Navy peers.

Having moved out of the classroom and into the field, we find these various sergeants and captains truly in their element as instructors (the Army is by no means a bookish discipline), and we increasingly out of ours. Personally, though, even in such a short time I feel my practical knowledge of infantry technique has grown exponentially. I do have something (albeit, quite minor) to build on, though. As a Civil Engineer Corps officer, my education has been almost exclusively land-based, which puts me and the few other CEC gents here at a (somewhat surprising) advantage over our blue-water brethren. However, I would propose that this fact merely makes us somewhat more receptive sponges for this new knowledge and not actually any real steps ahead. This is a whole new world for all of us — including the instructors, who certainly regard us as some alien race.

~

Interestingly, with the oft-mentioned new world battlefield, this training is a far cry from that of years past. It is increasingly urban-based and reflects a general movement away from the

Vietnam-era woodland training that was prevalent up until only a few years ago (my own limited SeaBee training three years ago was carried out entirely in the forests of central California). In short, it looks nothing like you've seen in bootcamp movies. It instead mimics police and S.W.A.T. style training, with emphasis on target discrimination (threat vs. bystander; newly important with non-uniformed combatants), building assault, and room clearing.

The choreography of small team movement is a feat in itself, and those that do this work professionally work within the same team for months and years in order to function as one element. But even over the span of a few days, these disparate people we are can begin to form together and accomplish some level of effectiveness. It is a beautiful and satisfying thing. Strangely enough.

And herein lies the flip of the carnival coaster; it is at one moment exhilarating and satisfying to correctly apply this training in practice, and I would be remiss to ignore the certain strain of machismo such athletic and military endeavors feed. Beyond even this, the orchestration of body movement in space is something that absolutely tickles that spatial itch that put me into Architecture. But, at the same time, the reality of what we are doing, what we are being trained to do, is sobering. It is one thing to knock over targets, and relish the mastery of a firearm (or even of your own body), it is quite another to eliminate living, breathing targets. This is something that no training can prepare for. I have no bloodthirst, I have no inkling towards violence. I have no concept of true, personalized killing.

And I wish none.

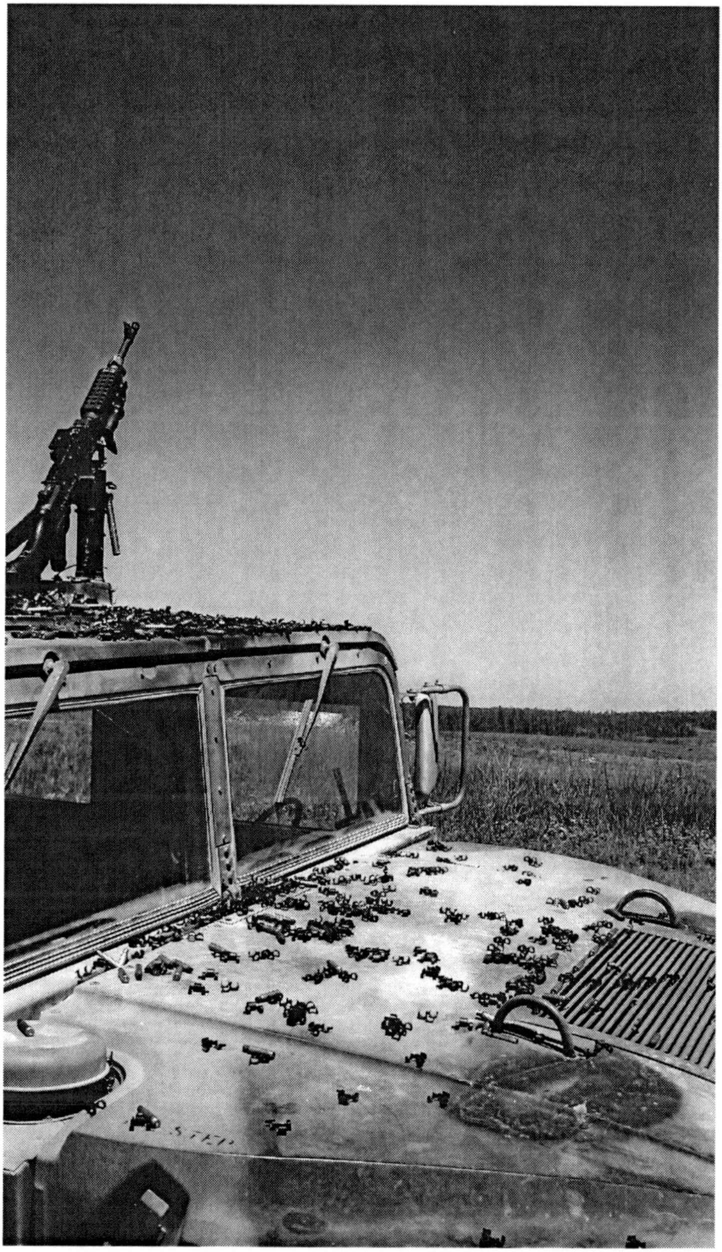

NOTES ON MARKSMANSHIP

19 April

I have a bit of an odd handicap. Despite all efforts on my part and the misguided assistance of many others, I simply cannot wink. Never been able to. A related consequence is, as the anatomically savvy among you might have correctly concluded, I am similarly unable to keep one eye closed. In normal daily life, this limitation rarely exhibits itself (but for the occasional amusement of others, particularly the lady, who is particularly amused by my eyelid's lack of dexterity).

Not so inconsequential, however, when one's new occupation revolves around gunplay. Not so, at all...

With both eyes open, I couldn't hit the broadside of a daytime talk show host. Fortunately there is an effective, if somewhat inelegant, cure for my malady. A strategically folded bandana makes one hell of an eyepatch, and like Superman's cape, somehow transforms me into an effective marksman (but without all the fanfare). Days on the range thus find me with some manner of improvised eyewear (a candy wrapper wedged behind sunglasses has also proved effective, and nearly as chic). Downside of all of this being, of course, the fresh attention brought upon my previously invisible disability. And the requisite humor.

"Arr matey."

Last weekend we tried on Crew Serve weapons (your various machine guns, so classified because they generally take more than one person to effectively operate). For those of you interested to know, we shot the M249 SAW and M240-B, two relatively lightweight guns, as well as the .50 Caliber, which is a beast of a machine. I picked the SAW for myself, as it is the closest to firing a regular rifle (it actually uses the same size rounds as an M16).

And we did the Navy proud. Our guys may have no grasp of Army doctrine or procedure, but they can shoot the damn lights out. We all qualified so quickly, in fact, that there was a load of ammunition left for our lighter machine guns. As a result of this, a few of us were given the chance to dispel the offending rounds on the long distance .50 Cal range, while our Army counterparts continued their attempts to qualify (our .50 Cal gunners had already qualified with high marks). The pop-up targets on this particular range were between 500 and 800 meters.

Firing a .50 caliber round at an 800 meter target is roughly akin to standing on the roof of a 160-story high rise [†] and trying to drop a softball on the head of a guy waving for a cab at the street corner. Firing the SAW's 5.56 mm round at the 800 meter target is like trying to hit that same guy with a marble.

Several of us did "qualify," and our best marksman managed a perfect score. Despite never having picked up a SAW before, the unassuming boatdriver made short work of even the 800 meter targets. Having not been trained on the weapon, no one had told him the maximum effective range of an unassisted SAW is 600 meters. So you can't really blame the man.

~

And in the midst of it all I had received a call from the lady. With all manner of explosions resonating in the background, I relayed my excitement over my quick qualification with the SAW machine gun.

To which she replied, "I'm not sure how I should feel about that!"

....

[†] *Editor's note: The tallest skyscraper in the world (as of 2014) is the Burj Khalifa in Dubai (United Arab Emirates) at 829 meters and 163 floors, nearly twice as tall as the Empire State Building. It was not yet built at the time of the original letter.*

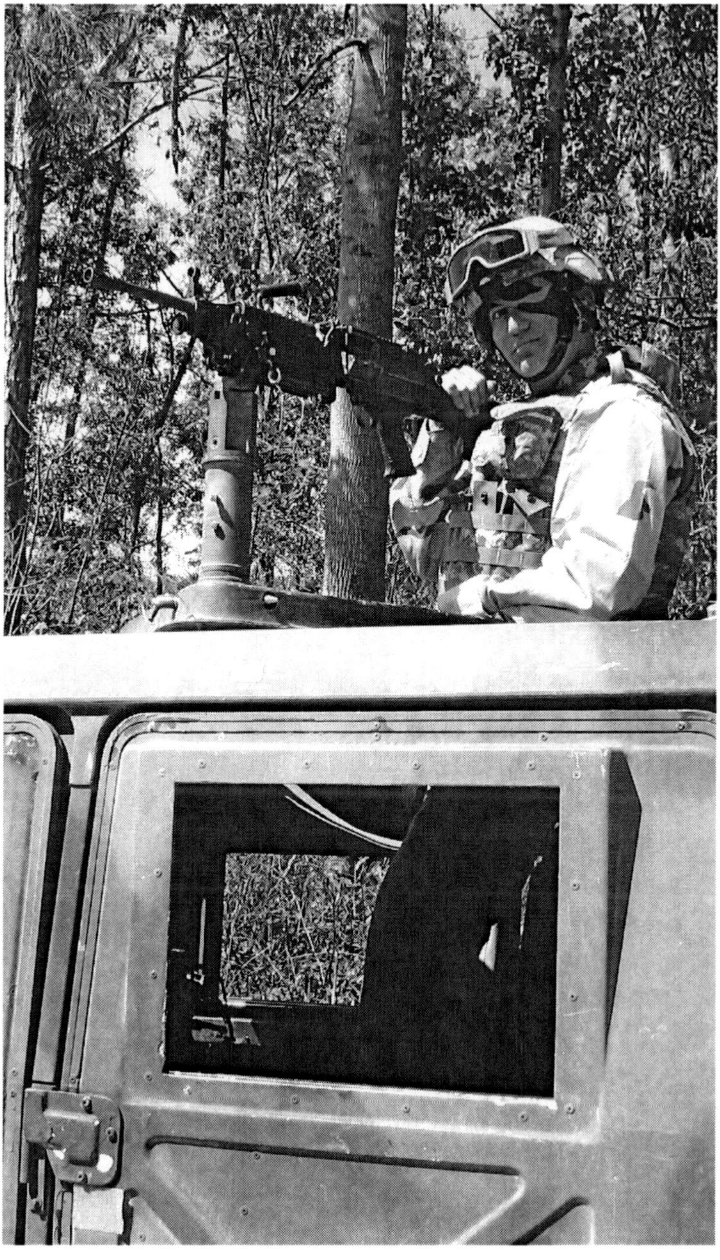

TODAY WAS A GOOD DAY

25 April

Up at 0500. Shave, brush the teeth, pull on the still damp uniform from yesterday (no point grabbing a new one, I'll be drenched within a few hours anyway), grab some chow — 2 over easy, toast, and some fruit. Climb into that wretched body armor (a good 50 lbs. of Kevlar and ceramic plates strapped around my chest and back), holster the 9mm, clip in the rifle (theres another 8 lbs. pulling down the shoulder), don the Kevlar helmet and requisite Joe Cool sunglasses, grab the backpack, and we're off at 0615 headed for the range.

Arrive around 0700, but no relaxing coffee this morning sitting on the hood of a Humvee (that was yesterday), I'm pulling gate guard duty along with Master Chief. Master Chief is a 30-year Reservist on his first mobilization. He speaks 3 or 4 languages fluently, but doesn't know how to stop talking in any of them.

An occasional vehicle enters the range, but mostly I read my book—and what seems like half of Master Chief's, as every few lines he's reading aloud to me because they are so very interesting. It's 0800 and the fog is first beginning to lift on the range below us. Gray clouds are rolling quickly by the as-yet unset moon. The range tower cuts a sharp profile in the foreground. I'm taking a long moment to breathe in the stillness before it is broken by the first convoy exercise (and the accompanying gunfire). 0900 passes with no watch relief as scheduled. We will wait until nearly eleven, minutes before the departure of our own convoy group, before we are able to give up the post. Meanwhile, the rest of our group is planning and discussing the mission. This might seem like an important thing to be missing, and certainly on some level it is, but today I'm just a gunner; tell me which way to shoot and I'll be fine.

Moments after I rejoin my vehicle, we are moving out. I am in the gun turret of the lead Humvee, armed with a SAW (borrowed and unmounted, but a SAW nonetheless). It is quite an unparalleled position to inhabit, here aloft, at once being pre-eminently powerful and markedly vulnerable. It is not a position I would relish holding on the back roads of Afghanistan, but for these purposes, there is little to rival it.

In the early stages of the drill, we are ambushed twice by different tribes of green plastic torsos.[†] Their will is strong, as is their resilience (their mobility... not so much). But our Navy-Army team (heretofore to be referred to as The Narmy) prevails. As I've mentioned before, we're pretty decent shots. We return to the clear. I am completely drenched with sweat. I've unloaded 200 rounds with an unmounted (thus, hand-held) machine gun and another 60 from the M16 on full-auto. It's hot work.

Upon our return and debrief, we find our next engagement to be five hours off. My ops officer and I quickly devise a plan to escape the imposed downtime and finagle lunch in the process (anything to avoid an MRE[††]). We reappropriate a spare Humvee and head back towards base. After some sandwiches, an errand or two, and a 2-hour wait, we return to the range with twenty fresh pizzas and cases of Coke for the well-deserving Narmy [our ground pounding associates had previously been quite impressed with our ability to procure ice, so this bit of self-initiative was well over the top]. Needless to say, our reputation with this particular group of Army folk is now rather cemented. Nothing feeds morale like pizza. Perhaps hookers, but we didn't have 20 of those to pass around.

Invigorated, our Narmy unit set out for the evening mission. Apparently, the Green Torso Brigade had also reloaded as they returned with gusto. We responded en force. Mounted .50 cal's. 240 Bravos, SAWs, and a gang of dismounted M16's.

It got a little loud.

To say the least.

I had found myself without a working gun and had switched to the rifle. I settled back in the turret, amidst the pounding fire of the .50 in the adjacent Humvee (which shook my truck with each burst), and calmly began sniping the rear line troops. I locked into a particular 250 meter target and dispensed my last magazine in a futile attempt to discover how many fatal blows would keep his green torso from reappearing.

Up. Bam. Down. Pause. Up. Bam. Down. Pause.... and so on.

So locked into this challenge was I, that I had not realized the entire convoy had run out of ammo. My last twenty or so shots had been the only ones taken. Instead, the rest of the battlefield had tuned into my single shot spectacle, though I did not find out about the audience until later. There are worse ways to draw attention, I imagine.

Again we debriefed, and were lauded for our team's performance— with particular praise directed at the Naval Infantry, given that we really had no business being there anyway. Although, remarkably, I guess we're beginning to look somewhat like we do.

Truck back to the barracks. Hot shower. Call from the lady. 2300 and I'm out. Six hours 'till tomorrow starts.

Today was a good day.

[†] *Editor's note: The targets used on live-fire training ranges are essentially mannequins bolted to massive, spring-loaded hinges. A computerized timing program randomizes their "pop-up" in accordance to scenario. The contraption is extremely pressure sensitive, hinging back into the ground upon impact with a fired round — even from small caliber sidearms.*

[††] *Editor's note: MRE = Meals Ready to Eat. Pre-packaged, field-ready rations.*

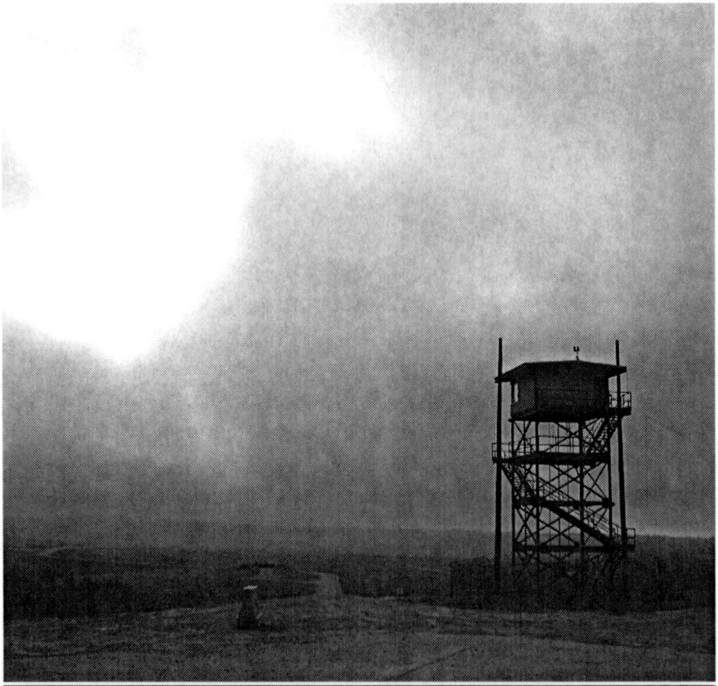

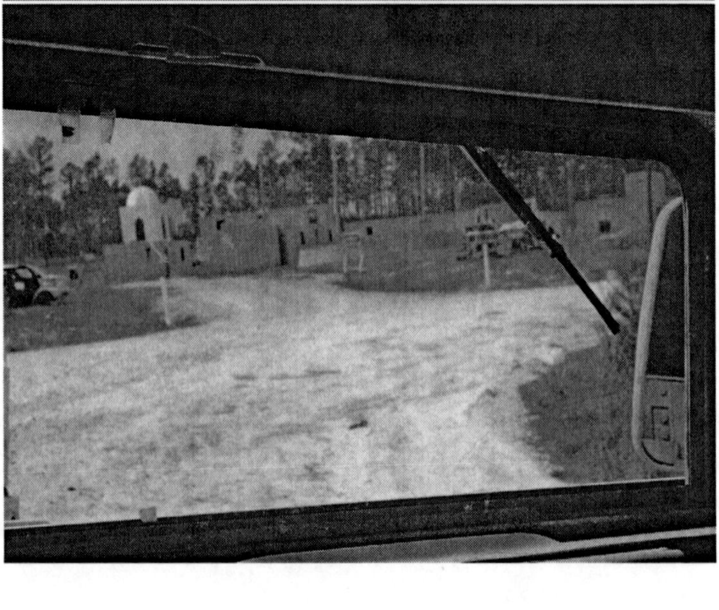

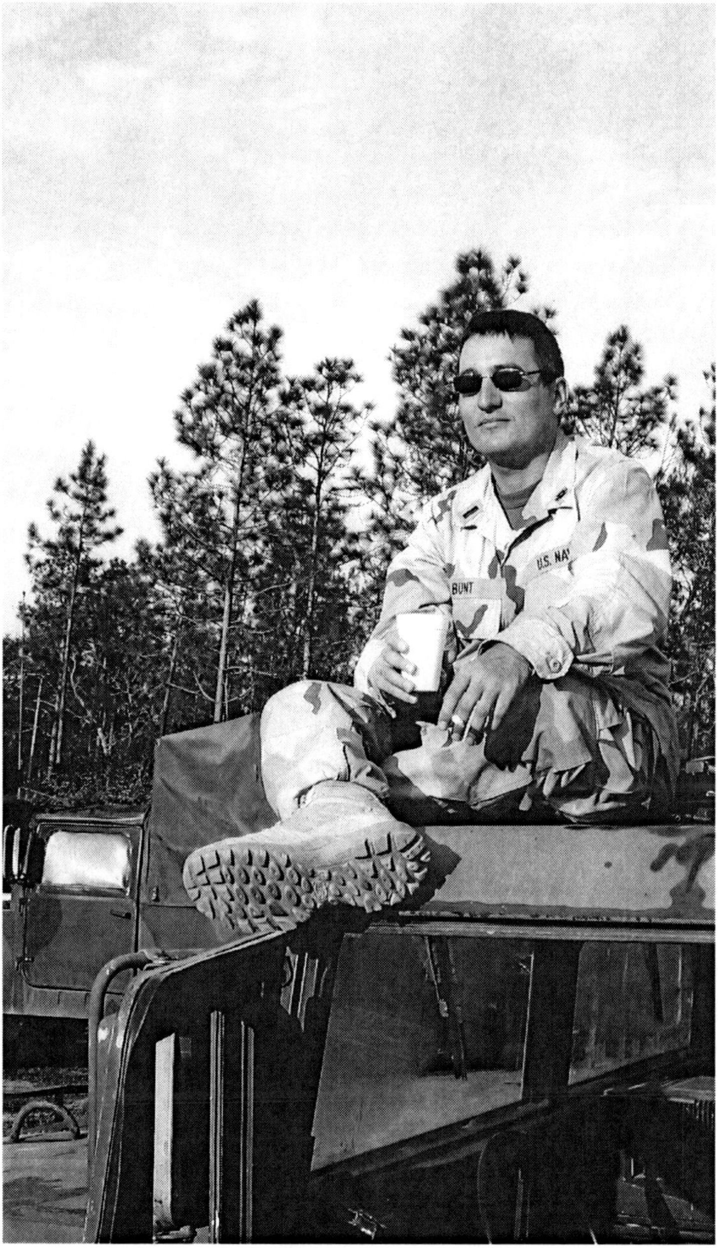
U.S. NAV
BUNT

AND THEN THERE'S THE NOT-SO-GOOD DAYS

26 April

Three hours as a rear gunner on an extended convoy mission is no way to spend an afternoon. The rear gun is responsible for covering the 180° zone behind the convoy and must keep any other vehicles from approaching or entering the convoy. It is no easy task. My back and legs are like Jello from constantly rotating the steel turret, back and forth. I am again drenched with sweat and worn from extended exposure.

I did manage to stop traffic on a major highway, however...

Not realizing that for the purposes of the exercise, I was only required to prevent a particular marked car from interfering, I followed training to the letter—and prevented ANY traffic from passing our slow moving caravan. The truckers weren't too happy with me, but it's amazing how persuasive a military uniform, arms waving, and a machine gun can be. Or maybe it's just the machine gun.

LAST DAY

10 May

"60 DAYS OF INTENSIVE ARMY FIELD TRAINING"

So said the orders. Whether or not each single day
met that requirement is debatable, the important
thing is that day 60 has arrived and gone.

The last two weeks did in fact live up to billing, with four
hours sleep nightly and the other twenty packed full with
all manner of remaining material necessary for our full
qualification (as well as random last minute additions tossed
atop by, uh, well-intentioned star-collared individuals).

We are battered, bruised, and exhausted...
and desperate for reprieve.

And for some reason unbeknownst to any and all involved, our
last hurdles—the last series of our extensive list of checkboxes
so requiring checks—consist of modules normally allotted for
the initial weeks of instruction. Having thoroughly satisfied
the tests of advanced training, the Army now handily supplies
the basics. We've qualified as Combat Life Savers, now we
learn First Aid. We've successfully run complicated operations
as full platoons and convoys, now we learn to cover, crawl,
and roll. The inanity of following 12th grade studies with
kindergarten enrollment is impossible to adequately express.

But nothing has followed a sturdy schedule here, let alone a logical
order. Such is the result of squeezing in a foreign service branch
upon an already taxed and thoroughly unprepared system.

That said, the efforts of individual instructors—these seasoned and knowledgeable sergeants—has been phenomenal. And well appreciated. What was a somewhat incoherent and out-of-their-element gaggle has adapted and excelled in this entirely unique situation, thanks in no small part to the skill of these NCOs.[†]

~

For those keeping score, we are now qualified in: Platoon Ops, Convoy Ops, Urban Ops, Base Defense, Checkpoints, Personnel and Vehicle Searches, Reflexive Fire, Public Drunkeness, and Organized Gaggling. And myself as an individual as: Sharpshooter in the 9mm, M16 Rifle, M16 Rifle with Optics, and the M249 SAW Light Machine Gun; Humvee Gunner; Humvee Driver (Up-Armored and Standard); Combat Life Saver (three days of training beats years of Medical School); Crawling, rolling, ducking, running, diving, getting muddy, sweaty, nasty, and tired.

And then we've also endured the specialized training in: "Ordering Humvee parts," "Rules of Engagement" (3 times), "Handling Detainees" (3 times), "Risk Management" (8 or 9 times at least), and any number of various uninteresting but I'm sure thoroughly valuable additional powerpoint beauties.

To cap off this comprehensive survey of Army Training, we ended in a most appropriate way... I would pose, in fact, that there could not have been a more fitting conclusion to these two months.

They gassed us.

....

[†] *Editor's note: A quick explanation of the various short-hands used for ranks in the letters: NCOs, or Non-Comissioned Officers (Sergeants in the Army, Chiefs in the Navy), are senior enlisted servicemembers who have earned their stripes through experience and demonstrated leadership. In most unit structures, there is at least one NCO paired with each officer, assisting with the functional leadership of the troops and/or sailors. At the top of the spectrum, the "star-collars" refer to the rank insignia for Flag and General officers, the most senior level of each respective military branch. Further musings on rank and structure appear in Book III.*

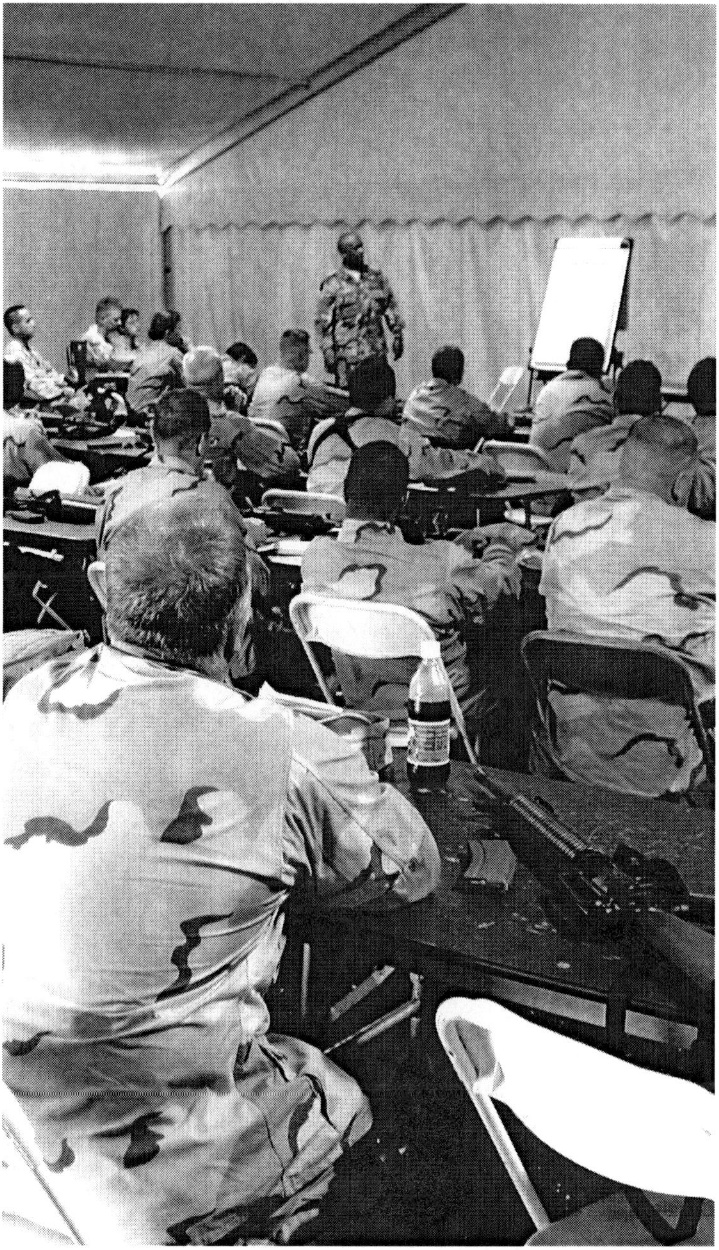

GAS GAS GAS

10 May *(Supplemental)*

As part of their efforts to "familiarize" us with the various gear we have been issued, the Army had us don gas masks and marched us into a gas chamber. The stated intent was to give us confidence in our masks' effectiveness. The result—for me, at least—was anything but.

~

I don't consider myself as one prone to phobias. I might hold some various healthy fears—say, that of cockroaches, or rich people, for example—entirely understandable and justifiable squeamishnesses, but by no means full-blown phobias.

I was content in my phobia-free life. But being gassed proved fairly effective at breaking this particular misconception of self.

~

Having made sure we had all properly applied our masks, a (presumably) well-meaning instructor led twenty of us into the chamber. Once inside, he prompted us through a series of sweat-producing exercises. Then, he issued the gas. Our pores open, the irritant set our skins afire—not too unlike a hot shower on a bad sunburn. Painfully aware of the gas' presence, we were now made to remove our masks, wait, and reapply them. To do this properly, and avoid inhaling the gas, takes some practice and some guided instruction (naturally, this would be given AFTER we had been gassed, per the Army's considerable foresight). I, already utterly uncomfortable with the whole operation, did of course manage to not perform the switch correctly. Realizing my particular error, I frantically tried to re-clear the mask (a beginner's mistake), which resulted in a full breath of the irritant. Inhaling a plate of wasabi could not replicate the intense burning within my throat and lungs.

It was at least an hour until I felt alright, which, oddly enough at the time, had nothing to do with the burning itself. Rather, it would seem the sensation of not being able to breathe is something I am not well equipped to handle. And upon reevaluation, I've determined that this is no new thing, but a consistent fear throughout my life. A fear that kept me from certain asphyxiation experiments way back when (as some of my childhood peers were fond of), made me particularly avoidant of kids who got their jollies dunking their juniors underwater, still makes me wary of swimming where things overhang or float just above the water's surface, and also makes me extremely sensitive to being touched around the neck. Congratulations, Travis, you do have a phobia. I feel so much more complete as a participant in the human experience now.

In any event, being gassed was, without hyperbole, a singularly miserable experience.

But, it was the last experience to be handed out by this place. Which makes it at least in some small way a positive event. Or, no, not so much really.

Not so much at all.

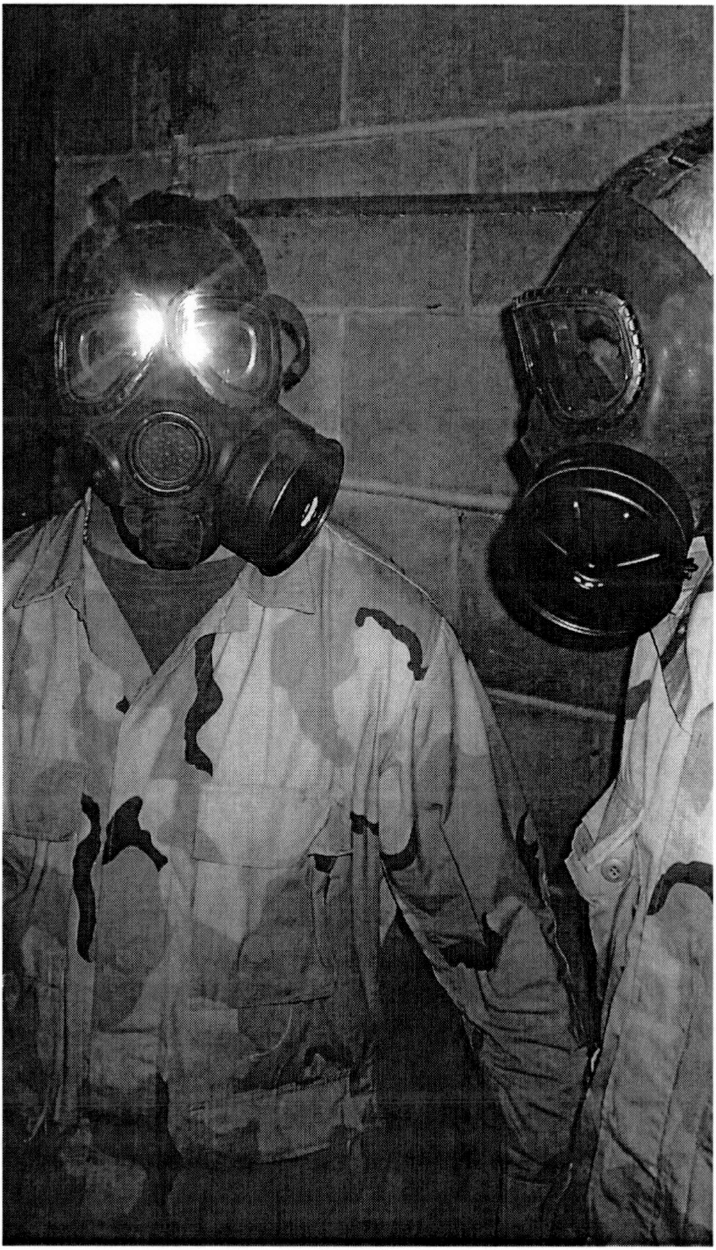

AN EXERCISE IN CONCLUDING PRELIMINARY COMMENCEMENTS

17 May

Five blessed days of leave with the family on a Florida island. Sat on the beach, imbibed, ate too much, evened out the "Army Tan" (face and hands darkened at the rest's expense), slept a little, caught up, and said goodbye. Days drive back up to Mississippi. Leave's up at midnight, we roll in with an hour and a half to spare.

28 hours to go...

Grab a hotel room with the lady in Hattiesburg. We're exhausted from the drive, and she's sound asleep by midnight. The NBA Playoffs are in full roar and my Suns are on. Game 5 against the Clips. It's all I can do to stay quiet and not wake her up through the double overtime thriller. Suns win, with the help of some last second heroics. Content, I roll over and fall asleep with her in my arms.

Not a bad way to spend the last night before I leave.

26 hours...

The next day is an odd mix of busyness and idle time. We rush around with last minute admin and packing, then take a leisurely lunch at the Catfish Shack. A couple more errands, a little more wasted time, and by four o'clock, everybody's bags are on the grass, staged to go.

13 hours...

All the ancillary functions complete, a dedicated group of us pile into a rented car like circus clowns (setting quite the example for a group of enlisted sailors who look on quizzically). We head up the hill to take care of the most serious final business — at the bar.

In this few hour flux, we loudly reminisce on the events of the past two months, poke some fun at each other, and have some hearty laughs. We joke and carry on like we've been doing such for years. The faces, the comments, the quirks, the chuckles are all so familiar, though in real time we've hardly just met. But no one is on real time here.

It is a strange interstitial moment, as we revel in the completion of this Mississippi chapter, knowing full well that the remainder of the book is yet to be writ. And in all certainty those pages will be set in a far different world from which we now sit.

Our short reprieve is at its end, and as we move into the final stages of departure, the lady must take her leave. It is a difficult thing to look into someones eyes to say goodbye, knowing there is no chance of seeing them again for at least half a year.

You are never held so tight than when it is time to go.

7 hours...

We and our accoutrements are weighed and we pack aboard buses to shuttle down to Gulfport, where we will await our plane. We sit inside a cavernous hangar lit twice as bright as the day. You cannot speak to anyone at a distance greater than ten feet — the echos drown out original words. The plane arrives, and we load several tons of equipment, gear, and personals into its bowels.

One hour...

Load ourselves onto the chartered bird and settle in for the long haul across the pond. Next stop, Ireland.

And then, into the shit.

Buckle up.

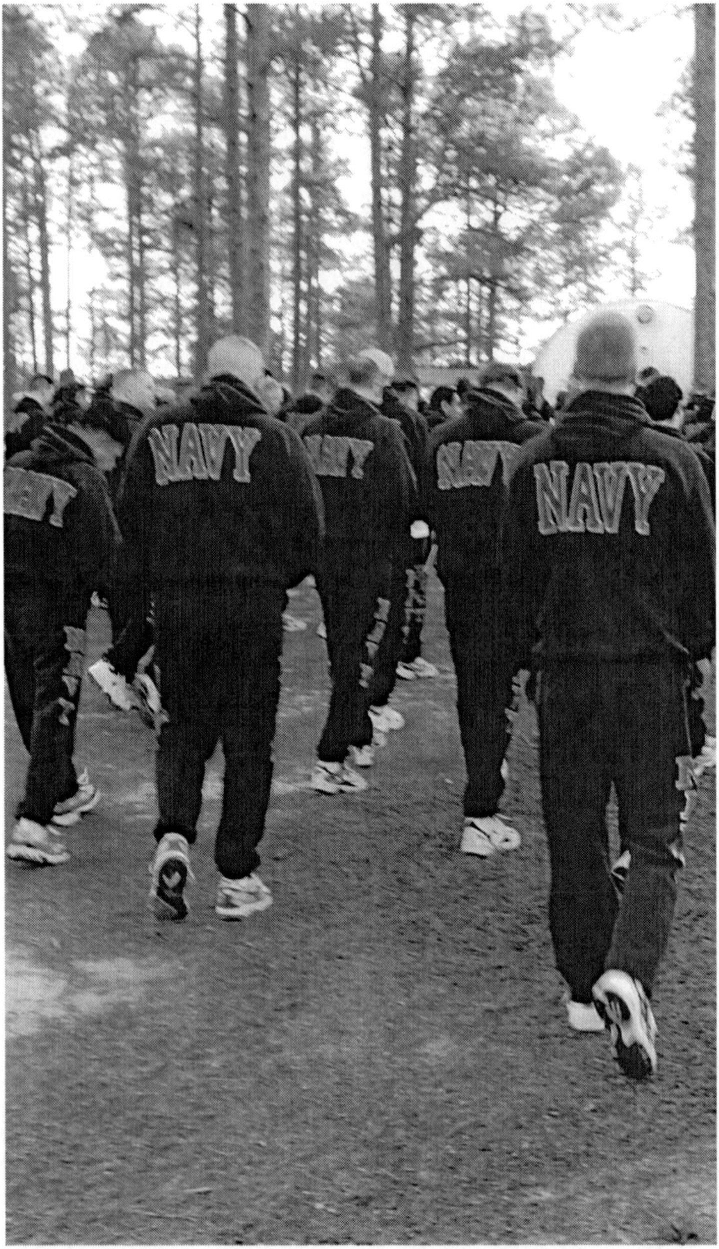
NAVY
NAVY
NAVY

Editor's general notes:

The convoluted training schedule (and confused training personnel) was the result of a command not yet equipped to handle the influx of "Individual Augmentees" being contributed by the Navy. Camp Shelby had been primarily a Reserve Activation center, transitioning existing Army units from Reserve status to battle-ready. The sudden addition of hundreds of another service's members was a great tax on the system. A "Shelby Horseblanket" was produced in haste, a quite colorful three-month calendar spreadsheet of training modules and training lanes (classrooms and field ranges) which was used to fit the Navy personnel in available slots — in whatever order they came available.

The process of exiting the country and heading towards the war itself was similarly haphazardly scheduled, with the date and time of actual departure not known conclusively until the last moment. Part of this is general security protocol, where even basic travel plans are kept on a need-to-know basis as long as possible to reduce the risk of accidental leakage of potentially useful information. The larger part was simple mismanagement.

~

Despite several notations to the contrary, the team was not heading to Herat. Several days before departure, each group received new destinations. This one was now bound for Mazar-i Sharif, in the northern region of Afghanistan.

BOOK II

Letters From Afghanistan

N
RUSSIA
KAZAKHSTAN
UZBEKISTAN
Manas
KYRGYZSTAN
TURKEY
TURKMENISTAN
TAJIKISTAN
CHINA
Mazar-i Sharif
SYRIA
Herat
Bagram
Kabul
AFGHANISTAN
IRAQ
IRAN
Lashkar Gah
Kandahar
PAKISTAN
NEPAL
SAUDI ARABIA
Doha
QATAR
UAE
OMAN
INDIA

THE LOST DAY

18 May *(Barely)*

SOMEWHERE BETWEEN VERY LATE WEDNESDAY
AND UNGODLY EARLY THURSDAY.

AIRBORNE, OVER THE ATLANTIC OCEAN — For all my wanderings over the last two and a half decades, I've somehow managed never to make it overseas (save Hawaii, though I don't think that counts). Ugly impetus aside, it is rather exciting to finally be making that trek. Even if it involves a 3 am departure.

Fortunately, I've trained myself over the years to sleep on airplanes — it is roughly eight hours across the drink to Shannon, Ireland from the lovely Mississippi Gulf coast. We're on a roomy commercial 767 replete with a full attendant team. It is the last taste of near-luxury we'll experience for some time.

I wake in time to see the clouds clear over the Irish coastline. The black cliffs cut sharp through the dark water and I feel as though I'm watching the front end of some Bondish cinematics. Just past the breaks, the rural countryside comes into view, and the "Emerald" moniker proves an apt one (if I previously assumed it to be more marketing hyperbole then actual description, I duly apologize). Shannon lays on the land like a thick patchwork quilt. Nary an inch of the fabric appears uncultivated — which makes for quite an unusual image to this denizen of the western United States, where wilderness is the norm and development the cancerous exception.

Irregular quadrants are carved out of the elevation, bordered by single lines of trees, resembling a sort of green cobblestone expanse — though in this case, the grout is squeezed higher than the stones in an interesting figure-ground reversal. Occasional farmhouses appear within various squares, and even from this height, their age is apparent.

Shannon is by no means a large airport, but it does have a pub. As such, I am enabled to check one important item off of my (unwritten) bucket list — drinking a pint of Guinness in Ireland.

Contrary to popular rumor, it seems to taste very much the same as that poured from American taps. Having fully expected this not to be the case, I am initially disappointed... that is, until a savvy compatriot points out this means we've actually had the privilege of drinking the real thing back home and not some bastard version. *Brilliant!*

I follow my official Irish indulgence with a Beamish for good measure.

Ah, but our tour of the Isle is a short one, as we're quickly reboarded and underway for the next eight-hour leg. Fortunately, my Irish sleeping aids take effect with a blessed quickness...

I awake somewhere over the various -Stans. Far below us is an endless gray and brown speckled floor, flat and wide. In its barrenness, it nearly resembles portions of west Texas and New Mexico — in the manner that a piece of heavily tanned leather nearly resembles a porterhouse. From 15,000 feet.

Harsh. To say the least.

~

Somewhere over Kyrgyzstan...

We've been flying above this mud-rock-sand plain for a few hours now. You might recognize the area as that tannish splotch in the middle of Asia that stands out on NASA's popular photographs of the globe. Seemingly from nowhere, a gargantuan mountain range — completely white — has popped up on the edge of the horizon. This is the northern border of Afghanistan. Mazar-e-Sharif (our ultimate destination) is directly on the other side of the range.

Essentially, we are all of a sudden, emphatically "here."

It is a strange and surreal moment when someday's eventuality becomes all-too-present reality.

~

Thirty-some-odd minutes later, we are on the ground at Manas Air Force Base, Kyrgyzstan. It is midday, Friday the 19th.

Somewhere in transit, we missed Thursday. Apparently, I'm told, we will find it a year from now.

Or thereabouts.

AT THE SPEED OF MOLASSES

19 - 22 May

ONCE BEYOND THE PURVIEW OF COMMERCIAL AIR, ONE'S PROGRESS DOES SLOW CONSIDERABLY...

MANAS AFB, KYRGYZSTAN — The best thing to be said about our arrival to Manas is that, for all intents and purposes, the countdown clock has begun — after being stuck indefinitely on 365, tomorrow the day ticker will finally drop a notch to read 364, a minor change perhaps, but an advance nonetheless.

The other notable attribute of Manas is that it is the last station we will occupy not beholden to General Order #1—that which prohibits alcohol in theater. The officially sanctioned indulgence of Manas is, however, officially limited to two beverages daily. Sharing is strictly prohibited. Such commendable behavior will be punished by a one week suspension of bar privileges.

Thankfully, we are only to be in Manas one night.

There is no greater-valued human commodity than a non-drinker in an overseas Armed Forces establishment operating under rations. I am convinced that this is the primary motivator behind the heavy recruitment of Mormon individuals into military service. But I digress...

~

We leave Kyrgyzstan behind the next afternoon on a particularly non-luxurious C17 — a bulbous gray cargo jet with Air Force markings on the tail and crew. Flying due south over the considerable Hindu Kush mountain range, we land at Bagram Air Force Base (Afghanistan) in about two hours.

Not long after our arrival, a dedicated convoy pulls in to transport the entire Navy group the remaining 60 miles down to Kabul.

They are 13 seats short.

13 happens also to be the combined number of personnel between the two Mazar-i Sharif teams. In an amazing coincidence, our "Mez" team is nominated to stay behind. We are to rejoin the main body the next morning.

This particular schedule turns out to be quite optimistic.

Two days later we find ourselves still loitering in the transient circus tent. This is not an entirely bad thing — Bagram is, after all, an Air Force Base with Air Force amenities. Porcelain toilets, hot showers, expansive Exchange (or shopping center for those not versed in military establishments), quality DFAC (Dining FACility), and even a pizza joint. Buildings are well constructed and comfortably spaced. There is landscaping and trees (Manas offered only gravel, acres and acres of gravel). But for the location, it is not noticeably different than any U.S. grounded base.

On the third day, our relaxed diversion is interrupted by the arrival of our transport convoy. Things seem to happen this way as if by design over here; we wait for ill-defined periods of time as scheduled event after scheduled event fails to materialize, and then suddenly we must move on a moment's notice. Anything placed more than an hour ahead on the agenda will not occur.

Plans duly changed, we quickly pack up and prepare to mount — a Bluebird schoolbus. Not very comforting...

~

We depart Bagram with a four Humvee escort, two to the front and a pair to the rear — all with mounted .50 caliber machine guns at the ready. Despite our initial concern, the complement is clearly an effective security screen.

As we exit the gate, two things become readily apparent. First, Bagram is at the dead center of nowhere in particular. The land is desolate and sightlines virtually endless. Small groups of nomads are the only inhabitants outside the base walls. Second, the powers-that-be have apparently decided that this specific region of nowhere is the ideal location for the heart of military operations. Bagram is rather large as it is, but a massive amount of construction is underway on its surrounding acreage — perhaps because there isn't much besides goats to constrict its advance, and they are not too terribly disagreeable most days (the land, I presume, is probably quite affordable as well).

It is a 60-mile trip south to Kabul. The landscape is severe, but impressive. There are occasional tents and occasional nomads. As we progress, the tents begin to be supplanted by smallish huts and adobe brick houses. Every so often we come across significant sets of aged ruins, with well-worn earth walls and crumbling passageways. Mesmerizing are these scattered remains of prior civilization... and at times I feel as though I have slipped through time's borders into Biblical realms.

~

About 15 miles outside of the city we begin to encounter walls. A lot of them. Acres of land cordoned off into square after square — strikingly similar to a southern California suburban development, only without all the houses. For all I can see, all that's being partitioned is dirt. In a minute, however, a clue is revealed as to this proliferation.

The next five miles are consumed with open-air factories of the brick-making persuasion. I see long rows cut into the earth and stacks of adobe bricks of all sizes. A little farther down, the smoke stacks of primitive kilns pierce the skyline where hardened bricks are produced. With nothing else above 10 feet, these smooth cones dominate the visual field.

It is unclear whether the factories were built to support a wall-building craze, or if the walls are the unintended result of a brick-making craze. I'm reminded of Douglas Adams' Shoe Event Horizon[*] and wonder if it doesn't apply. In any event, I am quite sure the bricks and the walls are somehow related.

~

As we approach the outskirts of Kabul, the scene begins to feel strangely familiar... as if I've somehow managed to wind up back in South Tijuana among the street vendors, makeshift storefronts, and raggedy bands of curious children. The graffiti and other signage are in a slightly less recognizable script, however. The bullet-holes scarring the stucco walls are a bit larger, as well.

I imagine that most any semi-urban third-world avenue must carry a similar pastiche.

~

We will be in Kabul for anywhere from a few days to over a week waiting for final transportation to Mazar. While by no means a speedy transition, it could be worse. 25 of our guys are still in Manas, waiting for a flight.

....

[*] *Adams theory, as articulated in the noted journal "The Hitchhikers Guide to the Galaxy," postulates that overproduction and overconsumption of a particular item (say, women's shoes) is a vicious cycle that can only result in the destruction of a society.*

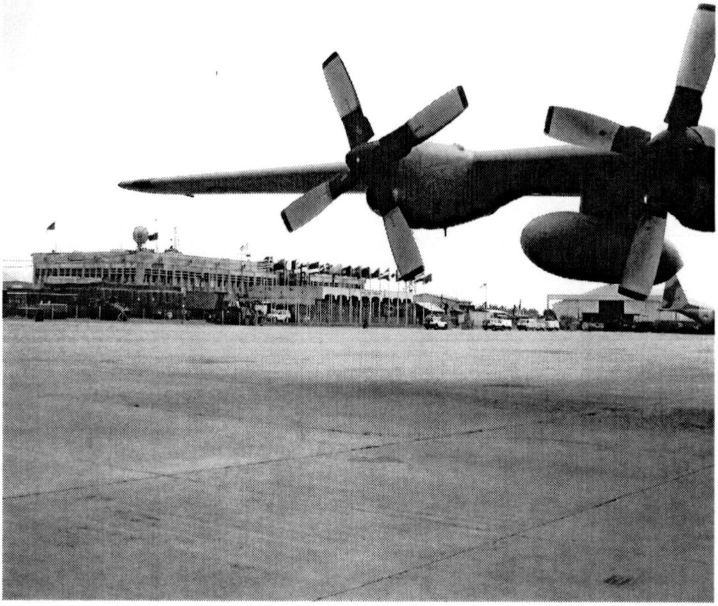

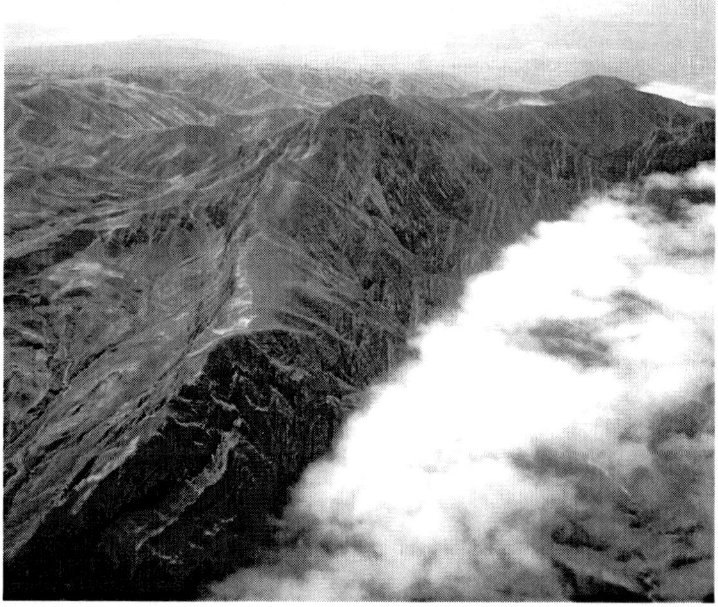

WELCOME TO KABUL

23 May

COMBINED JOINT TASK FORCE PHOENIX, KABUL, AFGHANISTAN — Not yet three hours on Camp Phoenix, and already confusion... Somewhere in the darkness of night, the emergency sirens were blaring loudly, interrupted only by a very official voice notifying us in stereo that we were all to be in the bunkers. Unbeknownst to the official sounding voice, someone had neglected to inform us as to the location of those bunkers. We put on our body armor over our t-shirts and shorts and grabbed our rifle-shaped paperweights (ammunition issue had also been neglected) and waited. In our tent.

Small arms fire echoed from the north, somewhere outside the walls of the compound. Just outside our tent, the four loaded Humvees of the Quick Reaction Force rumbled quickly by, throwing up clouds of dust in their wake. They seemed to be in somewhat of a hurry.

Thirty minutes passed. The alarm continued.

A pair of security types found us still inside the tent and gamely escorted us to the nearest "bunker." It was most definitely not a bunker. If somewhere a base plan made note of its intended existence, it undoubtedly would be signified with a dotted line and the words: "Proposed Location of Future Bunker."

It was, in actuality, no more than a Conex[†] box surrounded by formwork that might one day form the concrete that would make the box a bunker. But Army Doctrine said that it was a bunker and that, being a bunker, we should be inside it. There is no room in Army Doctrine for either logic or reality. And there was hardly enough room in the make-believe bunker for all of us.

At this very same time, similarly roused from their bunks, several hundred other individuals in varying stages of undress were also cozily enjoying several other bunkers in various stages of completion. And twenty soldiers were outside the wire quieting the threat.[††]

An informal survey reveals that we were not the only ones sent to Afghanistan solely for so-called supporting functions. Just about everybody else is too. Thousands of people at Camp Phoenix working in administrative positions so that five or ten percent can carry on the fight. Robert Heinlein would have a conniption.[*]

A few hours pass. A few of us doze off. The alarms subside. We find that the gunshots were part of a domestic dispute and were not aimed in our direction (through an inadvertent shot may have made it our way). Back to bed, and the comfort of our cots.

Only to be jarred awake some hours later by a large explosion outside the south wall. Round we go again... armor, weapon, head back to the bunker...

...where we are told to return to our tents. Controlled explosion of a VBIED (Vehicle Borne Improvised Explosive Device) by gate security. No threat. Thus, no alarm. No alarm means go back to sleep. Nice to know.

But there's no more sleep to be had tonight. Just anxious tosses and turns awaiting daylight, and our eventual departure.

Welcome to Kabul.

....

[*] *Author of Starship Troopers (classic book, unfortunate movie); he advocated that support functions be left to civilians and every uniformed soldier be active in the fight.*

[†] *Editor's note: Converted shipping containers, 20 and 40 footers. Conex is the eponymic brand of such boxes for military personnel (like Kleenex, Xerox, et al). "Chigo" likewise came to represent all the split unit AC's attached to them.*

[††] *Editor's note: "Outside the wire" is soldier's parlance for the areas outside of the protected confines of a base or outpost.*

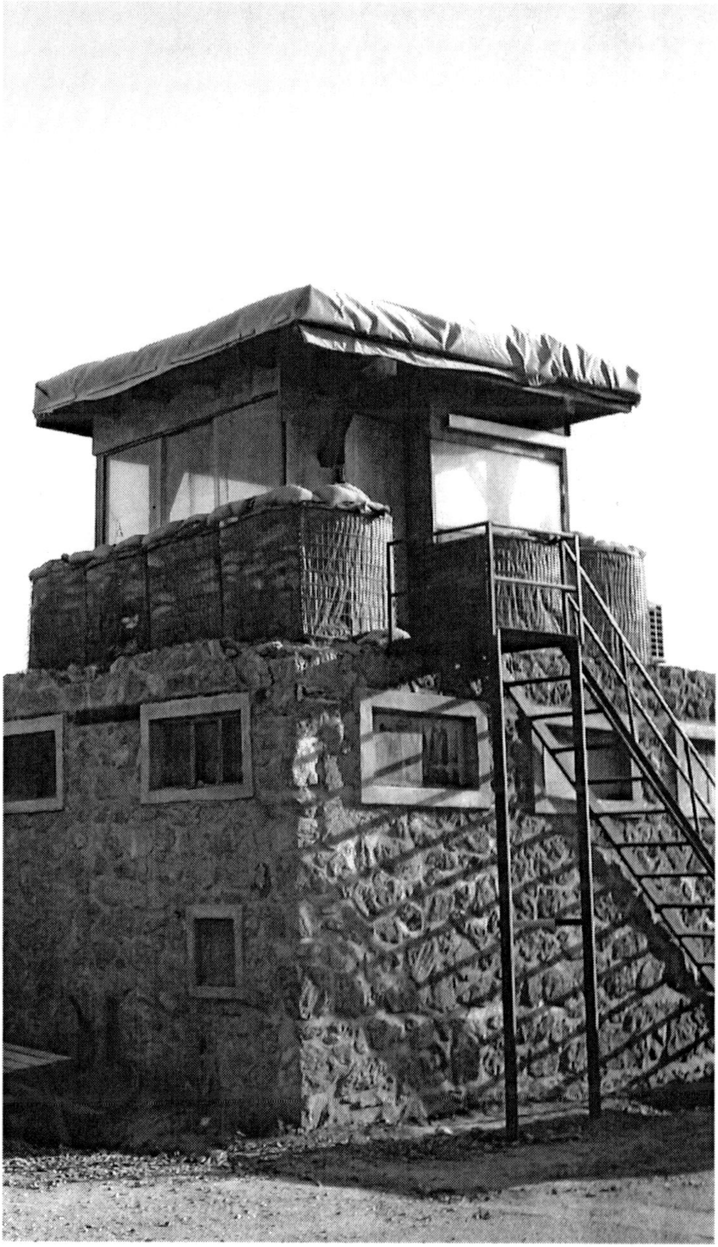

NOTHING DOING

29 May

UNITED STATES EMBASSY, KABUL, AFGHANISTAN —
There is something to be said for doing nothing. Given
the right environment and right assistance, nothing is an
art form. There may be a limit to how much nothing one
can do, but if I find myself on a beach with a good supply
of Corona and companionship, that horizon is far off. I've
spent unsuccessful weeks of dedicated research attempting to
discover it in the past... but it remained just out of reach.

Within the concrete prison camp that is Camp Phoenix,
Kabul, my limit of nothing-doing is considerably shorter.
Probably more along the lines of twenty minutes or so.

The period from Minute 21 to Day 9 was
thus, understandably, a difficult one.

Eat, sleep, read, write, play a little basketball. Great
schedule for a day or two (especially in a slightly more
chic environment), but after a week you might begin to
wonder why your flight keeps getting cancelled.

~

The one semi-notable non-event that did occur (or did not,
depending on your adherence to proper and logical English usage)
was the Engineering Conference at the American Embassy. In
one room was gathered each of the Afghan National Army base
commanders and a series of American engineering officers,
brought in from all corners of this Texas-sized country (no
small task); 15 or so Afghan Colonels giving up their day to be
lectured on facilities management by a group of American Navy
Lieutenants. Each Colonel sported a thick black beard and dressed
in their combat greens — looking every bit the revolutionary (or

war lord, depending on your perspective). All that was missing were the rows of self-awarded medals. After a second's thought, I realized that this practical omission hinted at combat-earned positions in a way that other imaginary honors can't replace. These war-darkened men had not seen peace or stability in decades. Military action was something they knew inherently.

Military maintenance, however, is an entirely different story. Which brings us nicely around...

The main thing I gleaned from the day-long conference is that we are far behind. There exists no Facilities Maintenance structure in Afghanistan (I imagine they've been too busy fighting to pay attention to reinforcing their fighting positions). For the last few years, the Army Corps of Engineers has simply built and repaired around them, with no mind towards implementing an Afghani-run system, or really involving them in the process at all. Cue the Navy's Engineers.

We got a job ahead of us...

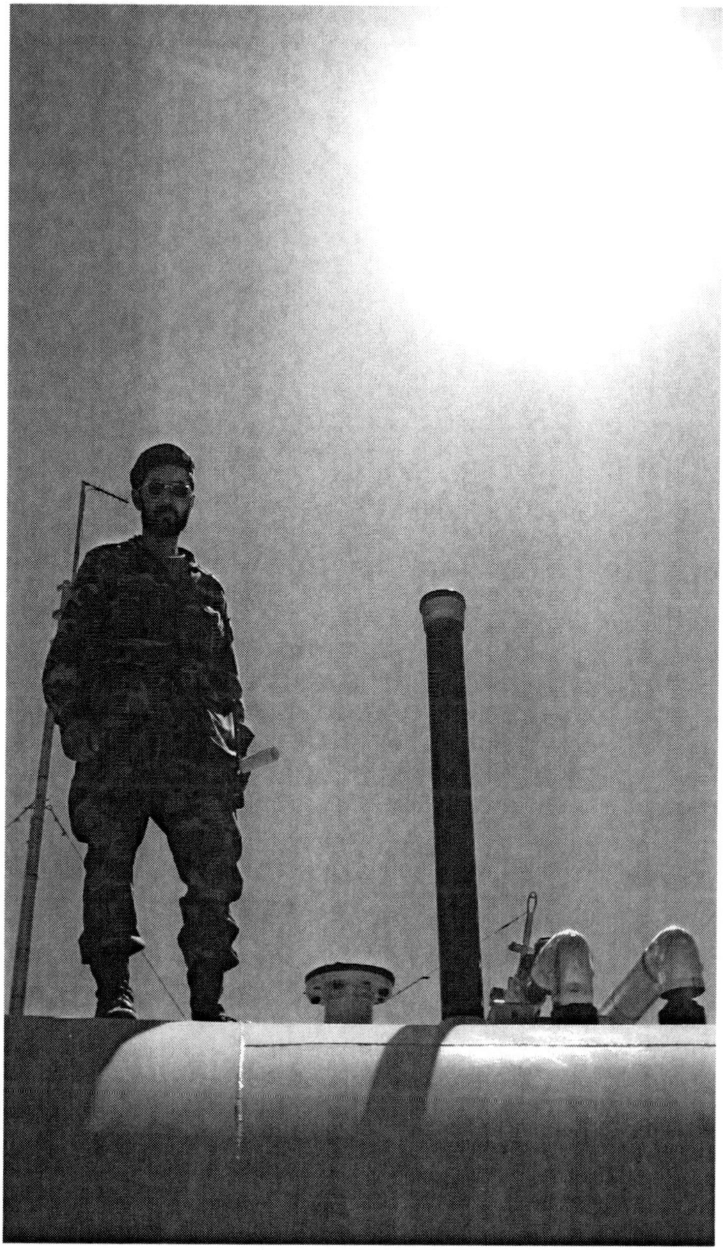

FROM IOWA, WITH LOVE

30 May

Middle America, it seems, is quite enthralled with the US military. Boxes chock full of all sorts of hygienic paraphernalia and tooth dissolving candies (an interesting combination, that) regularly appear at the local chaplain's office for distribution to unnamed soldiers. Some packages carry greetings from Middlefield Junior High, Middlefield, Iowa while others are the work of well-meaning individuals dutifully showing their support. There is nothing quite like receiving a tube of Crest with a bible verse or a country proverb taped to it. Really, there's not, I've checked around.

Care packages from one's actual home are a bit more effective. Given that the sender has a better idea of the recipients taste, this is not too surprising. Though I believe the real value is knowing someone back home is thinking of you—that is to say, someone you actually know is thinking of you. Personally, I find it rather disconcerting that Darryl in Sioux Falls finds it imperative that I have enough Sure® deodorant.

~

On an entirely coincidental note, my mailing address [†] for the next year is:

~~RCAG-North / U.S. NAVY~~
~~Camp Mike Spann~~
~~Mazar-e-Sharif~~
~~APO AE 09318~~

Seriously, though, I think the family has the care package arena covered (but cards and letters are always appreciated)

However, if anyone has a little generous itch that needs to be scratched, it's not me or the other service members who need stuff from the States, it's the Afghani kids. We're in the process of building schools and community centers for the locals and what I could really use are school supplies to give out. Crayons, pencils, notebooks, coloring books, whatever. These kids have nothing...

They need care packages far more than we.

....

[†] *Editor's note: This mailing address is, not suprisingly, now defunct. It may be of some interest to the reader to know that these addresses have an amazingly short shelf-life; as the mission evolves in changes in a region of conflict, so does the name of the operation, and thus the mailing address. Names of bases often change regularly, renamed for fallen soldiers from that locale. Only the last line of the address is relatively stable, as it is assigned by the US Postal Service. The first three letter code, APO, is a notation for Army Post Office. The next two letters are the equivalent of the state in a domestic address, in this case standing for Armed Forces Europe (the command head of the Afghan operations, and regional routing center for the Middle East and Africa). The five-digit number is, in fact, the zip code. In this manner, all overseas military mail is treated (and billed) as domestic mail by the USPS.*

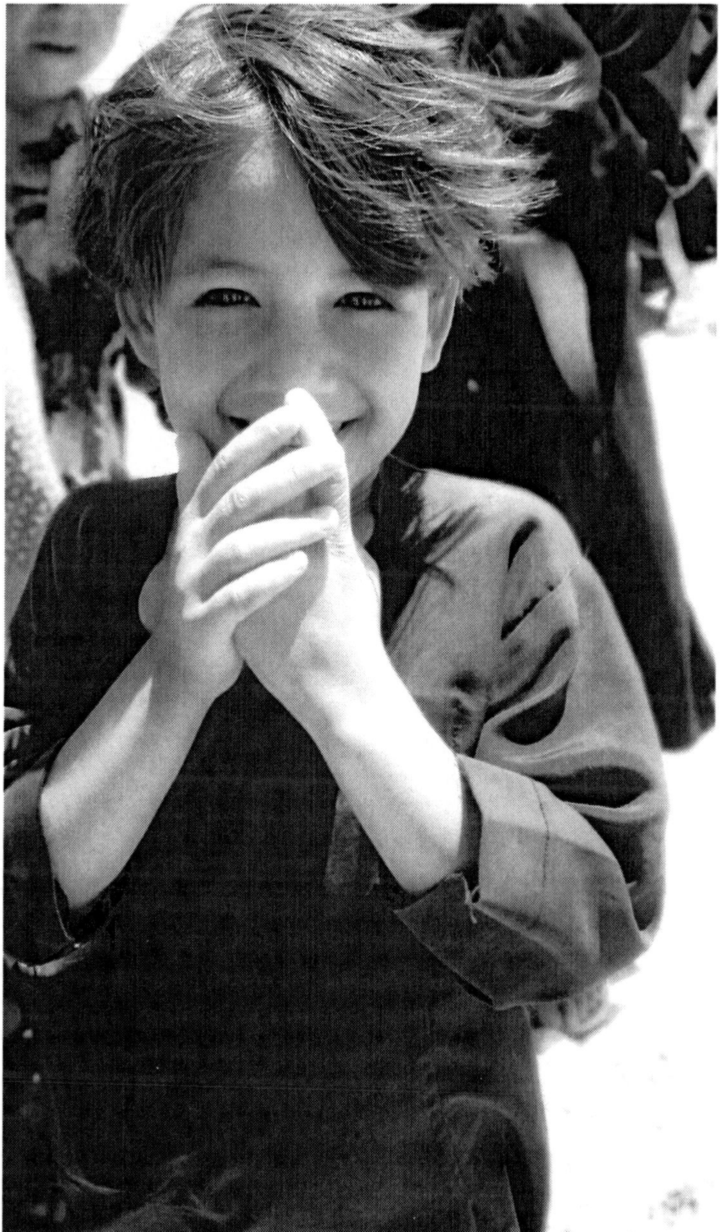

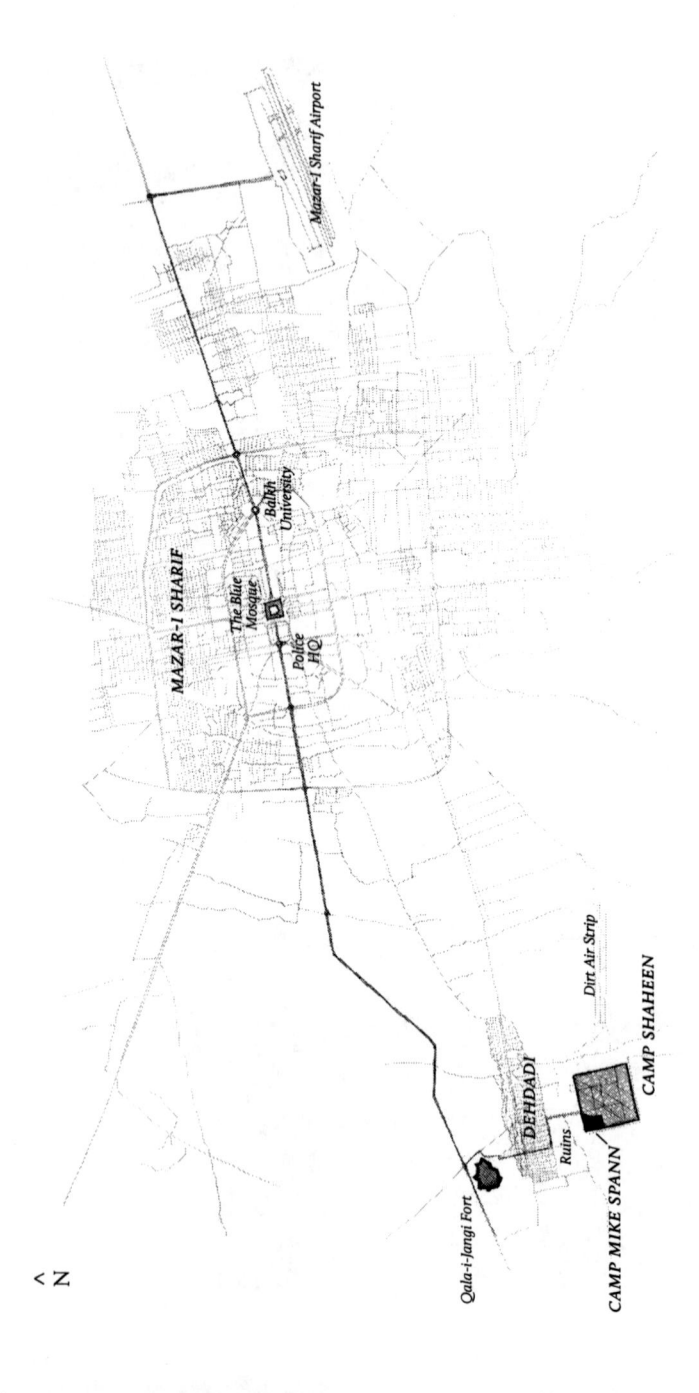

The Range

AFGHANI PICTURE SHOW

1 June

MAZAR-I SHARIF, AFGHANISTAN — Ten days it took us to leave Kabul. Such is what passes for efficient travel in theater. It was a short convoy over to Kabul International Airport, an airfield tagged with the rather disconcerting shorthand "KIA." Also disconcerting was our Vietnam-era transportation method: rag top personnel carrier. This did give us quite a parting view of the city streets, complete with trailing children — one of whom attempted to sell my commander a live scorpion inside a plastic bottle.

It's a short flight on a C130 up to Mazar-i Sharif, but not necessarily a smooth one. The takeoff involved a quick ascent followed by a series of sharp banks, skimming precipitously over the rocky crags that cradle the northern edge of Kabul and a dart through a tight valley into the open desert. These shenanigans presumably are proper procedure to avoid being a ripe target for an opportunist with an RPG* hanging out in the hills. That, or our pilot was unseasonably drunk. Either is quite possible.

The transition from overflowing urbanity into barren nothingness is crossed in a blink. Once in uncontested air space, we rose slowly above the sand and through the cloud layer. Within minutes, blue and white peaks began to nip and tear at the cumulus carpet. As the sky cleared, dramatic snow-capped ranges spread out below and around our capsule. Just as quickly, the cloud screen returned and again dissipated, leaving the severe tan hills of central Afghanistan in their wake. Staring at this geographical convolution through the 9" portal drilled in the C130 underbelly, the sensation is not unlike watching your neighbor's television set through a peephole — only he persists in changing the channel at entirely inconvenient and unannounced intervals.

Mazar-e-Sharif sits inside a wide open desert valley, ringed with massive mountain ranges that isolate it from the rest of the country geographically and culturally, much like the city of Phoenix, Arizona. On both counts. The airport (if one could call the airstrip and sentinel post an airport) lies far to the outskirts of town. Climbing down out of the plane, we were comforted — nee' intrigued — to see our arrival overwatched by an Afghan soldier manning a .50 caliber machine gun mounted to the roof of a tan Ford Ranger.

We were met on the tarmac by a lone Army sergeant and the query, "Do they know you're coming today? They'd normally be waiting here for you if they did..."

Standing at the doorstep of our final destination after two weeks and thousands of miles of travel, this question brought on the purest and most comprehensive look of bewilderment seen on a group of human faces since Columbus landed his barges on Haitian shores.

After a few phone calls and a fair bit of sitting around, it was determined that our transportation was indeed on the way. Some time later we were able to board our charter bus for the other side of Mez.

[To the scorekeeper, tally this the 4th out of 4 convoys that we've ridden the unarmored vehicle — at least on this trek we had a pair of Humvees as escorts; my trip to the embassy crossed downtown Kabul in a trio of Toyota Landcruisers][†]

Despite our load of gear, ammunition, weapons, and armor, the ride took on the feel of a tour bus as we transitioned through the agricultural outskirts and into the heart of Mazar-e-Sharif. This was perhaps due to the outgoing commander's insistence on standing in front and yapping for the entirety of the trip.

In short, Mez is nothing like Kabul. Where Kabul carries the degradative form of a third-world hodge-podge sticking to the remains of a war-torn shell, Mazar-e-Sharif does a fair imitation of a semi-modern central-Asian metropolis. There are people everywhere. Most of them are selling things. There are signs everywhere, splashed with colorful pictures and multiple languages. Most of these are also selling things. It looks every bit a trade center parked at the crossing of the transcontinental routes. I imagine that this is, in fact, what it is.

Past the urban climax and on to the other side's outskirts, we encounter series upon series of earthen ruins, punctuated every so often by bombed-out Soviet behemoths. As if by some temporal gradient, the rammed earth structures begin appearing less and less crumbled as we distance ourselves from the main city. At some point the cracked walls begin to be inhabited and we find ourselves in an outlying village.

The village is called Dehdadi. It envelops the military encampment and provides a very real protective skin for the base within. Children run after our convoy, laughing and showing us their "thumbs up." Elders wave from doorways. It is quite a welcome.

Minutes later we are within the gates of Camp Mike Spann. Home, as it were, for the next eleven and one half months.

....

*Rocket-Propelled Grenade, a shoulder-launched anti-aircraft weapon.

† *Editor's note: The reader may recall various "armor-plating" controversies in the news over the course of the Afghan and Iraq operations. Here, the team has been caught in flux — where their state-side training has indoctrinated them in the importance of maintaining 100% armament "outside the wire," but in-country practice has not caught up to the training standard. In defense of those in the field, available equipment always lags doctrine.*

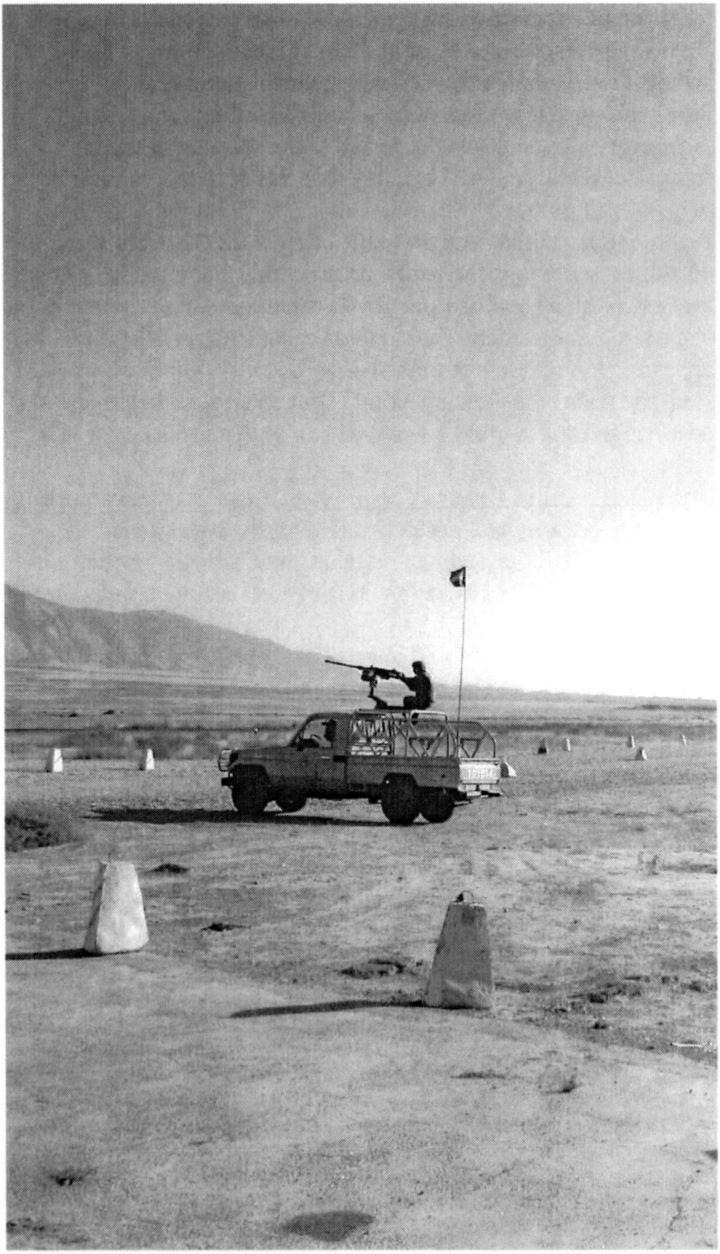

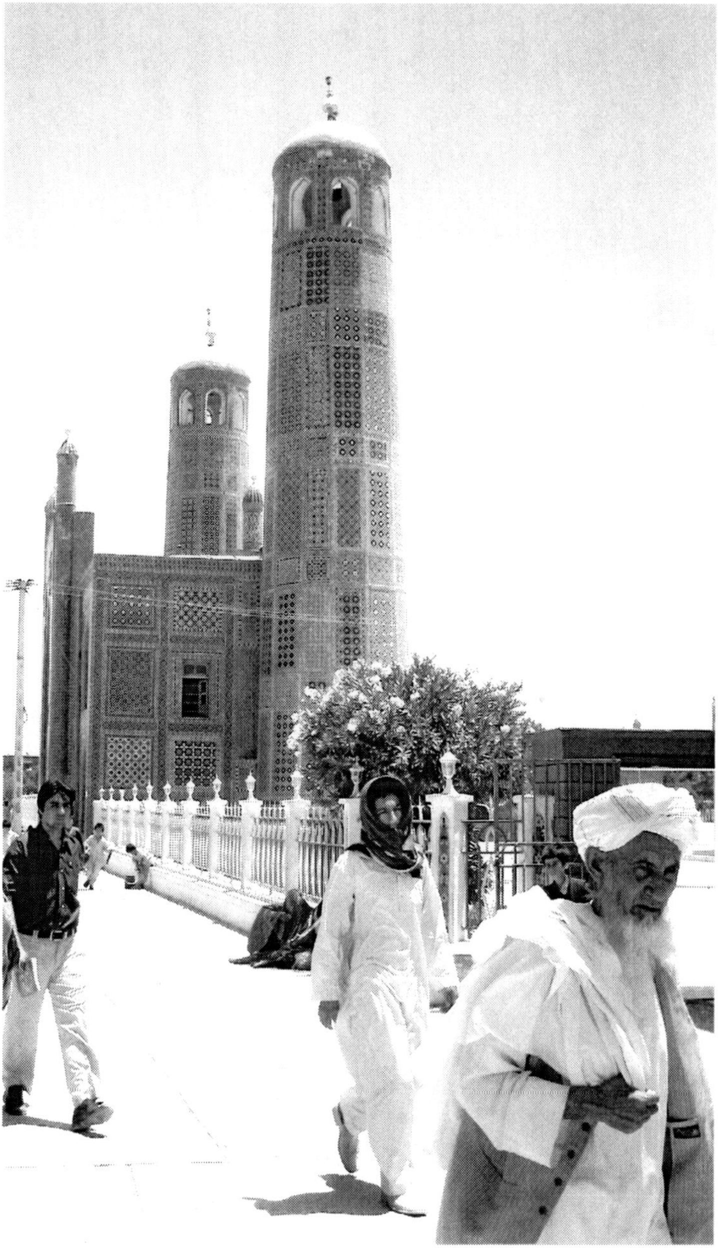

THE USUAL SUSPECTS

4 June

FORWARD OPERATING BASE SPANN, MAZAR-I SHARIF, AFGHANISTAN — It might at this point be advantageous to introduce the cast of characters involved in this little soirée. Not necessarily a great gain for you the reader, of course, but it will certainly be to my benefit to be able to refer to people in shorthand rather than interrupting some fabulous future anecdote to explain just who exactly I am referring to. This is by no means a comprehensive list, just a useful cheat sheet for my Navy counterparts here in the desert.

In no particular order....

Mr. Carlton J. Boatright... is a gentle giant of the first order. A deep thinker and deeper sleeper, he holds down the bass line for this group number. The ease with which he slips into the background belies his dark 6'4" frame. Born into the Deep South, he never strayed far from Savannah until the day he joined the Navy. In the eighteen years since, he's barely been able to put his feet down in any locale, let alone put down any sort of roots. This adventure is just another in a long series of deployments that keep him ever away from home.

Dwight "D"... is quite fittingly our communications offer, as his mouth only ceases to move in his sleep. Three days he's had his issued cell phone, and it has yet to stop ringing. A former Navy chief and current LDO,[†] he joined up 20 some odd years ago to get away from Maryland and take a break from school. Rather than let his tenure be the short diversion he intended, the Navy persisted in promoting him up the ranks.

The Coolman... has, in fact, been previously mentioned in my ramblings. It was he who joined me in the reappropriated Humvee to fetch pizzas for our Army brethren way back when in Mississippi. He's the Ops officer for this dog and pony show and, along with the previous two gentlemen, completes my group of roommates. Although he is one of those damn Reservists, we forgive him for his touristy ways because he did spend seven years on active duty driving boats around the world—and because he takes such pretty pictures.

Johnny U... is the honorary 5th roommate, because he uses our hut as his own, and rarely ventures into his assigned bunk area except to sleep. A submariner by trade, he is a natural fit for this desert deployment. Like myself, he came more than halfway 'round the world from a post at Pearl Harbor. Jon's only a converted Hawaiian, but with his Amer-asian* features and relaxed demeanor, one wouldn't realize to question his credentials.

The Boss... is too a Reservist, but we let it slide because he's the boss. He's on his second deployment in three years, having spent '04 in Bahrain. Laid back with a dry wit, but with a strong sense of obligation to his people, he's the kind of guy you'd want in charge of this far-flung outpost—and a marked improvement over his Mr. Magoo impersonating predecessor (though, in all fairness, a bowl of petunias would have been a decent upgrade).

Senior Chief Clark... is a fairly salty 30-something NCO plucked straight from a carrier and dropped off, rather unceremoniously, in the middle of this endeavor. Seldom serious in casual conversation and quick to perversely spin even the most mundane topic, local bookies have him the frontrunner to snag the first sexual harassment suit...

Big Minnesota... or Chief Wotzka, is the prototypical good-natured midwestern product. Though its true he speaks an entirely foreign language from the rest of us, I've been able to communicate with him somewhat due to the few phrases I picked up years back on a visit to Minneapolis. Such as: *"Goeh Goeh-Furrs!"* which is a common greeting, and also *"Yah Yoo-Betcha"* which doesn't apparently mean anything but must be tossed in regularly as some sort of verbal punctuation.

Senior Chief Volkl... is from Chicago.

Senior Chief McMahon ... is the only female NCO on the base, and she could definitely kick your ass if she wanted to. She won't, because she's very nice, *but cut the crap, alright, we don't have time for this shit.*

Mark the Caffeinated IT Guy ... starts each day with no less than 4 Red Bulls or 44 ounces of Diet Coke (whichever is available) and then hooks himself into the network to power the computers all over the base. He is also our Explosive Ordinance Disposal team.[††] That isn't frightening to anyone, I'm certain.

Dukes and Hazard ... form an inseperable, and most unlikely duo. A body-building African-American banker who hails from "The Great State of Missippippi" and a long-suffering Clevelander couch-potato ginger who cuts checks for vets, they run the Supply Office by day and do video-game football battle by night. Sadly, even the digital Brownies never win.

And me, well, I'm just happy to be here. Proud to serve. Etc. Etc.

....

[*] *Connotations aside, Jon prefers "Chinglish," as his parents are British citizens.*

[†] *Editor's note: Limited Duty Officer. A specialized type of promotion from Senior Enlisted to the Officer Corps which does not require a university degree (though most do posess them) and maintains some level of seniority in job placement over other commissioned officers which were not prior-enlisted. The "limited" notation refers to an ultimate grade cap at Captain (O-6), which prevents an LDO from eligibility for promotion to Admiral.*

[††] *Editor's note: Given a small base with limited manpower, but many roles that technically need filling, most of the team received several additional titles attached to their names (often irrespective of any particular expertise in the area).*

TURNOVERS

6 June

I was only fifteen minutes on the ground at Camp Spann when I inherited the wood shop. Serves me right for asking where it was.

Fifteen more minutes, after meeting the previous "Shop Guy," and it became abundantly clear that this was no side pursuit, but a full blown occupation.

And I hadn't even received the details of my real job yet.

~

The real job, that "challenging position" for which I'd been "hand-selected" (according to my most recent Fitness Report), was to be the Engineering Mentor for the Northern Corps of the Afghan National Army. This may sound like a prestigious and important station to hold, and given that I was allotted three entire days' overlap with the outgoing Lieutenant to learn the intricacies of the position, I'm quite sure the Army believes it to be.

The first day of turnover was spent mainly on introductions. The most important of these, of course, was with my Afghan National Army (ANA) counterpart in charge of Facilities Management.

The first thing I noticed about Colonel Ata was, well... I was at a loss to notice anything, for he was not there yet. Afghan time, they say (though every culture seems to think they have the patent on casual punctuality). The second thing I noticed, as he dismounted his Army-issue Ranger, was his Top Gun mirrored sunglasses. I was told that most traditional Afghani men refuse eyewear of any type (protective, corrective, or otherwise), believing it to detract from their masculinity. Of complete coincidence, welding careers are notably short in the country. Colonel Ata, it appeared, had no time for this foolishness—he was too busy being smooth.

He greeted me warmly and, through the translator, expressed his enthusiasm for our year-long partnership. Moments later we were sitting around his desk drinking chai and discussing whatever was new in the world of Facilities Management. This, I would find, is the bulk of my responsibility as Mentor. To talk over the issues as they arise, observe, and advise if necessary. The Colonel is quite sharp, however, and I imagine I will spend more time listening than advising over the next twelve months.

~

The second day of turnover we managed to repair and install a large key cabinet for the 1500 some-odd building keys Colonel Ata has sitting in cardboard boxes on his desk. We, of course, drank more chai as well.

~

The third day of turnover was a fair bit different. To begin with, the keys and responsibilities to The Shop were also in my hands. At 8am, I rolled my new beat-up Ford Ranger outside the gate to pick up our handful of Afghani woodworkers and learned to say *"sobh bah khai"* (good morning in Dari).[†] While I was opening up shop and setting them to work on various commissioned projects, I was interrupted by the strangest bit of Facilities news I'd ever heard.

There was, apparently, a dispute between two kandaks [battalions] as to who had the right to occupy a certain building. They were attempting to settle this disagreement by pointing rifles at each other.

We rushed out to assist Colonel Ata in resolving the situation.

As it turned out, one kandak had been reassigned to an entirely different region of Afghanistan. After their departure, the buildings originally allotted for them were otherwise utilized. This arrangement went quite swimmingly until the first kandak changed their minds about the whole deployment thing and reappeared, unannounced, early one morning.

It was as if a person vacated an apartment in Wisconsin, moved to Florida, got a job and a car, tooted around for a year or so, and then suddenly returned to the apartment in Wisconsin, stood on the doorstep waving a pistol and yelling at the new tenant to get out of his house. Then, blamed the whole thing on the landlord.

These are the kind of things an ANA Facilities Engineer must worry about.

We took off to speak with the kandak's leadership about the fiasco. Within moments of our arrival, Colonel Ata and some kandak Major were yelling pointed words in Dari at each other and flinging their arms about in the air. This continued, at various volumes, for about an hour. Then, like a tornado dissipating into thin air, the argument was over and the two men were shaking hands, declaring the problem solved. They kissed each others' cheeks respectfully, and it was done.

If we hadn't then all sat down and had chai together, I probably would have thought the whole thing rather odd.

[†] *Editor's note: Dari is the Afghan dialect of Farsi (or Persian), as distinct from the Pashtu language spoken by the southern half of the country.*

CERP IS FOR THE CHILDREN

7 June

INSTEAD OF WORKING TODAY, JOHNNY U AND I DECIDED TO GO AND PLAY WITH THE KIDS....

...So we loaded up three up-armored Humvees with some cases of bottled water, a pair of experienced turret gunners, and a fair complement of curious senior officers and headed out to check on two of our CERP projects. CERP, of course, is another of those popular Army acronyms which nobody actually knows what it stands for. What we do know is that it refers to the generous pot of money that funds the humanitarian projects we are trying to implement around the country. The above-mentioned seniority control this resource — prompting today's tourist expedition. On the docket we have a medium-sized primary school that is under construction and a nearby girls' school that we are about to begin repairs on.

Given that our convoy is limited to the three up-armored Humvees, Johnny U and I figured we had a decent chance of breaking our streak of riding in the convoy cattle car. Our bet is returned two-fold — we are both slated as drivers, Jon at the wheel of #2 and me taking up the rear.

The rural village of Bay Temor is only about 40 miles west of Camp Spann, but the road to get there quickly becomes little more than a goat trail past the outskirts of Mazar-e-Sharif. Rocks and trenches regularly disrupt the path. Last month's rain has carved deep ruts that have since hardened under the desert sun. It is all I can do to keep up with the convoy without bumping my gunner out of his post. The roads are, without a doubt, the worst I've ever seen since leaving southern Louisiana.

We cross large stretches of barren desert, every so often broken up by small adobe villages. But for the occasional displaced Nike t-shirt on a passerby, these rural smatterings appear completely left behind by time. I peek down alleyways looking for a film crew working on a "Ten Commandments" remake. Kids run alongside the convoy as grizzled old men look on. A group of women pass, all draped in silken fabrics, faces shielded from the beastly sun and our foreign gaze.

About two hours of rough driving brings us to the first school, where a large local work-force is on display. I watch with interest as a team builds a portion of the masonry ceiling. There are a series of steel ribs at about 16" intervals forming a skeletal roof structure. In between, shallow brick barrel vaults are crafted by two masons on a raised platform. On the ground, two men hand mix mortar in large bowls from gray cement and water. The water is brought in, bowl by bowl, by another man who must pump it from the well outside. Alongside stands a man whose sole purpose is throwing bricks up to the masons. He launches his projectiles one by one to the men above. They slather each with the freshly mixed mortar and tap them in place overhead.

As we tour the site, children begin appearing. It is just a few at first, but as word spreads of our arrival, a whole herd of munchkins converge on our location. Unfortunately, on this trip we don't have much to give them but our time.

We make the most of what we have, singing songs and entertaining the youngsters. We take out our cameras and snap hundreds of pictures. The children all fancy themselves movie stars. They gather around, climbing over each other to see the little digital images of themselves. They pose, they make faces, and they laugh in chorus when they see the results.

Johnny U puts on a Hawaiian culture class, teaching an impressionable group of young boys to say "Howzit Brah" and throw the shaka.* We then wonder how confused such things will make future soldiers and their interpreters.

We interrupt Jon's one man mission to supplant the thumbs-up among Afghani youth and head down the road to the girls' school. The pack of children follow us. As we tour the pair of small classrooms, a few of the bolder boys sneak in the back windows. Class is still in session. I smile at the mostly unnoticed faux pas, figuring ill-gotten education is better than none at all.

As the day turns to afternoon, we must leave behind our entourage and return to base. We do make two stops on the return, however. The first is to see a beautifully simple white mosque perched on a hill in a neighboring village. A few brightly dressed children sit on its several-hundred-year-old steps in picturesque fashion. Cropping around this scene of serenity, it is easy to forget the country's war torn present in favor of this juxtaposition of its exquisite history and the youthful future.

Our last stop is on another village's market street. We pick up stacks of flatbread and pouches of apple juice. The bread is baked fresh right off the street in fired brick ovens, the smoke of which wafts over our heads as we eat. It tastes somewhat like an unleavened version of Italian bread, thick and crusty. Surprisingly, it seems much closer to this European relative than it does to either pita or Indian tandoori naan. In any event, it is delicious.

At this same moment, friends in other parts of the country are ducking under bunkers to avoid mortar fire and rockets.

But we are a world away, breaking bread with the locals in the middle of a village street after spending a day entertaining Afghani children. Geography can have its advantages, I suppose.

[°] *Both are Hawaiian mainstays, the first a greeting and the second the classic "hang loose" hand signal adopted, then popularized, by southern California surfers*

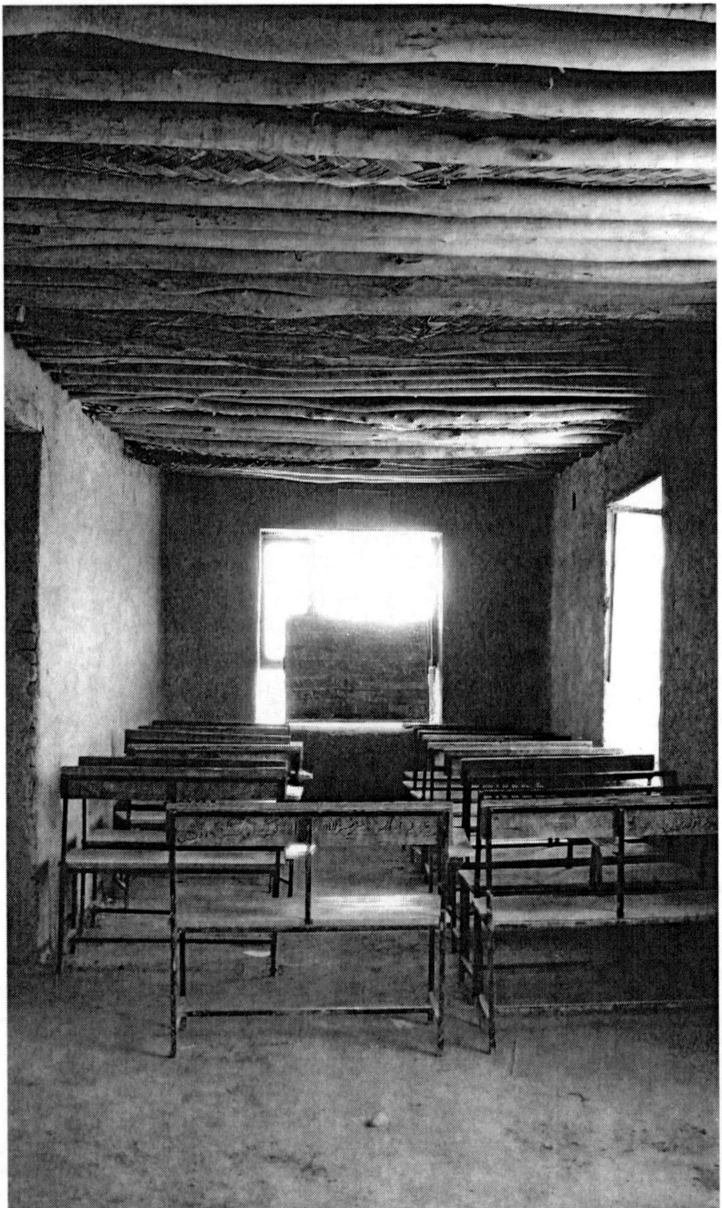

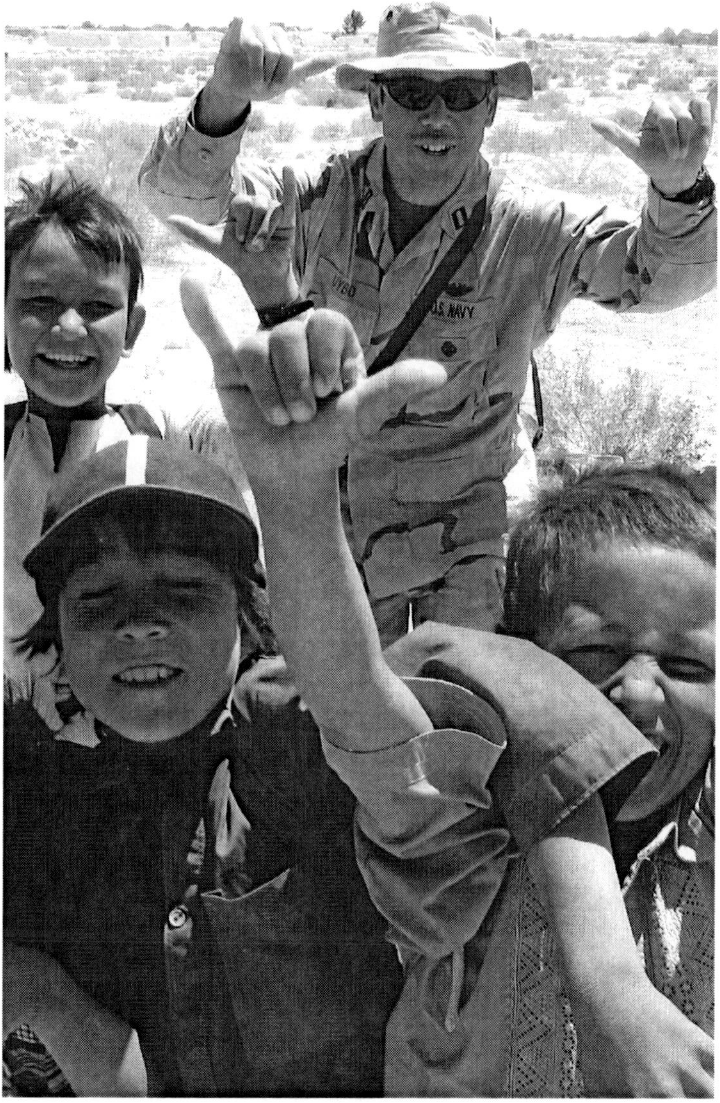

GENERAL DISREGARD

15 June

I must confess.

Blame my upbringing, blame my Navy training,
blame my incomplete military assimilation, blame
my damn rational brain, blame something.

I am completely and utterly incapable of understanding the
celebrity — no, *deification* — of the Army General Officer. The
hubris with which the office is carried, and the way in which
otherwise (somewhat) rational men fawn over these primadonna
personalities positively boggles my apparently inadequate brain.

Generally speaking, I try my best to avoid them. I
find it hard to breathe in reality-free air space.

~

There is a classic Looney Tunes short in which Bugs Bunny
dresses up as some famous maestro in order to hijack, as it
were, an orchestra. As he enters the auditorium, people in
the back row start whispering, "LEOPOLD.....LEOPOLD...." and so
forth. As he continues, the whispers grow to a medium-sized
murmur, "LEOPOLD. *LEOPOLD!*" By the time he reaches the
podium, every voice in the hall is repeating the conductor's
name. But, they are quickly snapped to quiet attention with an
authoritative glance from the rabbit. He's got on his Important
Man costume, and now he's got some showing off to do.

Visits from Generals are exactly like this,
except for the orchestra part.

We are in the middle of what is called a RIP, here at Camp Mike Spann, Mazar-i Sharif, Afghanistan. RIP stands for Replacement In Place. Essentially, the hundred or so Tennessee Army National Guard soldiers are being replaced by a hundred or so Oregon Army National Guard soldiers. We are busting at the seams. It is therefore the perfect time for the 1-star Tour to roll through town.

This morning there were two flights arriving at the Mez airstrip. The early flight carried 30-some-odd Oregon gents. The late-morning shuttle carried a couple of 1-star Generals (incoming and outgoing) and their entourage.

At 5 am this morning, a bus and two 5-ton trucks headed across town with a 3-Humvee escort to greet the three dozen newest members of Camp Mike Spann. Three hours after the modest early pickup, a twenty Humvee caravan armed to the hilt tore out of the front gate and across the city to engulf the little airstrip in the desert with a shuddering display of military might. Apparently the outgoing Colonel was dead set on impressing the visiting celebrities.

I, for one, am sure glad they were impressed by this gratuitous display of incompetence. Because every goddamn machine gun we had in Mazar-i Sharif went on that convoy. That's right folks, Convoy #1 was sent out to pick up the troops armed with nothing but M16s and hand guns. Even we received more protection than that on our various nail-biting excursions on old school buses. Meanwhile, the base itself was deserted during the whole charade, as every gun and gunner were otherwise occupied.

Oh, but what a show!

Dramatic display. Obligatory tour. Little speech. On their way again, with a dramatic display in reverse. Then everyone in Army greens breathes a little easier and gets back to work.

And I am left wondering why no one ever seems to notice the little gray rabbit legs poking out of their costumes.

117

ADVENTURES IN INTERPRETATION

25 June

As a necessary component of my job, I was assigned a full-time interpreter. He was issued in much the same fashion as any other item of equipment: "Alright, Lieutenant, here is your truck, your phone, and your 'terp.' Sign here. The Army expects to get them back."

I find this somewhat amusing.

This lingual lifeline of mine is named Ramin Amiry. He's a good-natured fellow, a jolly little balding Buddha. On his monthly salary of $800 USD, he supports 16 family members (brothers, sisters, cousins, children, brother's sister's cousin's children, and so forth). Jobs are hard to come by here... those that pay anyway. Ramin's brother is a math teacher, but that earns him barely enough cash to feed himself, and not enough to really contribute.

Ramin is my age, but like all his countrymen he wears a patina of ten extra years. A generation of war wears on a people.

His face is proudly shaven and he sports shiny sunglasses and a navy blue ball cap with "Cal" embroidered above the bill. When the Taliban were in control he was forced to maintain a traditional beard and appearance. Beardless men were kept in prison for their indiscretion; those with western garb were handled much worse. To be now in control of even just his appearance, and his daily life, is a badge of honor—a symbol that the Taliban have been driven out of Northern Afghanistan. And, I think, a representation of hope that they never are allowed return.

Ramin has very quickly adopted the role of personal assistant to my daily cacophony. He finds this preferable to being a mere translator. He carries the radio that connects me with my shop workers and brags to his fellow interpreters that he is an important man. Important men must carry radios, you see. I'd rather he carry it, as I carry my father's aversion to such communication devices. Besides, my shop workers speak Dari, so there's not much use in me answering it when it chirps.

What I do carry is a handy "Dari/English" dictionary in my cargo pocket, left thigh. It is very quickly becoming dog eared and inked over. I reach for it regularly in my attempt to learn this entirely foreign language. This book would barely serve as more than a paperweight without a guide, however. With Ramin, a former language professor, to explain the intricacies of grammar and to guide my pronunciation and usage, it is a fabulous tool. I've told him my goal is to make him obsolete, and his job is to help me do so.

Given the eclectic combination of background and language, our conversations can tend towards the absurd. Normally this is because one or the other has misunderstood something (usually me). That's no reason not to charge ahead with discussion, however.

This morning we were drinking morning tea in the office. Ramin mentioned that he was looking forward to seeing his girlfriend this weekend. Ramin is married with three daughters. I thought perhaps he was misusing the term and asked him to define "girlfriend." Somewhat surprised at my reaction, he asked me, "you don't have girlfriends?"

"Ramin... I don't think the lady would be ok with me having girlfriends."

    "Oh. Why is that?"

"We believe in a partnership, one man and one woman..."

    "Ah... In Islam we are allowed three wives, but there is no limit on girlfriends."

"Hmmm... How did Mohammed come at the number of three? Why not two? Or four?"

> "Well, really, it is more important that you can support the wives you have. Most people can only support one wife."

"How do you mean 'support?' Did Mohammed mean it solely in the financial sense? Or is he concerned with their overall well-being? Can one man fully 'support' more than one woman?"

> "Well, of course not! This is also why few people have many wives. For me, as example, one wife is more than plenty. But I prefer to have many girlfriends!"

Fortuitously, the Boss strolled into the conversation. The discussion of marriage and girlfriends shifted to an interesting practice he witnessed in Bahrain. Due to Muslim law forbidding sex outside of marriage, the brothels in Bahrain employ priests who will "marry" the night's couple and divorce them after consummation. It's an interesting way to avoid the sin of fornication. Ramin informed us that Afghanistan does not allow such tomfoolery (he didn't use that exact word), but desperate men will cross into Iran for similar ceremonies. It was in this discussion of Afghan sexual cultural that we discovered I had completely misunderstood Ramin's apparently platonic usage of the word "girlfriend."

Though a little embarrassed at the thought of many mistresses, I'm quite sure he relished the thought for just a second or two. I admit my mistake, but our best conversations just wouldn't happen without a little misunderstanding.[†]

As the other day, when Ramin expressed some fear of Taliban reprisals in the region. It had been publicized, he told me, that they had put a price on his head.

> "500,000 for an interpreter! They are angry that we help the Americans…"

"500,000? Wow. That's a lot of money Ramin…" I paused to eye him for a second. "And where would I have to take you?"

> "You would turn me in to Taliban?"

"I'm a poor man, Ramin, I could use that money... besides, they'll just assign me a new interpreter."

"And you are not worried I would turn you in? They are offering 10,000 dollars for Americans too!"

"10,000 for me, 500,000 for you? Who do you think they want more? If you took me there, I would turn around and act like I brought you, and they would reward me!"

"You are right about this. If you and I were walking down the street and a Taliban saw us, if he had only one bullet he would use it on me. They hate us more for helping"

"Ramin, he'd shoot at you anyway. He'd waste that bullet shooting at my body armor."

"This is true, I do not have protection. This is why I should have a gun."

"Have you ever used a gun?"

"No...I am not allowed."

"Then I will feel safer if you continue not to have a gun, Ramin. Especially if I have to turn you in to the Taliban."

It was only later, when I was telling The Coolman about our new plan to get rich, I found out that Ramin had meant 500,000 Afghani—which, at a 50-1 conversion rate, right about equals $10,000 US. My plan was doomed to failure. *However...* The Coolman pointed out, we could round up a whole bunch of interpreters to turn in. Then we would make some money.

Besides, they'll just issue us some more anyway.

....

[†] *Editor's note: Not actually a mistake.*

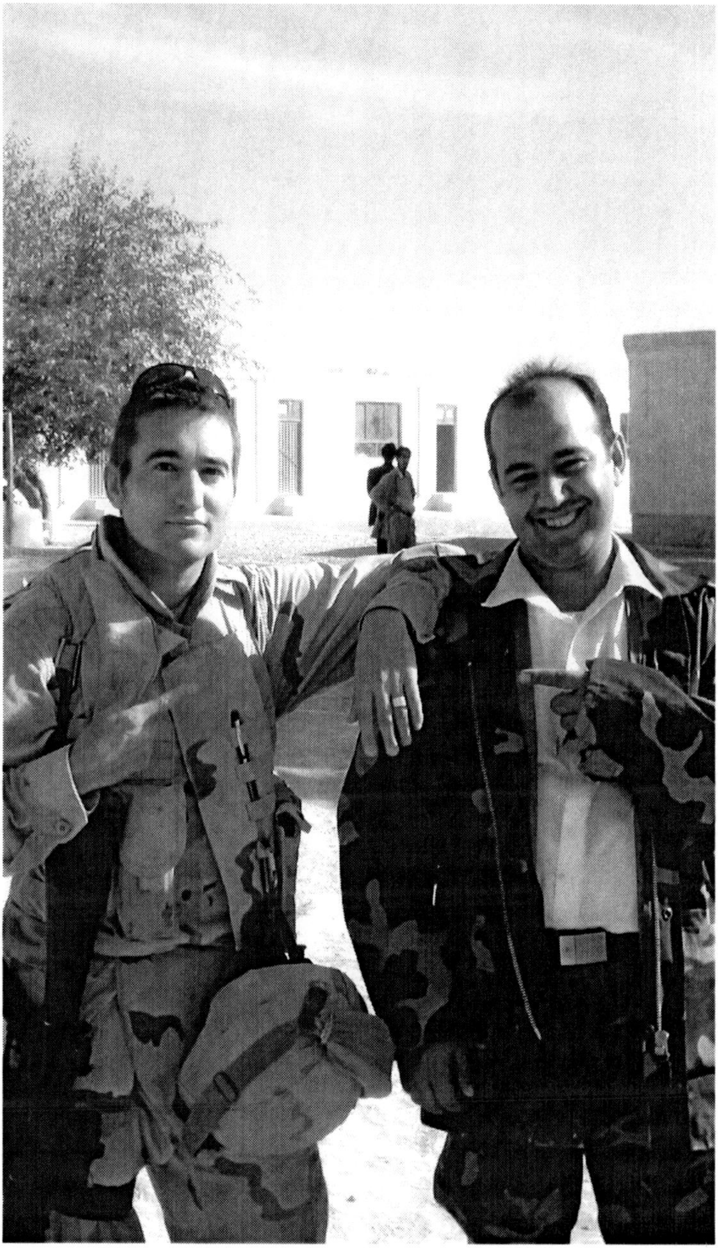

A LIFE AWAY

1 July

*THERE ARE GOOD DAYS AND THERE ARE BAD DAYS,
BUT YOU CAN'T REALLY TELL THEM APART...*

Each day blends into the next where their beginnings are muted semi-awakenings and their ends are missed somehow in the repetitive continuation of it all. The sun seems to shine ever whether through darkened glass or thin eyelids. Sleep is likewise not realized, though it must occur here and there, I'm sure. The calendar turns occasionally, but it is difficult to relate to reality as we mix our daily schedules with attempts to connect home. While you sleep, we are working. The NYSE opens at dinnertime, extra-inning baseball games stretch into breakfast. Straddling this duality of time seems only to accomplish a certain weightlessness. We have no roots.

There are no weekends, per se. Without the anchor of a traditional Saturday and Sunday, wayfinding within the week quickly becomes unbounded. Friday is a holy day for the Afghanis, so we typically are allowed that day free. It is mostly used as a catch-up time—catch up on rest, on email, on whatever has been pushed to the wayside during the endless work week. It comes and goes surreptitiously, in such that once you realized it arrived, it has gone.

Current manpower reflects the low priority our distant outpost represents. We each do the work that was recently the job of two or three predecessors. And more cuts threaten us with greater workloads. The swell of Military Might drifts southward, and though we count the blessing of relative safety, we become increasingly harried in this modulating environment. When danger does present, we stretch ourselves thin to compensate. When daily operations multiply, we double our efforts to keep up the status quo. There has been little free time.

When we do manage to steal respite at the same time as one another, the roommates and I play heated battles of Spades on a requisitioned table (it was quite clearly a spindle of Kuwaiti-made steel cable in a former life). Mr. Boatright, my ever competent partner in cards, comes alive in these competitions. Taunts and bickers fly between him and the man he's christened "Nervous" [Dwight]. It's rather entertaining, and it does distract our foes consistently enough to keep our winning percentage high. There are all kind of rules I don't remember using back when I wasted away class-time in the back row of high school religion class: Blinds and Nils and Two for Tens and Double-Secret-Around-the-Back-Big-Joker-Surprise (I may have made the last one up). But the competition is fierce, and the games are bona-fide events. Such as it were.

Though we have stolen a DVD player from a conference room (in the confusion of the turnover), we seldom have time for full-length movies. Instead, we have all grown a mutual addiction to the classic maneuverings of the 80's icon Macgyver. This is not a joke. Johnny U packed along Season One in his personal matters, and it was quickly adopted by us all. Every few nights we gather with our care-package junk food and predict plotlines.

"Okay, that line's going to break and all the bomb-defusing tools are going to drop into the ocean and he'll have to make something up.. maybe with a drinking straw...and...and...some bubble gum wrappers!"

—*SNAP!*—

It would be a phenomenal drinking game, were we permitted drinks.

As we watch the remaining episodes dwindle, we beg Johnny U
like sniveling addicts, "When's your wife sending Season Two?!"
These are the major diversions... in smaller stolen
moments we individually read, write, or sometimes
race cars on little portable game screens.

~

The food here is not the best, and generally worse than expected.
Particularly for a vegetarian, who must creatively compile meals
from meager offerings. Breakfasts do usually offer fresh fruit
and bagels, and are far and away the bright spot in my diet.

And for some odd reason, The Coolman and Johnny
U have sworn off meat for July. Apparently, I was
some sort of perverse inspiration. They assured me
it wasn't anything serious, they are just bored.

These are what pass for solid reasons in
the middle of the Afghan desert.

The accommodations, too, are slightly less than stellar. The
four of us, plus two temporary additions during the RIP, share
what is essentially a plywood shack. We've done what we can,
but in the end, it is still, undeniably and emphatically, a plywood
shack. I'm told the fire rating is somewhere south of five minutes.
To the ground in twelve. I think they are rather optimistic.

But, on the bright side, KBR[†] received an ungodly amount of
money to build them, so all is still right with the world.

The toilets and showers are plastic and temporary. Unfortunately,
"temporary" means something entirely different here. We
share these particular facilities with about 100 other
gentlemen, and we apologize daily to each other for earlier
complaints of cold showers. With the heat of the day rising
into the 120's now, the water in the reservoir reaches hellish
temperatures. I wish for cold showers. Though of course,
I will recant and deny when the snow starts falling...

There are really only two things that sustain
us here. The food is not one of them.

The first is satisfaction in working directly with the
Afghanis. Whether it is soldiers, civilians, or children, it is
easy to feel as though we are making a difference in their
lives. It is a very important thing to feel purpose. I'm not
so sure our brethren in Iraq are so lucky in this regard.

The second lifeblood is in our fleeting reconnects home. A
short call or an email makes all the difference in the world. I
live for the moments I can talk to the lady about her day, or
hear from my parents about how the horses and dogs are doing.
For oh-so-temporary seconds, you can feel almost home. It
is a sensation I don't believe I could ever adequately describe,
though I imagine every deployed servicemember understands.

I stared at pictures, yesterday, that had come in a care package
from home. The lady and I were waist deep in the blue-green
Gulf, off of Florida, fishing for some trophy dinner. I tried to
remember what it was like to hold her. I tried to remember what
that touch feels like... but it is so far from here, and I struggled.
I struggled, trying to capture that intimacy in my brain, to will
my skin to recreate sensations, to will myself back home.

But home is a life away from this place, and so hard to feel a part of.

....

[†] *Editor's note: Kellogg Brown & Root, subidiary of Mr. Cheney's Halliburton, and sole contractor for the bulk of troop-support services for the majority of the Afghanistan occupation. Such were the margins that a line-cook in a FOB dining facility could make upwards of 100,000 USD yearly, plus bonuses—multiples more than his equivalent military number. The heavy reliance on KBR and other service contractors (estimated at 60% total manpower in country) was ostensibly to reduce the war's cost.*

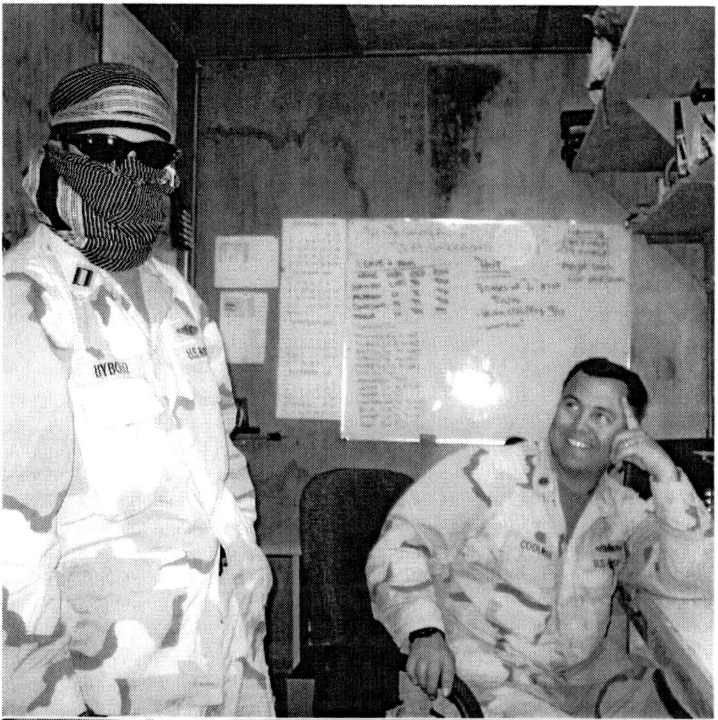

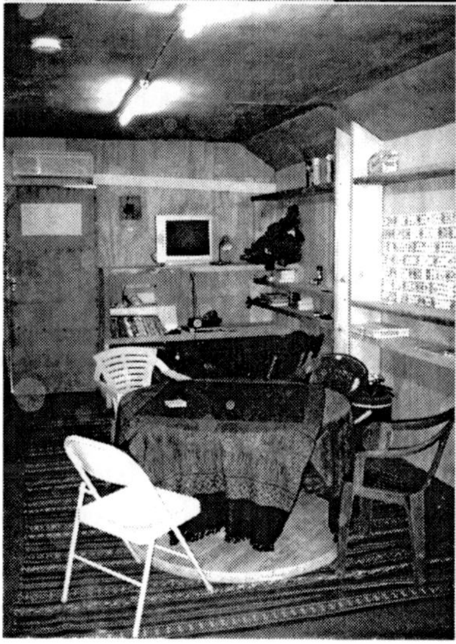

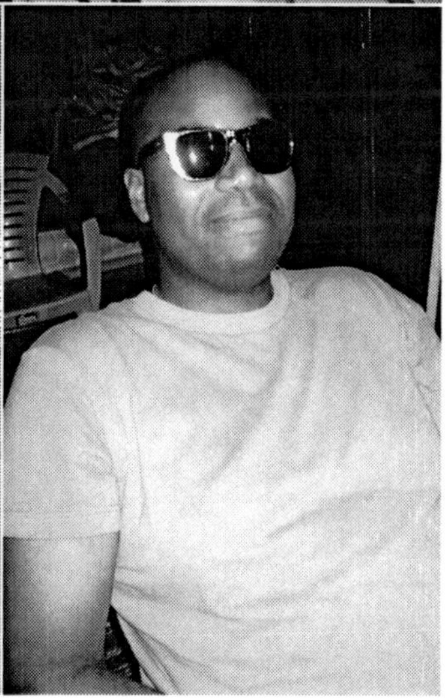

HAPPY INDEPENDENCE DAY TO YOUR COUNTRY

4 July

Ramin's wife is sick. Some time ago she was diagnosed with rheumatism. It flares up regularly, relegating her to the bed for extended periods of time.

She is only 22 years old.

Yesterday, while we were out mentoring in the ANA (Afghan National Army) camp, Ramin's cell phone rang. I could overhear a female voice on the other end. My Dari is thus far fairly limited, so all I could pick up was worry in the conversation.

"Is it your wife?"

> "Yes, sir... she is sick. Our friend will take her to the doctor this afternoon."

"Call her back."

> "What for?"

"Because you are taking her to the doctor."

> "It is alright, she knows I need to be here working with you."

"Ramin, call your wife and tell her you are on your way home. She needs you more than I do. And when you get back from the doctor, tell her you'll be staying home to watch the girls tomorrow so that she can rest."

> "You do not need me tomorrow?"

"Tomorrow's a holiday, I've decided that we aren't working."

"An American holiday?"

"It's our Independence Day."

"Ok, I see... Thank you sir...."

~

Afghanistan's Independence Day was 19 August, 1919. Like the US, they relieved themselves of British control. The next few decades were spent on a reasonable path to modernity, and by the 1960's the country was as progressive and prosperous as most any other nation at the time. In the 1970's it all started going to hell, first with some internal uprisings and then the Soviet's attempts at occupation. A decade was spent at war. When the Soviets eventually recognized their personal Vietnam and pulled out, a vacuum of sorts was left. The successful Mujahedin fighters fractioned regionally, and began to war amongst themselves for control of the nation. Civil war engulfed the country and stretched into the nineties, with no one group resolving uncontested power. In '94, an outsider group seized upon the situation, as the Russians had once attempted. The Pakistani-backed (and, lest we forget, American-backed) Taliban factions won out over the home-grown Mujahedin in most areas of the country and seized control, which they held on to rather tenuously until 2001.

The years since, though sparkled with direct military action, have been an exercise in reconstruction—rebuilding infrastructure and culture in a permanent fashion, and replacing the day-to-day survival ethos that has been necessary over the past two and a half decades.

Part of this is in crafting a functioning, standing military. Sustaining no longer regional militias, but a National Army, much like our own nation did as part of its transition from former-colony to recognized player on the global field. While the pacifist in me might reject out of hand this goal, I do understand the purpose. If this country can produce a functioning unified organization, it is a beacon of permanence and a reason for pride.

Moreover, I hope our work in the governmental organizations, in the police forces, in the communities, and in our day-to-day interactions with individuals, will provide ever more examples of functional permanence. And by "our" I mean the International community, for we are not alone in our efforts here.

I have allies here locally in my dream of Afghani self-sufficiency. I am blessed to be working with a person, in Colonel Atta, who has made that his personal goal in his sphere of influence. My interpreter, too, and his colleagues share this idealism. That is why they are here... well, that, and to feed their families.

I pray for a new Afghanistan Independence, that they will someday soon be independent of the graft and corruption that bind their organizations. I pray that they will someday soon be free of the chains of poverty and disease that shackle the lives of their people. And I pray that, ultimately, they may be free of us.

~

This morning my phone rang. It was Ramin.

> "My wife has told me to call you to say 'thank you' and to tell you *'Happy Independence Day to your country'* from our whole family."

I didn't know quite how to respond to that, though it did make me smile....

Perhaps someday soon, I can make that same telephone call to him.

RIVER CITY

6 July

The day after Independence Day was anything but
free... Communications were locked down for just over
26 hours. No phones, no email, no internet, no contact
whatsoever with the outside world. It is, of course,
very frustrating to have such connections removed, and
mutual feelings of isolation are accordingly amplified.

Many could not even work—those dependent on internet or
email for their day-to-day jobs sat idly by awaiting reconnect. A
number of these, I'm sure, whiled away many minutes mindlessly
tapping F5, waiting for some important website to come online.
I know I did, and I don't even need the net to do my job.

My work is fairly analog and local: consult with
the ANA Engineering Office and build shit at the
carpentry woodshop. Most everyone else, however,
saw their productivity come to a distinct halt.

It was reminiscent of those all too numerous Louisiana summer
afternoons where the electricity up and decides to take the rest
of the day off. The first two or five minutes, most everyone
pauses to wait for the power to reconnect. When it becomes clear
that it has no intention of doing so, they gradually drift outside
onto porches and the street and reconnect with the neighbors.
Impromptu block parties break out. Problem forgotten.

But that was New Orleans. Five minutes
is all it takes to shift priorities.

No such luck here. Those that drifted out of
makeshift offices simply appeared lost, and certainly
were not on their way to the corner pub.

Instead, a general air of confused frustration took hold. Isolated pockets of complaint arose, but quickly died. There are typically only two reasons for a gag order. When a sensitive operation is underway, comms are often silenced to prevent any security hiccup. Scattered grumblings among the troops are a common result.

Such lamentations quickly dissipate if this
is not the impetus for the order.

Not being able to call home suddenly seems very
trite when it is realized that someone else won't be
going home. And home doesn't know yet.

~

The military may not exhibit much concern for its live soldiers, but their dead are awarded commensurate respect. When next of kin cannot be located quickly and notified personally, the entirety of casual communication is put on hold until that family can be found. No one should have to lose a loved one to war, but still worse to discover that fact on the evening news.

~

The assignment of Afghan-network mobile phones to critical personnel does poke some small holes in the otherwise watertight policy, which I broke to sneak a message of explanation to the lady. No need for her to worry whilst we all waited on the delivery of someone else's terrible news.

I'm safe, we're all ok here... but somebody's not coming home, baby...

They're not coming home...and nobody knows it yet.

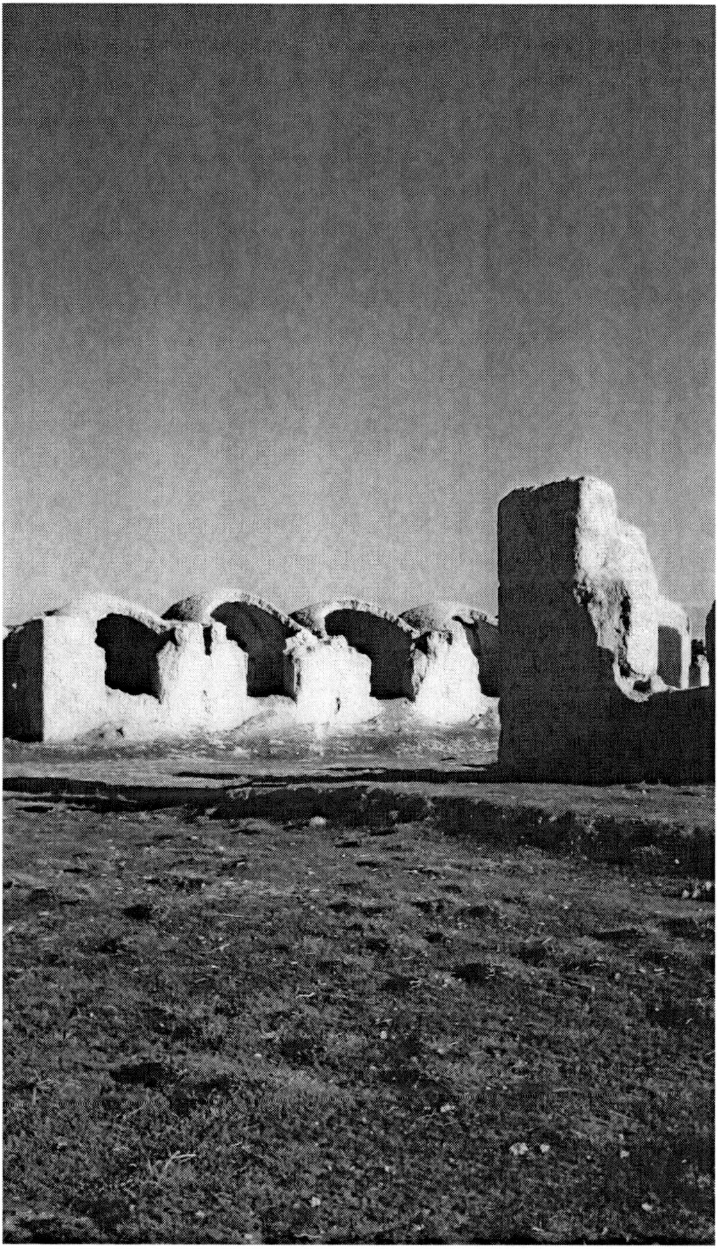

KELLER'S WOOD SHOP

8 July

Afghanistan is indebted to one David Keller of Chattanooga, Tennessee. They may not know it yet, but the nation owes him just the same.

He started with a few borrowed tools and a pair of local carpenters and built his wood shop in the middle of the desert. Drawing on his 30 years of carpentry experience, he worked side by side with these two apprentices, improving their expertise and their confidence. He recruited a few ANA soldiers and a few more eager civilians into the mix, and each day they worked together building skills and building a shop.

At a time when most of his Army colleagues were shying away from the local populace, David was visiting his workers in their homes, shopping for tools with them downtown, and teaching them everything he could about woodworking. Sounding something akin to a Dixie Mr. Rogers, he pleasantly bantered with his guys all day long. Though his syrupy drawl may not have been well understood, his sentiments were always clear.

When he introduced me to the workers, his confidence and affection were clear. I was told all about each man's family and what great workers they all were. It was not so much an employee introduction, but as if I was meeting his foster kids.

"This is Zuman... he's not much of a talker, but he's an excellent woodworker...huh, Zuman, you don't like to say much, do you?" After interpretation is made, Zuman dips his head and blushes a bit. He is quite a large man, but he is trying very hard to be invisible.

"Now Rahim, he's an electrician first. Then a carpenter. But Monan is a carpenter, and then an electrician…" And so on and so forth, while the men stand about somewhat sheepishly, their faces looking for all the world like kids about to be handed from the 2nd grade teacher to the 3rd.

~

There was no replacement scheduled for David, a fact which worried him. Because of that vacuum, interim ownership of the shop defaulted to me, as the "Garrison Engineer." I tried for three weeks to find a willing shop foreman among the arriving Army personnel. I made little headway.

During this time, I saw the payoff from David's efforts. Despite my absence from day-to-day operations, the shop continued to produce. And produce surprising quality.

When it became clear that the Army was not going to assist me in this endeavor, I called the workers together.

(I must confess that I fancied myself the football coach at halftime, issuing a moving speech about overcoming great odds, with each player's attention snapped in to my delivery. The surreal part of it was, my workers were visibly hanging on each word, as if the words could mean something before Ramin translated them. Odd. I can't say whether it was them sensing importance, or acting the part from politeness… but I digress)

Through my interpreter, I explained to them that there was no help coming. What was a temporary arrangement was now permanent.

However, I said, I think I have a shop foreman. Two, in fact.

My first official act as new boss was to hand out two promotions. Raheem and Monan, David's original carpenters, were now in charge.

~

Each morning I drive out the front gate to pick up my
workers. The five of them sit waiting at the ruins that separate
Dehdadi from the ANA camp, two sets of brothers (Monan
and Qasir, Rahim and Kasim) and Zuman. After the Afghan
soldiers search them, they pack the cab like a Tokyo metro.

Sohba-khai! Good Morning!

Inside the gate, a few of my apprentice soldiers jump in the bed
of the truck and we navigate the American checkpoint. They all
dismount and join the long line of civilian workers being searched
before entering the base. I sit back in the Ranger and wish it had
a radio. It's not much of a truck—and David did a good job of
banging up the nicer parts—but it's much better than no truck
at all. Most things in Afghanistan must be viewed in this light.

Once they and the truck are searched, we can enter the first
gate of the American compound (second gate, so far). Then
we turn into the interpreter village to add one more, because
there just aren't enough people hanging off the little pickup.
Most mornings I have to send someone to go wake up Ramin
(he's an important man, you see, so he is often asleep).

Habari now chist? What's happening?

Fully loaded, and then some, we roll our Beverly Hillbilly
jalopy through yet another checkpoint (2nd American,
3rd overall) of which I have yet to divine the purpose.
Once, though, one of the guards did flag me down to
ask if he could come by later and borrow a drill.

We open up the shop together, and Ramin and I discuss the days
work with the foremen, prioritizing projects and assigning them
accordingly. They'll bring up questions, and I normally bounce
them back. "Ask Monan how he wants to approach it..."

Ah... *Nazaré Auli Hast.* That's an excellent solution. *Sais.* Alright.

I have a few motivations for pawning off decisions. One, I'd rather not bother with edicts if I don't need to (this is the selfish reason). Two, I'd rather encourage self-sufficiency – it only helps them in the long run (this is the humanitarian reason). And three, they already know what they want to do anyway and are only asking out of misguided respect and politeness (this is the pragmatic reason).

Beeya-kay korra shoro koneem! Let's get to work!

The other motivational pull is that I have to get to my other full-time job.

Ramin and I will spend a few hours discussing business with Colonel Atta in ANA land, and then return to the shop by noon.

Nani Chasht? Goeshna Shadém... Lunch? I'm hungry...

I drop the soldiers outside the American gate, so they can eat at the ANA cafeteria. Ramin, Monan, Raheem, and sometimes myself, will eat at the interpreter dining hall. Their food is catered from a local restaurant, and with basmati rice and fresh fruit, it's a fair bit better than any other offerings around here.

Afternoons are spent between the shop and the office; emails, paperwork, planning, or laboring on some large project some random General volunteered off the cuff on some random visit and left for me to do.

At a quarter of four, I'll wander back into the middle of the shop.

Beeya-kay pak koneem...workshop basta shawad!
Let's clean up, the workshop is closed!

It is a completely unnecessary announcement, but everyone is so pleased I'm trying to learn the language that they don't mind being instructed to do things they're already doing anyway.

Everyone re-piles into the jalopy and we head back out through gate 3, gate 2, drop the soldiers off, and out gate 1. Packed in the seat behind me, their mood is always light on the ride home. And they're normally giggling about something or other. *Koon Kati Koon Kati*, the chorus cries today in laughter.

"They are making fun of Zuman and his large ass, it takes up two seats and crowds everyone out!" Ramin dutifully informs me.

A ways down the road, I pull off to let everyone out.

Khodafez! Fardo mebinem! Goodbye, see you tomorrow!

They all shake hands goodbye ("Everyone loves to shake hands," David told me more than a few times). And then they hop the wall into Dehdadi, disappearing over the adobe line. Tomorrow we'll do it again, and it won't be all that much different.

I'm really little more than a uniformed taxi
service, all things considered.

~

The workers have taken the changes (and the extra responsibility) in stride. I was left with a well-oiled machine, and the mark of my predecessor's work is in how well it all functions in his absence. But this is not simply a place to produce carpentry projects. What he started means self-sufficiency for these men—food for their families today, and a promising future tomorrow. That is the real responsibility I was handed.

"Keep trying to expand the shop the best you can..."
he asked me. I promised him I would.

David's back in Tennessee, and the shop is now mine. But the sign above the door still reads "Keller's Wood Shop," and as far as I'm concerned, it always will.

WE HAVE TO HAVE A PLAN

12 July

People often ask me how applicable my Architectural training is to the work I do for the Navy. I readily answer that it is not. Not at all.

This is not entirely true. There was one immensely valuable skill for management I picked up during those years:

"Instant Justification."

In architecture schools around the world, promising young students are regularly thrown to the wolves as acceptable practice. They've worked for weeks perfecting the design of some odd commercial building (a public bathhouse, say, or a columbarium, even), slaved over models and drawings, burned through six trees' worth of buff paper. They haven't slept in a week and they haven't eaten real food since Thursday two weeks past. But this morning, much like a morning three weeks prior, and another morning to come three weeks hence, they pin up their pride and joy and attempt to explain to said wolves what on earth they were thinking. Then, one of the more clever wolves will cleverly pose what is obviously a very clever question to demonstrate how very clever he, in fact, is.

"Why is the maintenance closet door here," he'll stand up and point for emphasis, "and not…. heeere?" At which point, he'll scrunch up his face in deliberation, pause for effect, and slowly regain his folding throne, awaiting the answer.

The difference between the prodigy and the "hard-worker" lies in this moment. It is not, as one might think, actually found within the project.

Where the hard-worker is caught surprised, and stammers some explanation, the prodigy smiles as if she's been waiting for this very question. Turning on a dime, she reinvents the entire project to center on the question at hand (*As you can see from the plan, my design anticipates the circulation paths of all important users, starting with the janitor...*). And she'll do it again to answer the next. Instant Justification.

The seasoned Architecture student can Instant Justify in his or her sleep, and often does (one is not necessarily awake during one's presentations). This ability to requisition an explanation from one's nether regions without blinking only gets better with practice, and plenty of opportunity is available in academia.

~

I've often heard people marvel, "it's funny how a plan comes together." But this exclamation isn't entirely accurate. Plans are more often invented on the fly based on the most abstract of ideas when one is forced without warning in front of an audience desperate to hear a formulated "Plan." It is at once debated, modified, debated again, modified for the purpose of additional debate, added to, taken away from so that other things can be added, argued over, agreed over, argued over again, modified once more for good luck, and set in stone. Then, once everyone is satisfied, the people who must carry out the plan can toss it aside and get to work.

Such was the context that turned an amorphous request for the construction of various interior walls in various ANA buildings into a town hall meeting with me at the pulpit. The leading NCO's from the Kandaks, Corps, and Garrison anxiously awaited the marvelous plan Colonel Ata and I had put together (not knowing that he and I had merely discussed loose objectives). Random inspirations and aspirations bounced together within my brain and coalesced into something surprisingly coherent.

"

I want 8 Afghan soldiers—two from each kandak—nominated to be carpenter apprentices. My senior carpenters will head up two teams of workers, and the soldiers will be split between them.

(break for translation)

We will start with a "test wall," at the Garrison building. This will give us a good estimate of how much wood will be required per wall, how much time each wall will require, and generally lay out the process. My carpenters will build this first wall, and the soldiers will observe the process.

(break for translation)

Next, the Facilities Engineering office—Colonel Ata—can field the various requests for walls and we can generate a prioritized list. Taking this list and the estimates from our test wall, we can put together a schedule and order materials through the ANA supply system.

(break for translation)

In the end we will have completed a substantial project that is planned by the ANA Facilities Engineering office, supplied by the ANA supply system, and constructed by ANA soldiers and Afghan nationals. We will have an entirely Afghan product, and we will have trained a whole set of soldiers in carpentry, to boot.

(break for translation)

"

The table nodded in agreement.

Colonel Ata stood and addressed the group. He re-laid out the plan I had just retrieved from my rectum, adding more specifics on the portion he and I would collaborate on. He also took my national pride angle and ran with it (as I hoped he would, it is one of his favorite topics).

The table nodded in agreement.

There were some satisfied murmurings. A few sidebars developed where mini-plans of action were discussed for others' respective portions.

The American mentors congratulated our master plan, and thanked Colonel Ata for his presence. The meeting had the definite scent of adjournment, and I marveled at how easy it all had been.

But a question of dissent came from the corner...

(break for translation)

> "The U.S. Embedded Training Team leader, Colonel Geren, promised us he would build this walls for us. We would not have to use ANA wood. Since he is now gone, it is your responsibility to fulfill his promise."

It was all I could do to keep my composure. Army "leadership" loves to throw out decisions without considering ramifications. Why not promise a huge project on your way out the door? It was not as if my level of respect for the man could drop any further, but the fact that this ignorant backwoods bubba was still throwing thorns in my side while he sat comfortably on his porch back home in the Ozarks made me absolutely livid.

I'd like to think I hid it well.

"

*I don't know what Mister Geren may have promised.
I'm not him. And he's not here anymore.*

(break for translation)

And it isn't the point. Certainly, we could waltz in here and build you 20 walls over the next few months. But what about the 21st wall, or the 40th? How do those get built?

(break for translation)

In eleven months, I will be back home. I'm not staying here, the United States isn't staying here. This is your country, what will you do when we are gone?

(break for translation)

At the end of this project, you could have 20 walls and that's it. Or, at the end of this project, you could have the ability to build walls for yourself. Which is better?

(break for translation)

My job, and the job of these other Americans, is to teach you. Not to give you hand outs. I aim to use this project to teach, otherwise it has no value to me. Otherwise, I have no reason to do it.

(break for translation)

"

Agreeable murmurs.

But the voice of dissent returns. He doesn't believe the ANA
supply can get the wood, he doesn't believe the project will get
finished if dependent on it. And, as I come to realize, he is very
concerned because his bosses (ANA Generals) are very concerned.

Colonel Ata reads my frustration. He fields the reply, emphasizing
that this is an opportunity towards self-sufficiency. What
departed American Colonels may or may not have promised
is immaterial in the face of such an opportunity. This
evolves into a sermon on such, culminating with a plea, née,
demand for responsibility now for purposes of the future.

The mood of the room falls behind him, and
the meeting is completed on this note.

I couldn't have said it better. Truly, I couldn't have
said it at all, my Dari just isn't that good yet.

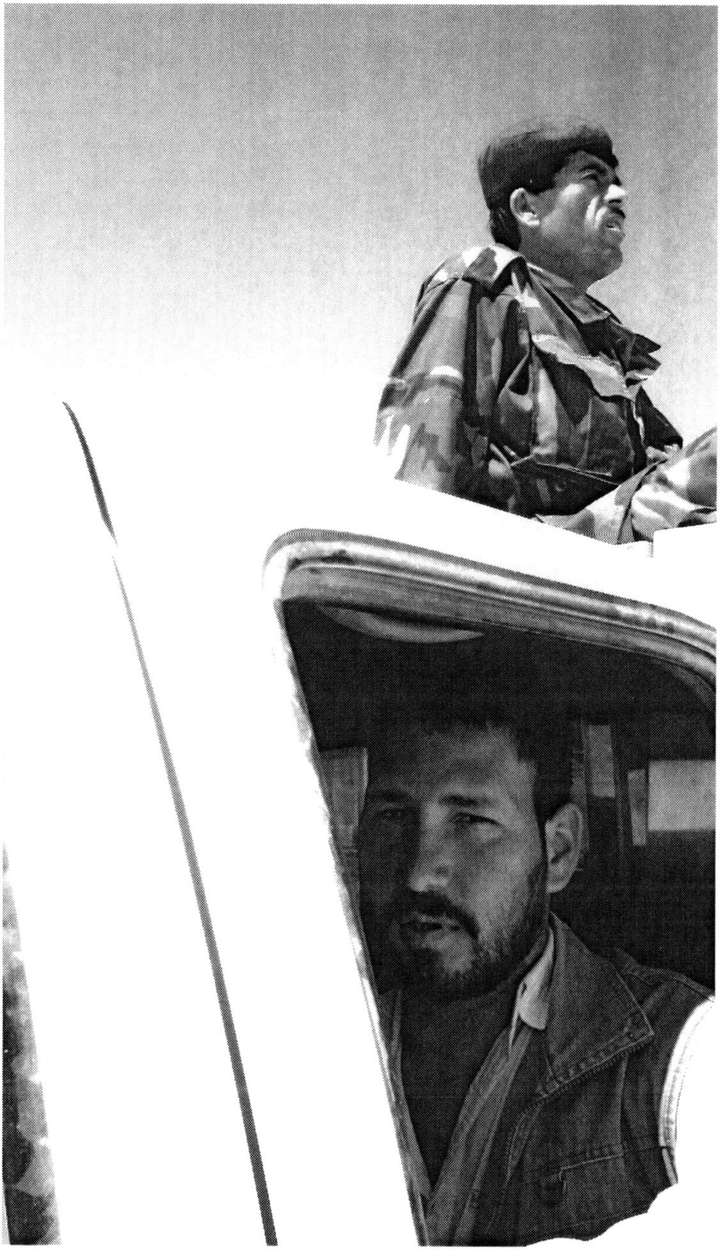

PUTTING THE SHOW ON THE ROAD

17 July

Pleasantries and planning completed, it was
time to toss both aside and get to work.

We headed out in the Ranger to conquer our first wall,
loaded up with 20 sheets of plywood, a bundle of 2X4's,
half the shop's tools, 5 carpenters, 2 soldiers, an interpreter,
and myself. It is not a large truck. However, the Afghanis
have a marvelous talent for over-utilization.

Our first location proved to be a difficult one — not so much
from a carpentry standpoint, but for the surrounding uniformed
environment. The large room in most dire need of partitioning
walls (housing a computer classroom, a training classroom, a
radio room, and an office in a single open space) was located
in the center of the Garrison Headquarters building. Damn
near every ANA officer and NCO on post passes through this
building at some point during the day. Or, they happen to
have their offices there. Not unlike their American military
counterparts, these festooned men have a wealth of opinion on
any subject, particularly whichever one happens to be at hand.

Worse still, the ANA Garrison Commander had his office directly
across the hall from our work area. Colonel Jabar is aiming
for General's stars I am sure, for the magnitude of unfounded
opinion he dispenses could fill a hundred Britannica sets.
Fortunately, the market for such preponderance is rather slim.

Needless to say — though I will — there was
constant interference on the job site.

Safety codes require that rooms over a certain occupancy and/or square footage must have more than one means of egress. This fairly sensible rule is intended to prevent people from being trapped if someone has inadvertently set the exit door on fire.

The ANA officers are a territorial lot (another similarity between them and their U.S. counterparts), and are apparently quite threatened by doors. No less than 18 individuals interrupted the proceedings to query, "why is that door there? We don't need a door."

To the first few helpful gentlemen I patiently explained the concept behind the safety code. Some seemed enlightened, others remarked that they would just lock the door after it was installed. By early afternoon, Ramin and my carpenters were dutifully reciting my explanation in chorus, again and again, without needing any prompting from me.

Jabar was particularly adamant about a no-door policy, which he distilled into a succinct twenty-minute Dari diatribe. At the end of which, Ramin simply looked at me and drolly summarized, "he also asks about the door." Then he turned back to dutifully explain its existence. Having received the answer, Jabar confidently exclaimed to the room that a door was absolutely necessary. He then commanded me to continue with the installation of the door.

Then he requested two more walls with doors in them.

~

We started the first day with eight new soldiers (in addition to my own two apprentices). Three were unable to find their way back after lunch. Two more wandered off somewhere between constructing wall one and wall two. Another hasn't yet returned from the restroom. By the time we finished the third wall, we were down to two new soldiers.

Colonel Ata surmised this as such, "These two remaining soldiers are hungry to learn, and they will be successful. The others are lazy and will never learn, no matter how much you try to teach them. Do not trouble yourself over these useless ones, we will find others who hunger to learn."

(This defeatist-optimism of Ata is quite intriguing to me.)

~

Despite all efforts to the contrary, the construction went quite smoothly. Three walls completed in three days, all with handcrafted doors courtesy of Zuman's efforts.

Proud of my guys, I had them all stand in front of the completed "test wall" so I could snap a picture. Fortuitously, Colonel Jabar strolled in to check on our progress at just that moment. Not one to resist a photo-op, he worked his way into the lineup, removed his uniform top (presumably to match the appearance of the workers), and mugged for the camera as if he were an integral part of the whole process. Which, I'm sure, he believed he was.

He will make a phenomenal General.

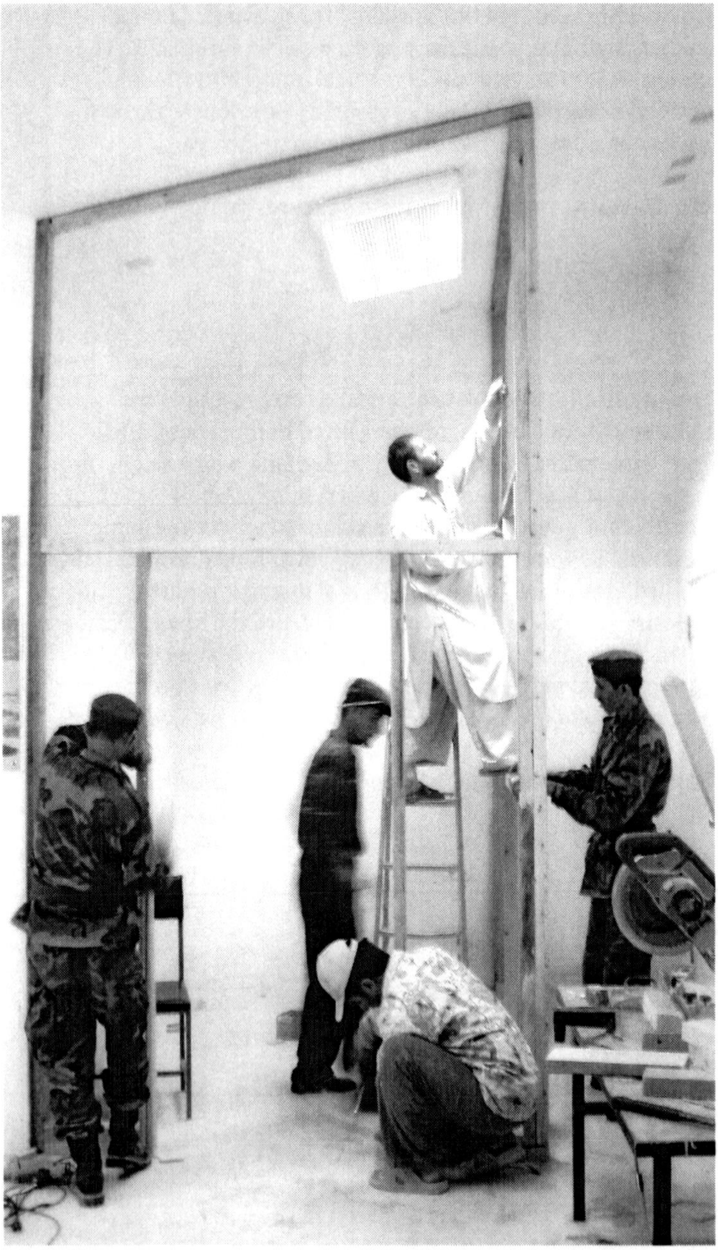

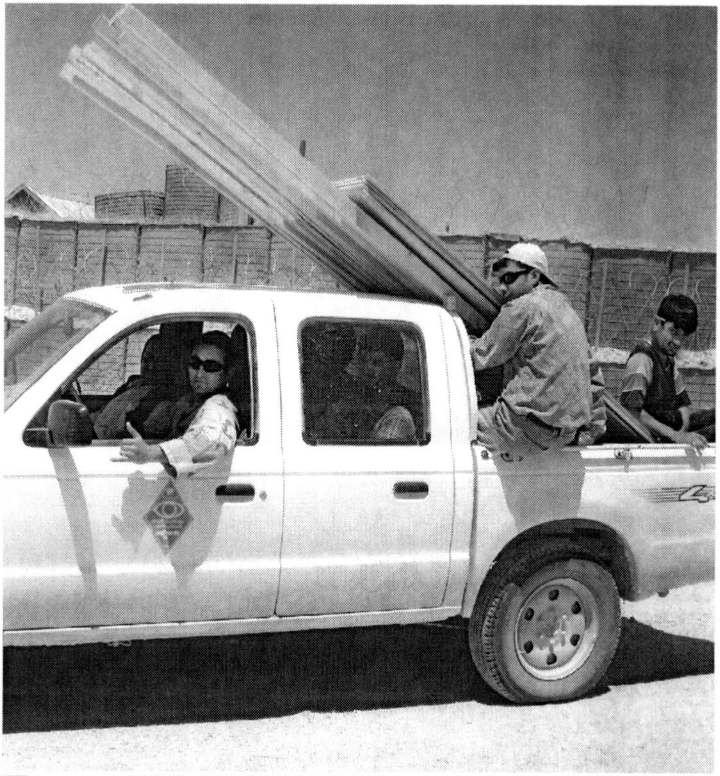

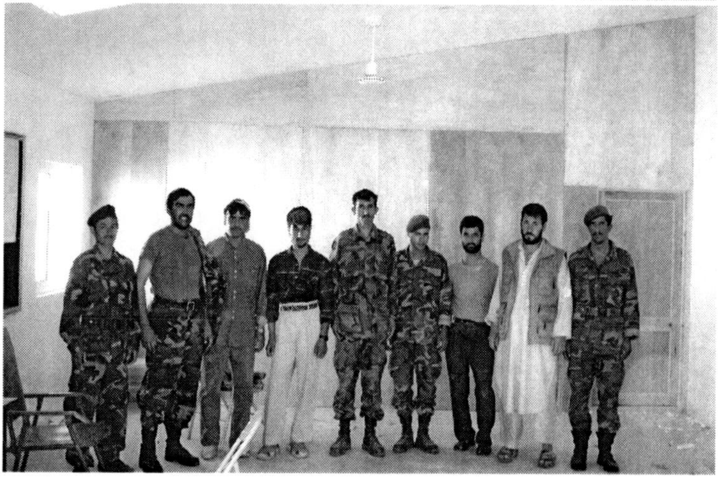

SHOPPING FOR THE SURREAL

22 July

In normal life, trips are delayed by things like weather, illness, or any number of perfectly normal interruptions. Here, plans get cancelled by bicycle bombs exploding on the city block we were supposed to be headed to.

Planning a shopping trip takes on an entirely different character when one must wait for routes to turn from "black" to "green" on the tactical map.

After four days of cancellations and delays, when it had become abundantly clear that we would not be heading out any time in the foreseeable future, The Coolman and I had our lunches interrupted by the news that we were cleared to go. In 45 minutes. Such is the miracle of the Army's probability scale, where sure things never happen and 12% odds guarantee a go.

Kudos to The Coolman for quickly rounding up a pair of Humvees and a Ranger pickup full of ANA soldiers (that's why he's "Ops" and I just tell people to build things). We managed to make it out the gate at more or less the assigned time, despite some technical troubles with Army communications gadgetry.

Our first stop was at an appliance store, where one of our number needed to purchase refrigerators for the base's makeshift Exchange (open 2 hours a week, and stocked with soap, shampoo, and everything in between). Coincidentally, the shop happened to be on the very same block as the exploded bicycle from three days prior. I dutifully examined the wreckage two doors down. It was as if the entire façade of the building had been ripped off by some belligerent Kong relative. Remnants of concrete beams hung limply at the ends of dangling rebar. Shards of glass filled the interior where streetwalkers combed the debris for salvageable bits.

While The Coolman looked on, I queried Ramin,
"So this is where the bomb went off?"

Ramin chatted for a moment with a somewhat-
friendly looking transient taking refuge in the hulks
shadow. He turned back to us, with a slight grin.

"Actually, it is that building across the street where the bomb
exploded... This building's condition is their own fault."

~

About ten minutes later, the three of us were following a
particularly enthusiastic sergeant into what appeared to be a
swapmeet crammed inside a tenant-home basement tossed
inside a parking garage. Underneath a subway. Through
steel grates above and below, the light patterns and noises
from foot traffic informed us that whatever we were in, we
were in the middle of many levels of it. On our left and right,
vendors occupied closet-sized cubbyholes, each crammed so
tightly with thousands of boxes of electrical paraphernalia they
appeared wallpapered. Wandering this cacophonic maze while
the sergeant debated the price of light bulbs, I turned a corner
and suddenly found myself outside on an idyllic side street. A
couple of boys rode by on ancient bicycles, trailed on foot by
a few others not so lucky. Old bearded men shuffled down
the alley, pulling old wooden carts piled with watermelons.

I stood there for a few minutes breathing in the scene...
until deciding that my armored, camouflaged, weaponed self
was demeaning it. It is an odd feeling engaging the surreal,
especially as you realize it is you that makes it that way.

Roughly one year ago I walked down a desolate Bourbon
Street, in the middle of a deserted New Orleans, seven
days after Hurricane Katrina. At my right was my good
friend Glen; we were both dressed in Navy issue forest
greens. I remember thinking what a peculiarly colored
splotch we must have made on the gray-toned scene.

I now find myself in these thoughts regularly.

~

Late afternoon found us finally where we needed to be, in the hardware alley. It looked strangely like a farmer's market, only with baskets of nails and door handles where one might expect tomatoes and cucumbers. Knock-off grinders and circular saws hung from overhead with Japanese brand names pasted upon their Chinese-made bodies.[†] I imagined it would take hours to sift through the rows of wares, but my carpenter Monan guided us quickly through the bustling bazaar. Ignoring the colorful displays, he led us to a corner shop with a "trustworthy owner."

And then we walked onto the set of a *Tool Time Christmas*.™

While The Coolman chuckled in the background, I stepped around the store pointing. "Monan, how about this drill press? Real or fake? Real? Ok, we'll take two." I showed the shopkeeper two fingers and repeated in Dari: "*du*."

"These grinders? Japanese? Four. *Char*."

Helpers scurried out of the store and down the market street. Minutes later, a second drill press and a pair of Makita grinders appeared.

"How many of these saws do you have?"

Through Ramin, I heard his answer to be as many as I wanted. If I wanted 40 saws, he would produce 40 saws. I began to understand the marvelous system before me. We wouldn't have to visit any other store after all— anything we desired would be found and retrieved.

Realization in hand, The Coolman and I took the opportunity to sit down on chairs that suddenly appeared for us. I could continue orchestrating from a comfortable seat.

It must be here noted that I have never once in my life had the opportunity to operate under a "money is no object" policy. Nor have I previously been blessed with such purchasing power. In a hardware store no less. It was like the adult version of those Toys-R-Us shopping spree commercials that interrupt perfectly good cartoons. I should be forgiven for thoroughly enjoying myself.

"Ramin, ask him to send someone to fetch Pepsi and cold water... we'll just put it on the tab."

I found myself asking prices first out of habit, then out of curiosity, then not at all. I continued pointing and ordering until I had run out of power tools to point out. Then I let Monan collect all the boring things — nails, hinges, bushings, sandpaper packs, and the like.

Icy cans of soda were sent out to pleasantly surprised gunners, still outside atop the Humvees. The convoy commander had established a defensive perimeter around the hardware shop, and let us know we had 25 minutes remaining before the show would have to be put on the road (security reasons, of course).

The refreshments arrived inside, as well, and in good time. The mercury read 120 degrees, with no appreciable difference on either side of the storefront door. As the shopkeeper began counting his career-making sale, he casually lit a cigarette and encouraged us to relax and do the same. Ramin and I obliged.

The Coolman looked over from his semi-reclined position and laughed at the scene we had painted. He was coolly drinking his Pepsi, as sweat pored from behind his extensive body armor. His M16 was leaned casually against his thigh, and over a million Afghani dollars rested inside the briefcase clipped to his chest.[††] In similar regalia, I sat a few feet to his side chatting with Ramin and tossing occasional instructions for Monan. A cloud of cigarette smoke and shop dust hung above our heads, slightly distorting the view of tightly packed carpentry paraphernalia on the ceiling high shelves. The dirty sunlight silhouetted an Afghan soldier standing watch at the door, AK47 just below the ready.

Steps away from the crowded busy-ness of the streetscape, we were isolated in this serenely absurd environ.

~

It took the better part of an hour for our tab to be counted. 120,000 Afghani—just under $2500 USD, for three pages worth of power tools and shop supplies. The ANA pickup was filled with our extensive purchase as we fired up the parallel-parked Humvees. Shopping over for the time being, we negotiated the evening Mazar traffic and headed back to our little slice of sunshine, the incomparable Camp Spann.

....

[†] *Editor's note: Monan's rough scale of value is as such: American/German > Japanese > Chinese, and is entirely based on his own evaluation of how long a tool lasts before needing replacement parts and how "fixable" they are. A Bosch or DeWalt may be incredibly expensive, but a good Afghan mechanic could keep one running for a lifetime. Chinese tools are seen as essentially disposable, good for taking to a distant jobsite because you didn't have to worry about lugging them home. Local versions don't quite make the scale, rather they create an entirely different category. Afghan tools are Kafkaesque composites of things that used to be parts of other tools and random pieces of material picked off the scrap heap. On one jobsite, I witnessed a local handyman repairing a metal fence with a homemade TIG-welder that consisted of (for best I could see) a dusty wooden crate, a large coil of wire, a spiralling web of dozens of smaller wires, and several battery cables.*

[††] *Editor's note: More on suitcases of cash in Book III.*

MISCELLANY, PART 1

1 **August**

When I was twelve, my father stole my bicycle.

Really.

One afternoon, I was playing basketball at the neighborhood park. When the games were over, I walked off the court to retrieve my transportation home, and was mortified to find the bike rack empty. No one had seen anything.

It was a long walk home.

My father was in the kitchen when I arrived. I sheepishly reported the theft, and (in my 12-year old mind) began cleverly dodging directly answering the stream of questions that ensued. After an interminable amount of time had passed, and the due gravity of the situation was well expressed, he finally let me off the hook. "Go look in the garage. Lock it up next time."

Such is the manner in which lessons were taught.

As I was walking back to my shop with an armful of tools last night, I thought about this story and grinned. Minutes before, I had been at the back porch of the Lieutenant who had borrowed them—under a special favor from me—for the day. I had arrived at the appointed time to retrieve them, but found no LT. In his place was a nicely stacked pile of Dewalt power tools, and a box filled with levels, hammers, and assorted paraphernalia.

With my dad's surreptitious ways in mind, I grabbed the pile and returned it to my shop. Then I went back to my card game.

A half hour later, there was a particularly frantic-appearing LT at our doorstep. He asked if I had come by to pick up the tools. I put down my spades hand to look at the time, "Shit— I'm sorry man, I totally forgot...I'll be there in a second."

It was a very long ten seconds that passed while he attempted to speak; understandably so, as his jaw was hanging down at his abdomen. I imagine this makes verbal communication difficult.

But I am clearly not the man my father was. My façade didn't make it a full minute before I admitted the ruse. Such relief is rarely seen on a person's face as was displayed on both of ours—his, for not having lost several hundred dollars worth of nearly-impossible-to-replace tools [there are no American tools for sale in Mazar], and mine for not having to hold a straight face for any longer.

I learned something yesterday. I am now convinced that "lesson-teaching" is no more than a quick rationalization for opportunistic foolery. A pious label for uncouth behaviour, if you will.

And now I wonder how hard my father was laughing in the kitchen while I was investigating the garage.

~

Now, for some completely unrelated snippits...

In my pursuit of understanding and experiencing proper Afghan culture, I have discovered that there are three national sports beloved by the countrymen.

The first, and most popular, is Kite Flying.

But this isn't your grandmother's lazy Sunday afternoon, after-picnic pastime, I promise you. This is "Bruce Willis starring in Last Man Standing" type cutthroat competition. A large group of otherwise genteel individuals gather on a chosen hill, toss a bunch of money in a pot, and throw their killer kites into the air. Once aloft, each man tries to down the others' prized wind wagons by maneuvering his steed about in fantastically strategic ways.

It deserves mentioning that the battles are won not by the fancifully colored apparatuses flitting about, but by their remarkably fortified leashes. Each kite string is laced with abrasive paraphernalia, like shards of glass or metal wires. The winning airfoil literally chops the heads off of its opponents.

Though this certainly may sound like a safe endeavor, these reinforced strings have been known to slice the necks of things that are not flying about in friendly competition. Small children, for instance. Accordingly, the sport has been banned in Pakistan. True aficionados don't discuss these things, however.

The second most popular sport, is a traditional competition called *Bozkashi*.

To the best of my understanding, the game functions somewhat like the game of Polo (which, incidentally, was invented in nearby Iran before being exported to Europe in the modern era). As in the contemporary version, players ride horses around a field attempting to prod a ball towards a scoring area. A minor difference, not necessarily apparent to the casual onlooker, is in the construction of the "ball." In England, it is

typically crafted out of bamboo or willow root. In Afghanistan, bamboo is in limited supply, so they use a dead calf instead. There is no scoring, per se; the first person to pick up the body and drop it in the scoring circle wins the game. A series of games will be played, with each winner acquiring a cash prize. On the final round, the winner gets the game-used calf.

The third most popular sport in Afghanistan is Volleyball.

~

Meatless July has come to an end. Johnny U lasted all of eight days—done in by a Slim Jim. He says it was by accident, an absent-minded snacking, but such excuses are difficult to believe. Particularly on the afternoon before Steak Night. Senior Chief Clark made it 3 weeks before being tricked by potato salad laced with sausage (how sausage ends up in a potato salad I will never understand). As the de facto judge of this impromptu competition, I offered amnesty, but he feared losing on this technicality. Or so he opined as cheeseburger droppings fell from the corner of his mouth.

After 31 days without even a hint of meat by-product, not even on the 4th of July, The Coolman triumphed over his compatriots. He declined, however, to attempt pursuit of my 16-year record.

Next on the docket: Sleepless September, Shower-free November, and No-Pants January.

~

In the midst of such foolishness, Johnny U has decided he needs a new hobby. He tried becoming a cigar connoisseur, but decided he doesn't really like smoking them all that much. Army personnel are ravenously collecting antique guns from the local economy, so he considered this briefly as well—until realizing he doesn't much care for guns. Vegetarianism? No, that didn't work so well, after all. I tried to help him brainstorm...

"Well...What do you like, Jon? What actually holds your interest?"

"I like my wife... a lot"

"Hmmm..."

"Maybe I should start collecting wives!"

"It *would* fit your interests..."

"I can't wait to try and explain it to her."

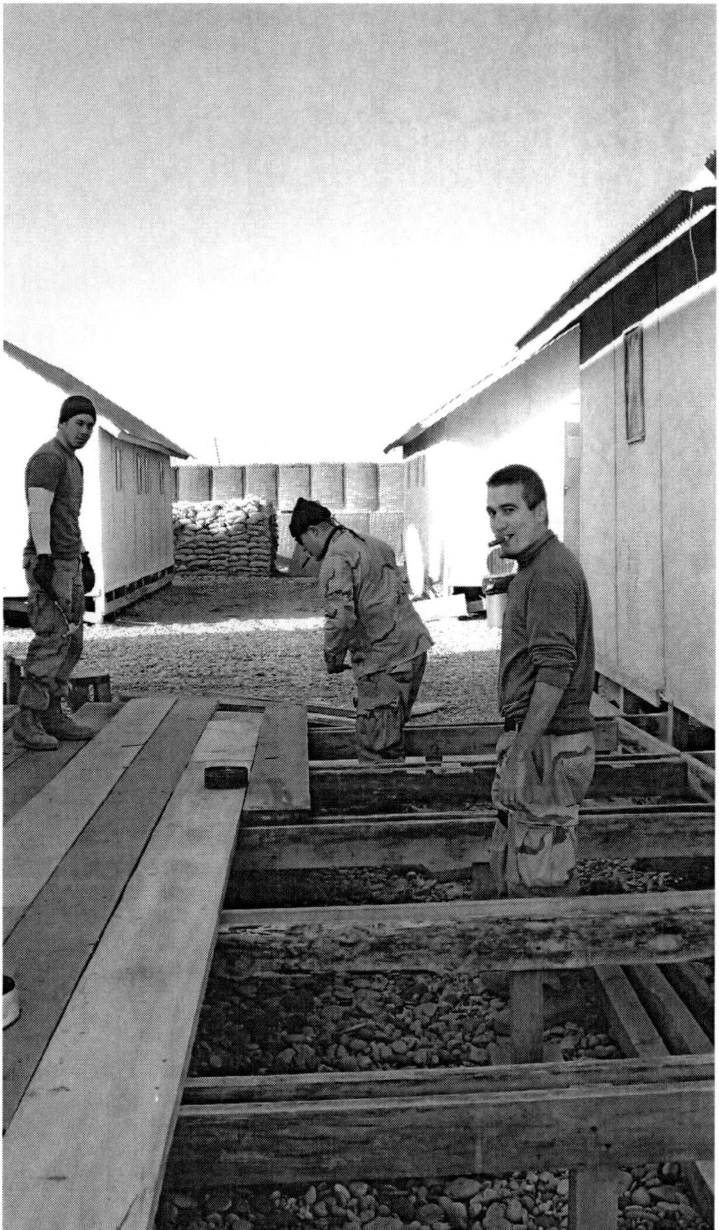

DECOPAGUE

17 August

My mother, bless her heart, was one of those "Crafts Moms." Never one to let a child sit around and be bored, she was continuously coming up with new and inventive ways to glue various colorful items together. One of her sponsored events of childhood involved the clumsily named technique of "decoupage."

This did not come from any craft book or anything of the sort, but from my mother's own childhood memories. Under her direction, I dutifully dipped magazine and newspaper clippings into a bowl of diluted Elmer's before pasting them upon a shoebox. Once covered, the glue dried clear, leaving a smooth surface of glossy images on the box. It must have been a raving success, for I only recall this project occurring once.

It's not a particularly important memory.

Or, more correctly, it wasn't properly one at all. Not until I found myself staring at a stack of maps trying to figure out how to apply them to plywood in a country that hasn't yet discovered spray-mount.

~

Some months ago, General Platitude swung through Mazar-e Sharif to check on his troops. Along the way, it came to his attention that the Afghan National Police Regional Headquarters was conspicuously missing a wall-size map of Northern Afghanistan. This was simply not acceptable. He promised them a map. On his way out of town, he notified someone of this promise. That someone notified someone else who notified someone else who notified me that I was to build a map for the ANP. ASAP.

It was an interesting proposition. Being that we would have to convoy to the headquarters in downtown Mazar, the project would have to be able to be transported easily and assembled within a single day. Nearly a hundred individual maps would make up the whole—far too many to piece together on-site.

I sketched an idea on a scrap of paper, to discuss with my carpenters. The basic concept was a series of vertical plywood strips, slid inside a channeled frame. The groove would be wide enough to accept a layer of plexi-glass in front of the map-faced wood strips. Simple. Elegant. The carpenters got to work crafting the pieces.

And so, a few days later, I was staring at these simple, elegant pieces wondering how on earth I was going to get maps on them. A minor detail, to be sure.

I tried a few different avenues, all of which resulted in wrinkled, not-fully-adhered maps. *My kingdom for a can of spray-mount!* There's not even a word in Dari for spray-mount.

I had in front of me canisters of white glue, some paint brushes, and a bowl of water for cleaning. After many minutes of intently staring at these items, and a cigarette or two, my mother's craftiness occurred to me. **Decoupage.** Amazed I even remembered the word, I tested a scrap piece. Seemed to work...

Thus began the epic struggle of men against paper, glue, and water.

~

With the help of Ramin, I dutifully applied our maps to the first set of boards. Another childhood activity quickly came to mind, as we realized we were working on what was essentially an oversized jigsaw puzzle—albeit one without a particularly recognizable image. Squares of a mountainous region scaled at 1 to 100,000 can be difficult to distinguish from one another, especially if your time in said region was measured in weeks.

It didn't help that we were putting the puzzle together without
the privilege of having the photo on the box. Our only guide was
the number printed on the corner and a small grid that showed
the six adjacent numbers to that map. Suffice it to say, I had
no concept of the big picture, only a passing familiarity with a
hundred small pictures that somehow fit together one at a time.

And it was soon apparent that such maps were never intended
to be pieced together. Due to their meticulous adherence
to the Earth's curvature, none of the maps actually line
up with their neighbors. It was here that Ramin learned
from me a new usage of the English word, "cheat."

~

It was an intensive job. There was no interior area large
enough to house the operation, so we worked outside in
shaded 120 degree heat. The process was messy, with strips
of paper and wet glue everywhere, and it was slow.

Fitting in blocks of time to work on the project between meetings
and mentoring was fairly difficult. Days would pass between
sessions. At the end of these interims, we would discover that
time and materials were not the only things working against us.

Altogether, 18 strips of plywood (8' by 17") had been prepared
for mounting. The morning we began our second map-pasting
session, we had 12 boards. Apparently someone had found
them perfectly prepared for their own personal project.

We wrote it off to simple ignorance. New boards were
purchased and prepared, and we moved on with the project.

A few weeks later, while setting up to do another session, we found
three of the partially completed boards (i.e., boards with maps
already glued to them) partially cut through with a saw. This could
hardly be accidental. Stupid, perhaps, but certainly not accidental.

I cannot claim to have been calm, but The Coolman flew off the handle for me.[†] In the next daily Base meeting, he laid into the respective Army leadership, holding the broken map boards up like Moses coming down from the mountain with the tablets. The behaviour was inexcusable, he said, soldiers were treating the "self-help shop" like it was a "help-yourself shop." He went on for a time, closing with the reminder, "...and this was *The General's* project."

Such things grab the attention of the Army.

But apparently not the attention of our thief. Within hours of the impassioned speech, a completed section of map board disappeared from the prep area. If ever I could claim to have been peering over the brink at a nervous breakdown, this was it. I was livid. As were a number of other gentlemen of far higher rank than I. The Commander ordered the shop closed to the public until I completed the project.

I guess we can't expect kids to be men simply because we throw uniforms on them and tell them to be.

~

A substantial amount of work (and re-work) followed. My glue-spattered prep area was occasionally visited by individuals expressing their sympathy for my losses. I was a widow, of sorts, for them. In part due to the way in which group isolation amplifies incidents into dramatic interludes, and in part due to the sheer incredulity of the events.

Others avoided the scene entirely, afraid of crossing paths with the accursed project.

Three weeks past the promised date of completion, we were ready to install. No one mentioned the lateness. I imagine the leadership hoped the Afghans wouldn't query either. How would one explain to their hosts—the ones we are to be mentoring, after all—that the project was delayed due to the thievery (or mischievery) of our sterling U.S. soldiers?

The irony was not lost on me.

~

We loaded up the project and convoyed to the Regional Headquarters building. It took the better part of the day for my carpenters to install the map. But by late afternoon, the appointed wall had been transformed by a framed and glazed topography, twenty feet wide and eight feet tall.

Army leadership having already made their appearance and departure much earlier in the day, I presented the completed wall to the ANP Colonel. He was gushing with gratitude, much more so than I had expected. Knowing the historical context, I offered the map as a symbol of continued partnership between the Afghan National Army and the Afghan National Police.

(Since the inception of a police force in Afghanistan to complement the army, the two forces have been at odds. They have been on opposing sides of numerous coups, including the April Revolution [that unseated the monarchy and ushered in the communist period], and have even engaged in open warring at certain points in history)

The large man grinned under his thick moustache as he gripped his left and right hands together, fingers interlocked. "The past is no more. We are like brothers now."

He may, in fact, mean it.

In truth, it is difficult to doubt a man so earnest. Time will tell if the Afghan Army feels equally cooperative.

....

[†] *Editor's note: At this point in the deployment, The Coolman has earned from his compatriots a second nickname, "Right Full Rudder," for his propensity to get spun up, like a ship making a hard turn at high speed.*

GATHER ROUND THE FLAG POLE

20 August

COMBINED JOINT TASK FORCE PHOENIX, KABUL, AFGHANISTAN — Though just days ago spread thin far across the Afghanistan desert, the motley crew of Navy Engineers has reformed upon Kabul like some kind of khaki Voltron knock-off. We sit on a wooden picnic bench near the center of the prison compound that is Camp Phoenix, throwing our stories of downrange around the table.

Big John, Uncle Mike, Penny-Lover, Junior,[†] and myself, trading barbs and outlandish tales that could only happen here—very much like we once did in the intermediate lifetime of Camp Shelby, Mississippi. Very much so, except for the distinct lack of beer. So, not much so at all, actually.

Of the more entertaining stories, we find that there is an epidemic of makeshift swimming pools popping up across the country's ANA camps. At one base, the fence around a fire-fighting reservoir is repeatedly broken through by a group of midnight waders. From another, we hear the story of a pipe breaking in a utility building. When the engineer arrives on scene to investigate, the room has filled with water... and Afghans. A number of soldiers have stripped to their undergarments, and are relaxing in the newly created swimming hole. Still elsewhere, a continual problem occurs with large above-ground water tanks losing their lids and gaining swimmers.

(I can pass no judgment here, having once taken refuge in a shaded water barrel while working in the heat of Northern Mexico—for which I was duly reprimanded, despite my obvious ingenuity.)

It is also during this round-table I hear for the first time the term "Fobbit." They tell me Fobbits are curious creatures whose purpose is shrouded in mystery. It is assumed they serve some function (due to their prevalence across the country), but as to what that particular function is, no one really is quite sure.

[The moniker comes from the shorthand FOB—for Forward Operating Base—and is christened upon those who never leave their walls, hiding out, if you will, within the confines of the FOB]

Then there was the story of the two unluckiest ANA soldiers in all of Afghanistan. On a desolate road out west, a pair of military Rangers were convoying across the desert. One of the trucks was hit by a hidden explosive in the road, throwing its occupants. The Ranger was destroyed, the soldiers mortally wounded. The soldiers in the first truck loaded the two bodies into the bed of the surviving truck and continued down the road. Minutes later, it too hit an IED and the soldiers' bodies were again tossed from the vehicle. Rough day.

Presumably, this is why the Americans drive armored vehicles.

Except, apparently, on the streets of Kabul, I wryly observe between Camp Phoenix and The Engineering Conference (Take 2).

But for the increase in attendance, there is little to distinguish this new charade from the one that preceded it three months ago. The room and the podium are the same, and from it the same idealistic speakers lay out the same idealistic plans and promises as before. Discussion yet again degenerates into non sequitur topics and complaints from the Afghan Colonels.

It quickly becomes clear that here at the heart of the operation, not a soul has any idea of the reality down range.

We are lectured at length about complex and comprehensive organizational structures for these regional Public Works meccas, built upon a professional civilian work force. Over an hour is set aside for an Afghan Colonel from the personnel department to describe the perfect civilian hire, and to outline the idealized hiring process.

Having already navigated his starry road to civilian hires, I have ten professionals awaiting final clearance to begin working. The only hurdle to their employment? The Ministry of Defense hasn't figured out how to pay them yet (a minor detail, to be sure). This long-winded Colonel is the man ostensibly in charge of making that happen. I take the opportunity to ask the single question I have traveled here to ask, "What is your timeline for fixing the pay system? These plans are all well and good, but when do I have civilians on the ground?"

The personnel expert pauses a moment, shifts his weight, and launches into a detailed explanation of...something or other. After a few minutes pass, Big John turns to me and whispers, "It's not looking good, man."

Nearly ten minutes pass, and the interpreter has had enough. He suspends the Colonel's ramblings and exclaims to the audience, simply, incredulously, "He doesn't know."

Dios Mio.

A fancifully complicated system, built upon a civilian work force—but no civilians.

My official reason for being in this country, my primary mission, is to mentor an Afghan Colonel on how to manage a Public Works office. But there is no office for him to manage. And the magic silk spinners in charge of this whole operation can't even provide a timeline on when they might wish for the important pieces to be in place.

In designing their wonderfully perfect forest, the rangers have forgotten to plant any trees.

Perhaps I should count my blessings. I can discuss Facilities Management concepts at length with Colonel Ata and we can simulate functionality. It's somewhat like playing house, only it's huge, strategically important, cost a hundred million dollars to build, and we don't pretend to be married.

Meanwhile, two of my counterparts downrange don't even have any ANA personnel to mentor. Hard to play house by yourself, I imagine.

So why are we here, again?

~

Realistically speaking, the most valuable portion of this extended weekend was not the Engineering Conference that mandated our attendance, but the opportunity to get a clearer picture on the situations of our far-flung compatriots.

Down in Khost—if not directly in the middle of the shit, certainly well within its boundaries—Big John and company are putting their Shelby training to work, defending positions, planning movements, and running their own convoys. In John's primary occupation, he's finding an entirely different set of rules in place then he's used to. A disagreement with a contractor this afternoon verily ensures rocket attacks tonight. Area control ebbs and flows between tribe and Taliban interests. Interpreters wake up to find "night letters" on their doorstep, threatening the death of their families if they show up for work that day. American Humvees and soldiers are peppered with rocks, thrown by the children of those children who hurled stones at Soviet tanks two decades prior.

On the other end of "Rocket Alley," Uncle Mike is having his own series of problems. To anyone querying on the status of his base at Lashkar Gah, he offers a steep wager. "I'll drop you off at any point within the city of Lashkar Gah — any point you choose — and I'll give you one month of my salary if you walk from there to the gate of my base."

Forty miles of hostile desert lie between the city and the outpost, a fact continuously overlooked by the leading minions of Kabul. There are no surrounding villages from which to draw contractors or supplies. They are, quite literally, in the very middle of nowhere.

This in it of itself creates a number of logistical problems, but the scattered Taliban strongholds in the region further exacerbate the situation. What contractors can be gleaned from the area seldom possess the longevity necessary to complete a project (let alone follow-ons), given the severe penalty imposed for working with infidel forces. I imagine construction activities could be difficult sans one's head. Likewise, supply trucks regularly find themselves mysteriously relieved of cargo and driver en route—if not simply destroyed outright.

With little support and little oversight, Uncle Mike, Big John, and their disparate counterparts find themselves going it alone more often than not. The old SeaBee mantra "Can Do!" has effectively been replaced by the more realistic "Make Do."

~

And despite the odds and the isolation that pervades down range operations, every last person is itching to get back. Escape from Phoenix is priority.

Like the disaster that is Engineering Central, Camp Phoenix is veritably abuzz with inactivity. Mid-level officers roam its concrete paths very obviously collecting salutes, having nothing more important to do but attempt to reinforce how important they, in fact, are. Senior officers try to justify their unnecessary positions by inventing superfluous policies and imposing them on their constituents. In turn, they circulate the crowded complex investigating the fruits of their misguided labors.

There is a cancerous aura that hangs over this center.

It is the very antithesis to Lord of the Flies anarchy — a place where authority and order are piled again and again upon themselves ad nauseum, becoming so dark and sticky that barest movement becomes impossible.

Thus we all push to return to our forgotten outposts, where the tentacles of misplaced priorities can't quite reach. The farther from the vacuum, the easier it is to breathe.

"Despite all the shit we have to deal with," opines Uncle Mike, "At least we're far away from the flag pole out there."

....

† *Editor's note: Mutually agreed upon nicknames during the pre-deployment period in Camp Shelby. Square of jaw and of body, and every bit the crusty North Carolina construction foreman, Big John (The Steel-driving Man) was a former enlisted-Seabee turned Navy Engineer. Uncle Mike, a ginger-topped, red-faced Navy pilot with far more blue-streaked energy than comportment, was so-named after everyone's crazy uncle from the Thanksgiving table. Junior, a baby-faced Salvadorian Lieutenant a half shade over 21, was far and away the youngest officer in the entire deployment. Penny Lover was given his semi-derogatory moniker by his commanding officer — the reasons for which I can't now, for the life of me, recall.*

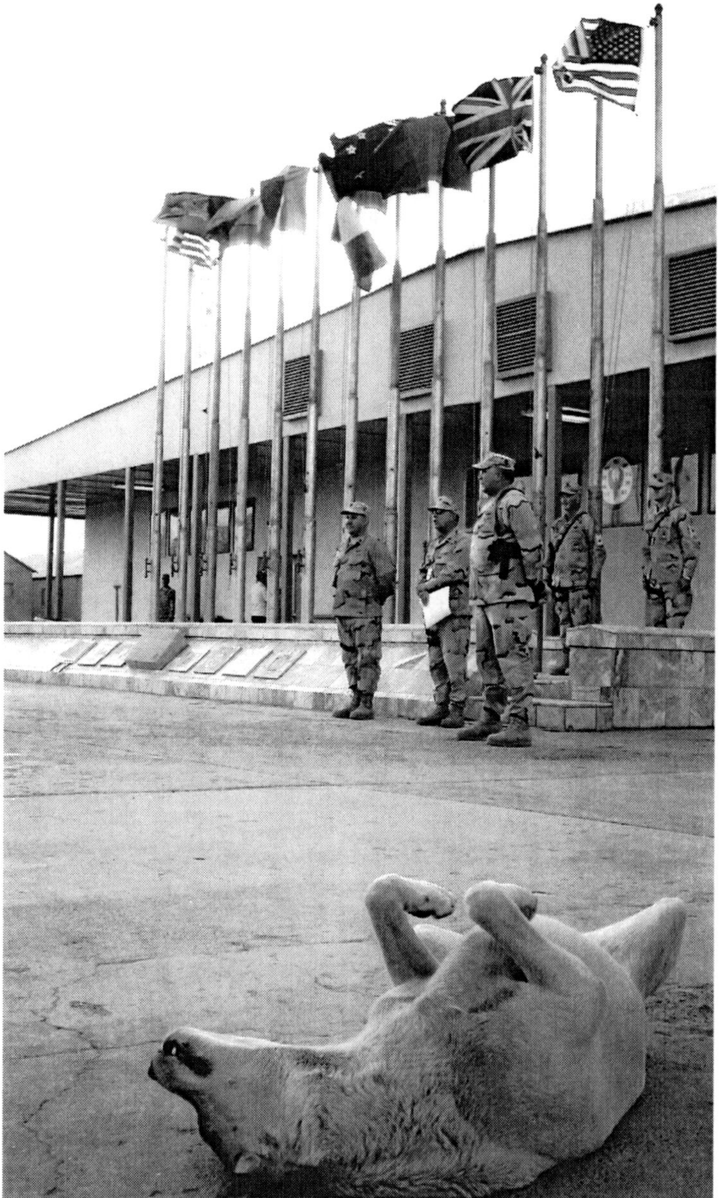

MICELLANY, PART II

30 August

FORWARD OPERATING BASE SPANN, MAZAR-I
SHARIF, AFGHANISTAN — Ah coincidence...

The other day I received a thoughtful care package from the lady that included, among other things, a mix CD she made for my listening pleasure. It just so happened that the morning I opened this special box was the first day of a two-week period driving a loaner vehicle.[†] A new Ranger with, glory of glories, a cd player (we've previously discussed the lack of any such device in my normal daily transportation here). I had a CD, I had a place to play it. Simple pleasures.

We could now taxi with a soundtrack, even if just for two weeks. The infectious Cee-lo Green track, "Crazy," became the running music for our daily excursions. By request, no less. Each afternoon when my workers would pile into the truck to head home, someone would request "that crazy song." As Monan explained (in Dari), "I don't know anything about what he's saying but I know this is good music."

Navigating the desolate dirt roads between the ancient stone and adobe ruins to these modern funk-soul rhythms could hardly be more surreal. Next to me, in thickly accented vocals, my interpreter Ramin attempts to sing along with lyrics. Some of which he may understand. And in my mirror, I can see four Afghani heads bobbing along with the music. I couldn't invent such a scene.

Ramin, for his part, has decided that Barry White is the pinnacle of American music.

~

Speaking of my adventure-stricken interpreter, I
must mention his recent clash with nature.

The details are a bit fuzzy, but it seems that one night a fairly large
scorpion found a rather cozy sleeping spot. Unfortunately for
both him and Ramin, that spot happened to be inside the latter's
pants. I can't really determine who was more startled of the two,
however, for the scorpion did not survive to tell his side of the story.

Ramin showed up for work the next day wearing a left
leg that was clearly too big for him. Before I could even
query about the swollen appendage, he reported:

"A scorpion has stung me—I was supposed
to die, but actually I did not."

I could nearly have mistaken this for an evaluation of the
weather, for all the affect he gave the announcement. No
need to be excited now, he felt. The whole show — the sting,
the temporary paralysis, the rush to the hospital, the death
predictions, the intensive care, the survival by slimmest
odds — was in the past now. Coffee or tea, this morning?

It took nearly a week for the swelling to subside, but Ramin's legs
are now no longer mismatched. Luckily, he's had no ill effects.
Johnny U and I were waiting to see if he would turn into a mutant
or a superhero, but unfortunately, this also did not happen.

~

On to other less life-threatening subjects...

Despite my all-consuming efforts with the Carpentry Shop,
my real job, again, is in mentoring Colonel Ata. As previously
mentioned, his office is currently sans staff. He does however,
have a Deputy Public Works Officer to manage the employees

they don't yet have. Though his engineering qualifications
are questionable at best, Major Salim is eminently qualified in
public relations. Too much so, perhaps. For the first couple of
months, I was entirely unclear as to what his job was—other than
bringing fruit to the office in the morning. Mangoes, grapes,
melons, piles of fresh fruits from the downtown markets. His
favorite, like most Afghans, is watermelon, and he delights
in showing up with a fresh, ripe example for all to share.

I hate watermelons.

But he's so happy to bring them, I force myself to eat
and look grateful. I guess I should thank my mother
for training that skill into me. Though life would be
much easier if she just brought me up rude, I think.

The funny thing is, everyone else knows my disdain for melons.
Each time the Major rolls in, excitedly exclaiming that he's
brought watermelons, Ramin will laugh and Colonel Ata will smile
mischievously, but neither will ever tell him the truth. I think they
prefer watching me suffer through the snack. It's just wrong.

~

Further on the subject of inedible food... I have given up on KBR.[†]

I have sworn off entirely the hot food they serve
at our dining facility. Most of it has meat in it
anyway, and what doesn't, they destroy.

There is a minimal salad/sandwich bar, and I've been relegated
to it. Breakfasts are the best meal, with fresh fruit and bagels
every day. But after that, I find myself piecing meals together.

I'm eating with Ramin at the interpreter's mess hall more and more.
It's catered by a local restaurant and I'm guaranteed fresh bread and
tasty rice. Having done some projects for the facility, I have been

essentially given a free pass to eat there whenever I want. Ramin, for his part, is happy to invite me. It means double meat for him.

The food is best described as midway between Greek/Middle-Eastern and Indian, which shouldn't be too unexpected considering the geography and history. There are numerous stews that approximate the look of curry, but the dishes tend to be much more mild than either of the periphery influences. Of the highlights: a pico de gallo like concoction called *salata* — finely chopped tomatoes, cucumbers, red onions, and cilantro — and a chile yogurt sauce they spread on flatbread with shish kabob strip meat (much like a gyro).

I've also got Ramin grocery shopping for me these days, bringing back fruit, cheese, and bread from the local markets [see picture]. Occasionally, his wife sends along special treats. An excellent dish is called, no joke, "*baloni*." Thankfully, it has nothing to do with ground up pig ears. Rather, Indian-style naan (thin, crepe-like bread) is stuffed with savory fillings like potato, leek, or spiced lentil.

Even with this outside help, I'm having difficulty making consistent meals and I'm losing weight. There is junk-food and processed food galore, but fresh stuff is hard to come by. I miss eating good food.

~

Break for an unrelated message from the Goat Locker:

"My lawyer's secretary must have really big tits, because she's dumber than a box of hair."

(Overheard from Senior Chief Clark while checking his email)

Speaking of legal problems, Mazar-e Sharif has
officially seen its first court martial.

One of the many bureaucratic elements being taught to (or
imposed upon) the fledgling ANA is the establishment of a legal
corps. Part of Afghanistan's historical problems with its own
defense forces has been the lack of a consistent internal justice
system. In years past, the needle swung wildly between anarchy
and Stalinist clearcutting — even within the same regime.

Establishing a uniform code of conduct and prosecution is an
important piece in the long-term functionality of this Afghan
Army. By extension, this preliminary step of holding a legal
trial is an important precedent; a certain weight of history lies
upon the inaugural proceeding. Undoubtedly, the decision
of just which defendant deserved that honor must have been
debated and pored over, deeply and thoroughly considered.

And they sure picked a doozy of a flagship case.

There were a couple of soldiers making a bit of a ruckus outside
their barracks building one afternoon. It seems that one had
stolen a belt from the other's personal effects. Or, perhaps
more accurately, the other soldier was merely quite convinced
the first had robbed him. In any event, they were having it out
over a green, woven, Army issue belt. I'm sure it was a very nice
belt, but let the record show it was quite certainly just a belt.

Tempers accelerated over the disputed item. One soldier
grabbed something resembling a baseball bat. The other soldier
responded by grabbing something resembling a service pistol.

Presumably fetched by a bystanding soldier, the
unit sergeant rushed out to resolve the altercation.
Solomon, admittedly, he was not.

"If you do not stop fighting," he ordered, brandishing his pistol, "I will shoot you both."

No change.

"If you do not stop fighting..." he yelled louder, "I will shoot you both."

Not a hint of compliance.

"STOP FIGHTING NOW!" He screamed with all the volume a trained sergeant can muster.

Amazingly, still no response...

...so, he shot them both.

At his court martial, witnesses emphasized that he had always been a man of his word.

....

[†] *Editor's note: The more accurate explanation is that Colonel Ata and I swapped trucks, his new khaki-painted military issue version for my beat-up, unmarked one. Ata was taking two weeks' leave to drive back home to Badakhshan (and his other two wives) and would be crossing some hostile territory. Using my truck was part of his attempt to do so incognito.*

[†] *Editor's note: "The Goat Locker" technically refers to the Chief's Mess on a Navy vessel, apparently so named because in times past, when livestock was kept aboard sailing ships, the goats slept in the Chief's kitchen.*

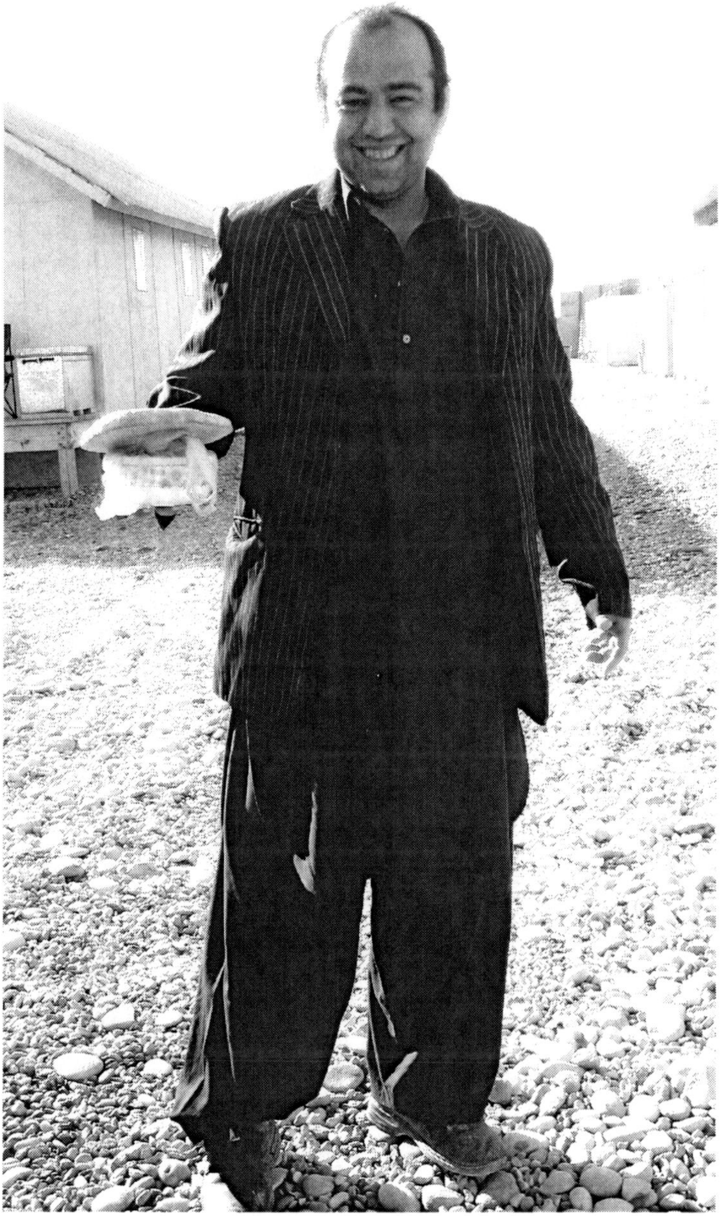

THE DUST BOWL

1 September

For lack of something more pressing to do, the Air
Force challenged the Navy to a football game.

So early one Friday morning, twenty or so of the services' finest
groggily appeared on a barren soccer field in ANA land. All that
distinguished this particular patch of scraggly dirt from any other
abandoned dusty lot was a pair of white rectangles, 75 yards apart,
roughly approximating goal posts. The soil was packed hard, and
mostly free of debris. There wasn't a hint of grass to be seen.

It would do fine.

Separating the players out according to service, the Navy team
quickly realized a distinct disadvantage. Johnny U and I, the
youngest Navy personnel at 29 and 26, respectively, were older
than nearly every player on the Air Force side. And they had subs.

It was sure to be a tiring morning for the Navy's elite.

~

Big Minnesota took quarterbacking duties for the Navy
squad, and like most corn-fed Midwestern boys tend to, he
set out to do his best backyard Brett Favre. Unfortunately,
at first, the most accurate portion of his imitation
was of Mr. Favre's propensity for interceptions.

The first half, itself, was rather Midwestern in feel
— little noticeable offense, and no score.

In the second, the Navy team began to put its age to its advantage. Realizing that the Air Force squad was limited in football knowledge, we began to mess with their heads. We shifted our offensive game plan, rolling out multiple different sets, employing screens, pitches, and even a flea-flicker. Not quite knowledgeable enough to adapt their defensive scheme, we began to shred their zone. With Johnny U and I running deep routes to spread the defense, Big Minnesota was able to hit Dwight "T.O." Taylor again and again in the middle of the field. Then we'd run Johnny U on a reverse just to keep them honest. It wasn't long before talk in our huddle consisted of, "Hey, let's try this!"

Meanwhile, as defensive captain, I employed similar tactics. While starting all plays from roughly the same set, each defensive player's responsibility changed snap to snap. I would send a blitz from any position, and shift coverage accordingly. Our opponents had no way of knowing who was going to rush, and from where. Overwhelmed and unable to properly adjust, the Air Force offense was dominated for the remainder of the game.

It was easily the most productive two hours any of us had spent in Afghanistan, thus far.

Though, I can only wonder what the crowd of curious ANA soldiers thought as they observed the spectacle from lawn chairs.

Dust Bowl I Final Score: Air Force 0, Navy 14.

~

Unwilling to accept such humiliation, and for lack of something more pressing to do, the next week the Air Force again challenged the Navy to a football game.

Short of players, Big Minnesota went on a recruiting mission. Among the ISAF[†] troops he found a Croatian Sergeant Major who was interested in playing.

"Have you ever played American Football before Dreyzden?"

"I watch few minutes on TV other night,
I think I understand playing"

We decided to make him a lineman.

Again outnumbered early on a Friday morning, our motley Navy crew (plus one Croatian) set out to embarrass the cockiest service once again. At the dirt patch, the Air Force team was poring over hand drawn plays, and predicting our utter defeat. We complimented their newfound studiousness.

Carrying over our "keep calling crazy plays" strategy from the previous game, we jumped out to a quick lead. In between series, Big Minnesota would lean over and explain rules and strategy to our Croatian teammate. Dreyzden would nod his head intently, thoroughly focused on absorbing this foreign pastime.

On defense, I found such coaching to be unnecessary. Handing out assignments before each play, I simply told the athletic Croat, "Get the quarterback." And on each play, he would. The Air Force linemen had no answer for our Croatian terror.

By the end of the first half, he was running to me before plays, excitedly asking, "Get the quarterback?"

I smiled, "Get'em."

He'd grin and run to the line, ready to inflict more damage.

In the end, our international coalition's effort and play-calling trumped their youth and numbers. As well it should.

Dust Bowl II Final Score: Air Force 7, Navy-Croatia 28

Dirty, bruised, and scraped-up, we headed back on base. At the gate, the guard mistook Johnny U for an interpreter and tried to search him.

Just another day in paradise.

....

[†] *Editor's note: International Security Assistance Force. Essentially, the collective name given to the sub-group of NATO countries participating in Afghan operations.*

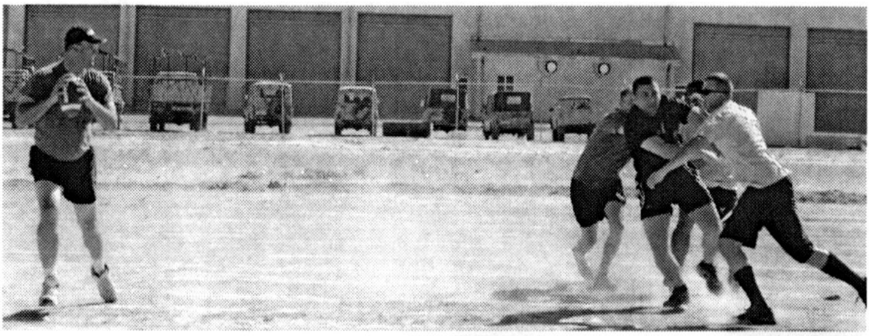

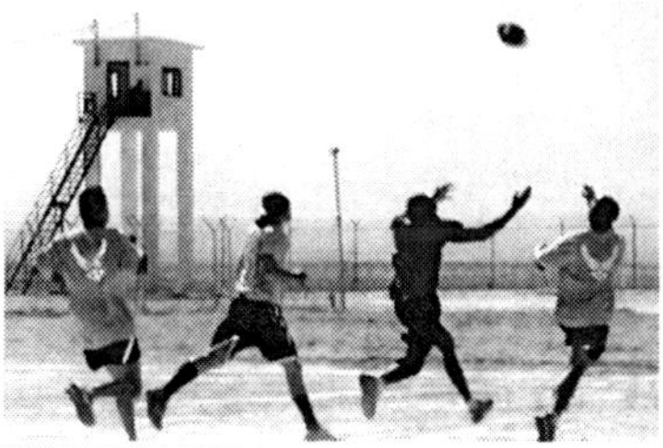

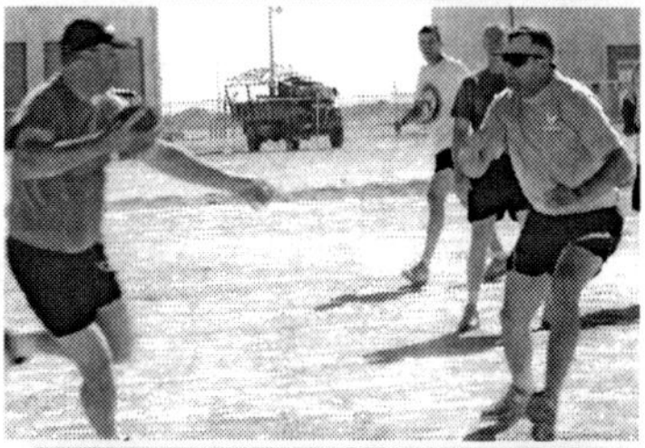

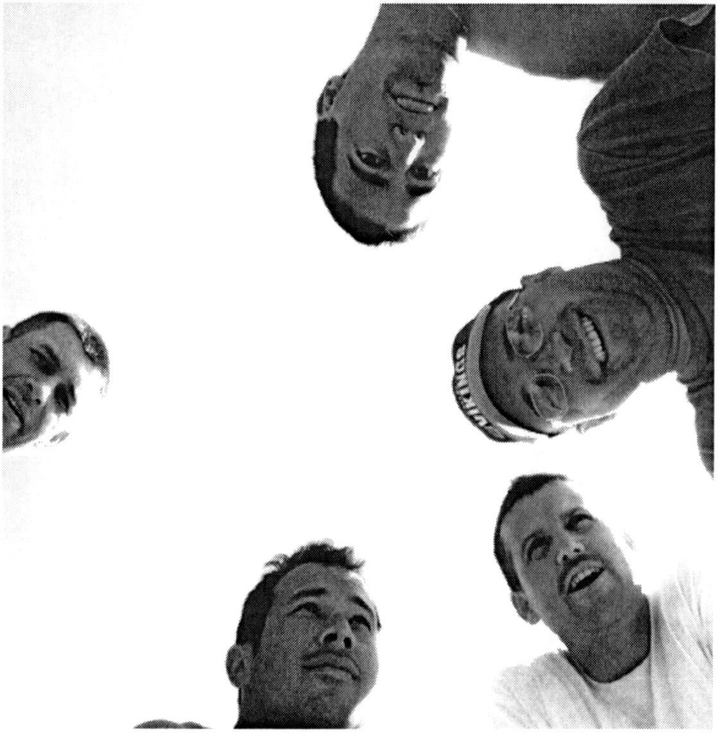

THE LION OF PANJSHIR

9 September

Having laid out our living quarters with a maximum of extra space, our berth has served as an occasional hotel for wayward soldiers, awaiting bigger things downrange. One such pair were temporarily stationed as such for upwards of eight or nine weeks. Those old Army roommates were deployed down to Kandahar a few months ago with a Kandak of ANA soldiers. The combined unit was originally intended to perform a few missions, supplementing the deteriorating Afghan forces in the southern portion of the country. They were to return within a week or two. They're still down there.

The locally based units are sparse, battling leadership issues and climbing desertion rates. Our 2nd Kandak, by comparison, is arguably the most experienced and best trained unit in the nation, comprised of several hundred former Mujahadeen. Fighting side by side with our veteran US Army training team, the Kandak has successfully completed mission after mission in the region.

Their success rate and their professionalism is to their detriment, however, as Kandahar can't afford to release them back home to Mazar. Weeks on end they spend in the field, limited in supplies, sleeping in vehicles and fighting positions. The proverbial tip of the spear in this war are these men, American and Afghan alike.

~

The ninth of September is a supremely important date to local history, and truly, to the so-called War on Terror. Two days before the World Trade Center attacks, Al Qaeda operatives, posing as members of the press, assassinated the Afghan revolutionary leader Ahmad Shah Masoud. He was the unifying head of the various Mujahadeen forces and instrumental in the ongoing rebellion against the Taliban. The valley where Bagram airfield now sits was wrested from them under his command.

The man is venerated as a hero, especially in the Northern provinces. Billboards, banners, framed photographs everywhere across the country commemorate his life. In Mazar's shops and streets you can buy rugs and blankets woven with his likeness. The anniversary of his death is an Afghan National Holiday.

It has been said that had Masoud survived the attack, he never would have allowed international military assistance within Afghanistan. But conversely, were he not assassinated, there is little chance Osama bin Laden could have managed safe harbor within the country's borders. Without bin Laden, outside forces never come to Afghanistan.

The actions of September 9th indelibly link our two nations. The murder of Masoud was the first movement in a two part play of terrorism, a movement that even the most fervent flag-wavers in the States are oblivious to—even in the very midst of their "Remember 9-11" refrains. Here, however, the people of Afghanistan never ignore the duality of the attack. To many, it is a blood bond that unites us against a common enemy.

As a student of history, I've struggled to understand the difference between this effort and the British and Soviet led occupations of the previous century. The surface similarities are many, but somehow the character is substantially different. All that I can come up with is this: We, the Americans, have not limited ourselves to being simple overlords or distanced advisors. Our boys are lying in the same muddy trenches, side-by-side, with their boys—brethren in a shared fight. The importance of this, culturally, can not be overstated.

And today, on the ninth of September, it was one
of our boys that died in that fight alongside his
Afghani brothers in Kandahar province.

Minutes ago, we stood at the half mast flag in somber formation,
his empty boots and rifle before us. We listened to the recital
of his distinguished career, and we tightened reflexively with
the mention of the wife and young children he left behind.

Two hundred rigid salutes in memoriam.

May he be the only fallen soldier needing remembrance
at Camp Mike Spann, Mazar-e Sharif. *Inshallah.*

TIMELY INTERNATIONAL NEWS BULLETINS

23 September

The British are coming! The British are coming!

As are the Germans, the Poles, the Norwegians, the Swedes, and the Croatians...

(You might also trip over some Fins, Romanians, or Cheks in your travels. So be careful.)

Around the country, members of the International Security Assistance Force (ISAF) are increasing their role. Soldiers from all the world's armies are converging on this relatively minor piece of real estate to put their mark on the fledgling Afghan National Army.

Slowly, the U.S. is moving out of the lead position in both military and mentoring operations. In the South, the Brits have taken command, the Italians are running Herat, and here the Germans have just been handed the baton. Integral to the nascent plan, such a turnover is ostensibly part of a larger effort to relieve the increasing strain on American forces. As the bulk of forward responsibility is taken by ISAF, the U.S. military is to shrink back into a supportive role.

Leave it to the Army to f' that one up.

As I've relayed previously, most of us in the 209th (Mazar-e Sharif/Northern Provinces) have been tasked with multiple full-time jobs. Each position now has a combination of mentoring and support responsibilities. Under the new organization, the mentoring duties will be handled by ISAF personnel, leaving only the relatively minor supporting duties.

Naturally, now that (technically) only half a job remains, the Army is belatedly increasing personnel levels. Two or three will handle the duties full-time that one previously did part-time. Such is military logic. Meanwhile, the ISAF nations are contributing about three people for every individual mentoring slot vacated by a U.S. counterpart. It's going to get crowded around here. Quickly.

In the last month, our camp size has doubled with the influx (doubled in personnel, not in capacity, let's not overlook), as the international community arrives to do its due diligence.

It does make for an interesting environment, however, with a myriad of languages being spoken on post and several levels of translation to get lost upon when conducting business. Indeed, the Afghan interpreters only trade in one European language—English. This sets up notorious translation chains, spinning from ANA soldier through Afghan interpreter to whichever German (or Croat, or Pole, or...) speaks the best English, who then more or less conveys the message to his compatriots, listens for the answer, and reverses course through the chain. It's quite an intriguing process—especially considering that the main link is conducted between people speaking what is generally their second, and often their third, language.

Given the difficulty a complex message has in surviving even one translation, it is truly amazing that anything resembling original intent is sustained through the cascade. But, if one forgets the serious nature of such discussions, the image of these grown-men daily playing linguistic "telephone" with each other is rather amusing.

~

In other international news, the ninth month of the Islamic calendar (which we begin today) is the month of Ramadan. Like the Christian lent, it is intended as a month of prayerful focus and relinquishment of earthly things. Unlike the Christian lent, the Muslims give up damn near everything.

From sun break to dusk, during Ramadan, no Muslim is to introduce any substance inside his body but air. No eating, no drinking, no smoking—nothing enters the mouth during the day. A moratorium on sexual relations is also observed. The good Muslim spends his Ramadan month in prayer and rest. Until sunset, anyway.

Ramin, my interpreter, is fearful of the coming month.

It will be his first Ramadan as a fat man.

~

And from the Colonel Ata allegory vault, an anecdote of international borders...

Some years ago, a somewhat younger Ata was serving as a Mujahadeen Lieutenant in the Northern provinces, protecting the border and tracking down Soviet supply lines. In their sector of defense, they discovered that the Soviets were utilizing a particular bridge to cross the Oxus river into Afghanistan. Intelligence reports warned of a large contingent of reserve troops approaching from the North, planning to enter the country at this point.

There was a fairly animated discussion amongst the leadership to resolve a course of action. One faction strongly advocated awaiting the Soviet crossing, attacking them as they attempted to reform ranks on the Afghanistan side. Another vehemently argued for a pre-emptive movement, meeting the Soviets on their side and not allowing them ever to cross. Others proposed delayed ambushes or even attacking while the Soviets were still on the bridge.

The argument raged for hours, with no side gaining significant advantage. Unaffected by such internal theatrics, the Soviets continued their advance towards the Oxus—and invasion.
As weariness of verbal combat began to set in amongst the seniors, a junior soldier requested a chance to speak. Given the little progress made up until this point, he was awarded this rare opportunity.

Though he was somewhat overwhelmed by the sudden spotlight, the soldier quietly suggested that rather than worry about when the Soviets would cross, they could simply remove the bridge and make crossing impossible.

He was greeted with silence.

And then agreement.

Heeding the advice of the younger, the Mujahadeen destroyed the bridge that crossed the Oxus. The coming invasion was averted, and the Afghans were able to buy time for their own re-supply and replenishment.

Such is proof, tells Colonel Ata, that important ideas do not come only from important men. A good leader must understand that wisdom can come from unexpected sources; he should learn from everyone that crosses his path.

~

If such an attitude is adopted by the Colonel's compatriots, there is truly a wealth of international knowledge here at their disposal—a myriad of tactical and technical experience that today crosses Afghanistan's path. Will all these cooks ruin the stew, or will the innumerable individual contributions result in a deliciously eclectic "Stone Soup?"

Such a question can only be answered at
Time's personal convenience...

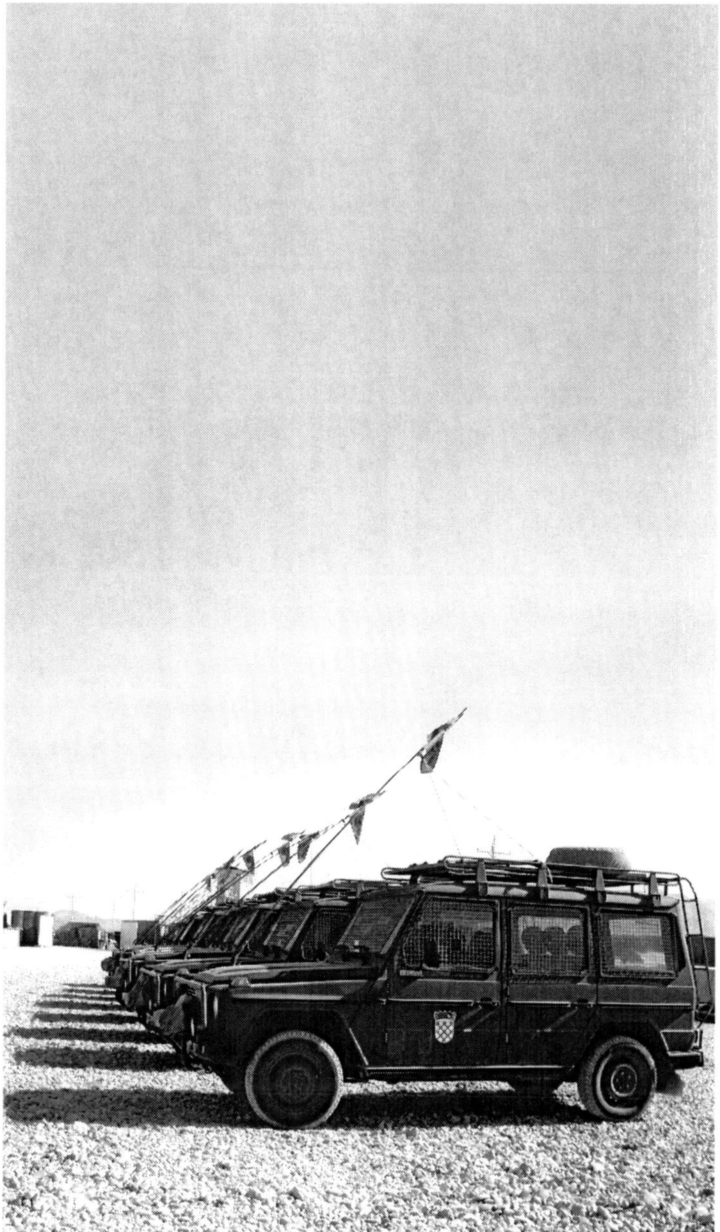

DIVERSIONARY TACTICS

26 September

9:30 on a Sunday night... the camp is dark and quiet, but
for a small room carved out of a modest plywood structure.
Inside that room, a large TV blares out the final minutes of
precursory banter. A crowd of displaced men are sprawled
about on derelict couches and mildly broken chairs. The air of
anticipation is stained with strains of microwave popcorn.

Seven thousand miles away, an odd-shaped
leather ball is kicked from a plastic tee.

And all is suddenly right between the world
and these collected vagabonds.

~

Deep through Sunday's nether hours and into Monday's
morning, we escape into this pigskinned diversion. The plays are
dissected, the announcers ridiculed and corrected, the officials
berated. Lively banter arises between various American refugees,
advocating their hometown representatives. The Chicagoans are
particularly irritating. No one is particularly surprised about this.

Cheers and jeers ring from different portions of our small crowd
on each play. Unflattering comparisons are made between
certain players and certain parts of the human body. Strategies
are debated, predictions are made, and the outcomes are
most certainly dependent on our intellectual involvement.

With the doors closed on this windowless viewing room,
attention centered on the games and camaraderie, you can
almost forget that Afghanistan is outside. Forget that it's the
middle of the night. Forget how far away everything familiar is.

For ever fleeting moments, normalcy is in grasp.

And you can almost imagine you're back home again, taking in the games with your football buddies down at the pub.

Just, uh, without the beer.

~

As the light of dawn draws closer, our pool of spectators will dwindle and thin. Eventually, I'll be alone in this temporary sanctuary, critiquing the events to myself. I'll hold on to my blessed diversion until it can no longer hold my interest, or the caffeine runs out. As the sun submits its early purple warnings, I'll reopen Afghanistan's door and stumble off in the direction of my bed.

I'll be little more than worthless for the day that is soon to start, but such a price is easily paid for a stab at familiarity.

~

The psychological value of diversion is widely underrated and too often overlooked. There is a redemptive power in diversion far and beyond its quantifiable benefits. This is particularly true when core emotions have latched themselves to a diversion.

On the 25th of September 2006, a little more than a year after the worst of nature and governance had left it a symbol of despair, the New Orleans Superdome reopened anew. For a football game. Louisiana's Saints were scheduled to be beaten handily by the powerhouse football franchise from Atlanta. So said every sportswriter in the country. Repeating this confident prediction, of course, was my Georgia-native roommate, Mr. Boatright.

"Carlton," I queried, "Do you know where they're playing?"

He said that he didn't, as we slipped out of the hooch
at 4am Tuesday morning, headed for the TV room to
catch the live broadcast of Monday Night Football.

"They're playing at the Superdome. First game since
Katrina.... Your guys don't have a chance."

~

When Katrina rolled through New Orleans, my life, like so
many others, was spun off in an entirely different direction than
previously planned. I had been scheduled to leave, for good, on
the last day of September, but that day of departure extended
indefinitely. I found myself trapped within its unmoving
hours, unsure of what was to come. I was not the only one.

The fabric of normal time was rent, leaving behind
an ethereal in-between where we stumbled around
picking up what life we found strewn about.

The life I chanced to pick up lay intertwined with another. As
if continuing an unread novel from someone else's bookmark
midway through, we slipped together into a new paradigm.
From this point on, she and I lived as if we'd always been.

But, without the pause nature placed on my timeline,
every experience we shared onward never happens.
The shift never occurs. The surreal nature of our
companioning well understood, between us, a silly little
pop song became our anthem of that interstitial life.

And this Tuesday morning, worlds away, I watch cameras
circling overloaded stadium seating. The crowd noise
is deafening, but guitar strummed notes begin to peek
out from beneath it. Strains of "When September Ends,"
burst out into recognition, and I nearly succumb to tears.
Unexpected symmetries can carry unexpected weight.

Through this extended reopening celebration, 70,000 people remain on their feet, the dome shaking under their collective voices. The scene fades to black, and pauses a beat, before commercials break my introspection.

I exhale slowly.

"No chance, Carlton. Not tonight."

Only now do I notice we've been joined. KBR's lead carpenter, a Louisiana Creole generations deep in New Orleans, catches my eye and nods. His weathered face gleams with pride.

Our faith is rewarded. The perennially underachieving Saints dominate the favored visitors, from start to finish. It isn't even close.

And though it shouldn't rationally make any difference, several hundred thousand people feel better about their current lot in life. Even if only for a little while. Diversion has that power. For three hours, these over-trodden souls find escape. Outside the Superdome's safety lit exit doors, they can almost imagine that the 9th ward was never flattened, that Chalmette wasn't washed away.

And maybe, in picturing what it was, they see what it can be again.

~

After enduring thirteen months of disaster and crippling loss, the city and its people today have something to be proud of. A large piece of New Orleans' identity rebuilt and headed in a positive direction—an internationally broadcast symbol of rebirth.

Good news had been hard to come by, of late. But, if their beloved Saints can rise from the soggy decay, despite every indication otherwise, how too can the overridden city be reborn?

People in Iowa and Delaware will write condescending letters about the misguided priorities of this wayward city (glorifying football, by God, when people don't have houses!) it will be because they don't understand. They don't understand that the Superdome is the economic engine that drives tourism (to borrow from the Times-Picayune's Chris Rose) and key to New Orleans' survival. They don't understand how much one publicized success means to a city that's been infamously failure-ridden over the past year. And they certainly don't understand the psychological lift of an immaculate diversion. For nothing but diversion offers the relief of familiarity to the displaced.

Perhaps it takes being displaced to recognize that.

THE ROOKIE WALL

20 October

In professional athletics, there is a common phenomenon that repeats itself season after season, regardless of the sport. So common, in fact, it has its own catchy nickname: "The Rookie Wall." It is the generic prediction that, no matter how strong and talented, first year players that are made to contribute full-time will peak early and break down somewhere in the third quarter of the season. Every year the scenario repeats itself with high-profile rookies thrust into starting roles. The reason for this is quite straightforward. In addition to the higher level of competition, professional seasons are simply longer than their college and high school counterparts—and significantly so.

Last year's NCAA Basketball champion played 39 games, including the post-season tournament. The worst team in the NBA this year will play 82. The best will play over a hundred. No amount of practices, wind sprints, cross-training, or other extra-curricular activity can adequately prepare a rookie (phenom or otherwise) for the rigor of an entire professional season. At the point where his body is about to give out, ready for the break, half a season will still remain.

~

The standard Navy deployment is six months.
Seabee or sailor, half a year is it.

Until now. Until two entire branches of our military became irretrievably stuck in the tar of Iraq. Until the Navy and the Air Force realized they needed to throw numbers at the ill-named War On Terror to justify their budgets in the new American era.

We are pioneers, of a sort, we wayward sailors and grounded airmen; the first wave under the new year-long paradigm. Our predecessors were packing up and preparing to go home at this point, 5 months into the deployment. We, conversely, sit with more months still to go then months left behind.

You can see it on the faces of these seasoned Chiefs and Commanders; their bodies are telling them it's time to go home, and their minds are for the first time really grasping how ungodly long a year away is. Oh, certainly they had their ideas prior to now, but never with such clarity, never with such weight of reality behind it.

Without the luxury of prior deployments under my belt, I am certainly much less prepared than they. All that really means, though, is that I didn't see the wall coming as I ran headlong into it.

We are all beginning to exhibit the signs of one concussed.

~

My family is quick to point out my look of fatigue on those occasions they see me on a video-call. The mirrors here can't quite reflect the change — they don't remember how you used to look quite as well as the people back home do.

But I am tired. It's been seven months since I've had what could be called a weekend. Longer since I've been able to go home for one. A minor thing, it may seem, but five years of Architecture school taught me not to take weekends for granted. The cumulative effect of skipping due recharges for so long leaves energy levels precipitously low. And apathy begins its creep in.

I've accomplished the things I've set out to do. I've met the attainable goals, and damnit if I don't feel like making new ones right now. But it's a moot point, anyway. Realistically speaking, further progression requires large scale changes on the part of individuals above and away from here — changes which make no appearance of happening soon, if ever. There's not really anything left for me to do but go through the motions, to continue in the incomplete system I've been able to construct within the limitations.

Such are the fertile seeds of apathy, and this isolation the water that makes it grow.

~

No one back home would believe the stuff of my daydreams these days... such simple, simple things. Sitting on my patio with a coffee mug, watching the sun rise above the backyard on a lazy Saturday morning; going out to grab a beer with friends on a whim; eating just one fresh, delicious piece of sushi, driving the smooth rolling hills on a tree-lined Alabama highway; actually feeling the touch of a loved one.

I've been separated from normal life now longer than ever before. I'm worn down, sore, and ailing, ready to be done. I've reached the bottom of what I have to give.

But they're picking me up off the floor, saying "43 more games to go, rook. We're just getting started."

MERRY EID!

23 October

A welcome respite from our daily routine comes in the form of Eid, the nearly weeklong feast signifying the end of Ramadan and its accompanying fast. The entire country shuts down—from government offices to street corner watermelon vendors—and takes a celebratory holiday.

Bosses give bonuses to their employees, workers bring treats (aptly named Eid cookies and Eid cakes) to their colleagues. Soldiers and migrant workers return home to their families. Every household is caught up in entertaining guests and traveling to be someone else's visitors, often at virtually the same time. It is both hectic and relaxingly slow.

And it all feels rather familiar.

Johnny U and I take to wishing everyone a "Very Merry Eid" and handing out brightly decorated Eid cookies. We may or may not have put up an Eid tree outside the office window. It is also unconfirmed whether or not we attempted to sing a song beginning with the words: "On the first day of Eee-eeid, my true love gave to me…"

~

Despite any potentially disqualifying shenanigans, Colonel Ata gracefully invites me to his home to celebrate the first day of Eid. I take The Coolman along so that it will qualify as "A Mission." We grab Ramin on the way.

The Colonel lives with one of his families in a modest adobe structure adjacent to the ceremonial entrance of Camp Shaheen [I say "one," because he has two other homes, with two other wives at the helm, elsewhere in the country]. He greets us at the door and brings us into the receiving room, where some other guests are already seated. It is a cozy space, with blankets and cushions lining the perimeter. Colonel Ata apologizes for the lack of western seating. We chuckle at this remark, sinking into the crimson pillows, and respond that we weren't exactly here for a western-style event. He next chides us for not bringing the rest of the Navy. Unbeknownst to me, Afghan dinner invitations apply to you AND everyone you happen to know.

The ubiquitous green tea appears shortly, along with candies, pistachios, and Eid cookies. Our host disappears into the rear room for more preparations. Ramin also leaves to answer his cell phone. The Coolman and I are left to share an odd silence with some extended Ata family members. Greetings having already been exchanged some time ago, we are well past the usefulness of my Dari proficiency.

So, instead we smile, and sip tea.

Our compatriots do the same. This goes on for some time. Occasionally someone has an Eid cookie. Colonel Ata reenters and finds a comfortable seat at the head of the room. More smiling.

Thankfully, the Important Man eventually returns from his phone call so that verbal communication can resume. Just behind him, more guests arrive. They are faces we recognize — other ANA officers from the Garrison. More pleasantries are exchanged as everyone settles in for an afternoon of socializing.

Stories are told, tea glasses are emptied and refilled. After a time, our host clears the serving area. A boy appears with a pitcher of water and a bowl. He pauses in front of each guest, pouring water over their hands and into the bowl. Ramin explains that this practice allows the guests to continue socializing, rather than breaking conversation to wash up for the meal. Every element of entertaining is constructed to prevent unnecessary activity for one's guests.

Colonel Ata again disappears into the back rooms of his home, returning with platefuls of food to place in front of his ready visitors. The center of the room quickly fills with dishes of mutton, rice, greens, and flat breads. For her husband's vegetarian mentor, Mrs. Ata has specially prepared a dish of spinach dumplings, garnished with yogurt sauce and kidney beans. Complementing our Eid meal are traditional Pepsis and orange sodas imported from Dubai. It is delicious, if somewhat mixed, fare.

After we have eaten our fill, we are encouraged to eat even more, in accordance with customary Afghan hospitality.

More green tea and candies appear, as does a very sweet pistachio cake, for dessert. A few of Colonel Ata's small children also appear to meet the guests. His wife, though, stays hidden in the back.

We are regaled with more stories from our dinner partners. But, after a while, the blood begins to flow to our stomachs, and the cushions are perhaps too comfortable, so we must graciously take our leave. As we say our thank-yous and goodbyes on the Colonel's doorstep, no less than ten new visitors are on their way in. Doubtless, it will continue to cycle as such for the rest of the day, until he closes the door to begin his own round of visitations.

THE SPACEMAN COMETH

9 November

It is so obvious a concept that I surely should have realized it sooner, rather than continue to get overrun with the stress of the day-to-day. When overwhelmed with one's duty, sometimes the best thing to do is to step back and do something that reminds you of your real purpose. This is particularly apropos in a situation like this, far from home and in servitude of an—at times—ambiguous cause.

Some months ago I requested of you dear friends and family to send donations for schoolchildren in lieu of care packages for us. After a number of boxes had piled up in response, Ramin and I took to filling backpacks, 50 of which had been sent by my ever-charitable mother for the purpose. It turned out to be a much larger job than the two of us had anticipated, taking the better part of two weeks to accomplish.

Very much on the fly, and with fairly amusing discussions on relative value [*"Hey, does 3 gummy erasers, 2 big magic markers, and kiddie sunglasses sound about even to a watercolor set, smiley face ring, and a Hotwheels® car?"* and *"Okay, we're all out of rubber bouncing balls, should I give him some extra pencil sharpeners or what?"*] we managed to stuff the canvas containers full of all manner of educational supplies and extracurricular goodies.

Every kid received a couple packs of crayons, a package of pencils, a coloring book, a drawing pad or notebook, a folder or binder, a package of either watercolors, markers, or colored pencils, a "How The Grinch Stole Christmas" pencil pack with matching sharpener and ruler (courtesy of some overstock sell-off my mother found), and, of course, a grab bag of toys, fun trinkets, games, and candy to rot their teeth. The arduous labor of equal appropriation behind us, the more important task of actually handing out the bags still remained.

An unanticipated mathematics problem arose, however, when we attempted to plan this portion of the activity. We had 50 wonderfully overstuffed backpacks, yes, but no school in the area had less than a thousand students, Senior Chief Volkl (the CERP coordinator) tactfully informed me. We certainly couldn't show up at an impoverished school and give to only a relative handful of the students. The classic starfish proverb ("Matters to that one!") didn't exactly apply, either. We glumly predicted: "Even if we were to give the bags to the top students, the dumb ones will just beat them up and take the bags!" The last thing we wanted to do is start fights, which is unfortunately the typical response to inequitable distribution. Instead, we waited until a reasonable opportunity would present itself.

When the general donation stores had filled, Mr. Volkl called to say he was planning a supplies drop. Though we still hadn't developed a specific plan for the bags, he figured the school headmaster could make the decision on how it should be handled. Besides, Senior Chief pointed out, with all the other donations, it won't look so unfair. He'd let me know when a mission could be scheduled.

A few weeks later, two days before I was to go on leave, he caught me at breakfast. "Got those bags ready, Sir? We're going to do the drop today."

With so many unfinished and urgent things swirling, as they tend to do right when you're trying to leave some place, I waffled. I didn't think I had the time.

"I gotta know right now, Sir, yes or no?" He laid it on the line in that pleasantly reassuring Chicagoan fashion. I almost said no, so consumed with the hectic atmosphere my upcoming departure had brought, figuring it could always be done when I returned. No hurry, the school would still be there in a month. But guilt at the thought of so many useful supplies sitting unused simply because I was busy changed my mind. Thankfully. A few hours later, we were on a convoy heading into Mazar-i Sharif. Ramin was of course at my side, excited at the opportunity to do some charity—and play with the kids.

Just outside of the main city, we pulled off onto a side street. We were lead inside a large courtyard where a number of tents bordered a makeshift volleyball court and playground. Across from the tents, an older brick and stucco building L-ed around the open area. Every room and tent was filled with dozens of young students. Most of them sat on the ground, as only a few classrooms had desks or chairs.

Senior and I talked briefly with the principal and headmaster to determine a course of action. Without hesitation, the headmaster declared that the top students from each class would receive the specially prepared backpacks. He yelled a few commands into the air, and the faculty scattered to retrieve the select.

Almost immediately, a line of rather frightened looking young boys began to assemble in the courtyard, undoubtedly unaware of exactly what they had been grabbed for. When all had obediently arrived, I began to hand out the backpacks one by one. Sensing their nervousness, I became rather self-conscious of my appearance, decked out as I was in armor and armament. I shed my helmet and sunglasses, in what was probably a vain attempt to look human. Regardless, I still felt like a Spaceman making handouts, and was probably perceived as such—especially considering the somewhat mythic reputation American soldiers seem to have among Afghani children.

While I was having these internal existential debates about my role and presence in this event, Mr. Volkl disappeared to conference with the principal about a proposed school expansion (his primary reason for the trip), leaving me in charge of the drop. After my personal delivery, there was still another truckload of supplies to distribute.

As thoughtfully arranged by Mr. Volkl, this was a joint operation with the Afghan National Army, and a dozen ANA soldiers had accompanied us on the mission. It was time to turn the show over to them. After a brief discussion with the headmaster, he began to bring out each class, one at a time, to receive the donations. The ANA soldiers, to their credit looking much less like Spacemen than I, opened up the boxes in the truck and began handing out armfuls of notebooks, pencils, and candy to each of the students. The Americans present did our best to fade into the background. For reasons of reputation, it was important that the effort appear as much an ANA mission as an American one. Community service is, of course, a very effective means of endearing the soldiers to the local population.

When it was clear that the process was running smoothly, Ramin and I left to tour the classrooms. We made simple conversation with the young students, asking what they were studying and so forth. Most of the teachers, surprisingly, were young women. A few were noticeably unsettled by our sudden arrival, others gratuitously receptive. We thanked them all for their efforts in educating the young generation, and although I felt rather clichéd in saying it, I stressed to the students that what their teachers were offering was much more important than the pencils and candy we handed out that day.

Smiles, apologies for the interruption, then on to the next classroom... *Azwakt tah-tahn tashakor.* (Thank you for your time)

Far too soon before it was time to head back to Camp Spann. The load of supplies had quickly been exhausted and despite the joy of this charity, upon our departure it was still difficult to feel that we had really made much of an impact. The truck that had seemed overflowing when we headed out now seemed so inadequate, so... not enough. Such is, I imagine, the overriding theme of charity.

Meanwhile, the drive to fill the need continues. My aunt in Washington has mobilized her staggering list of contacts and created somewhat of an Afghan Charity Central in sleepy Walla Walla. Other family members scour the internet and newspaper for clearance and wholesale supplies. Boxes arrive weekly, and we'll soon arrange another visit to another needy school.

Thanks to everyone who's sent packages. Every crayon box and pencil is much appreciated.

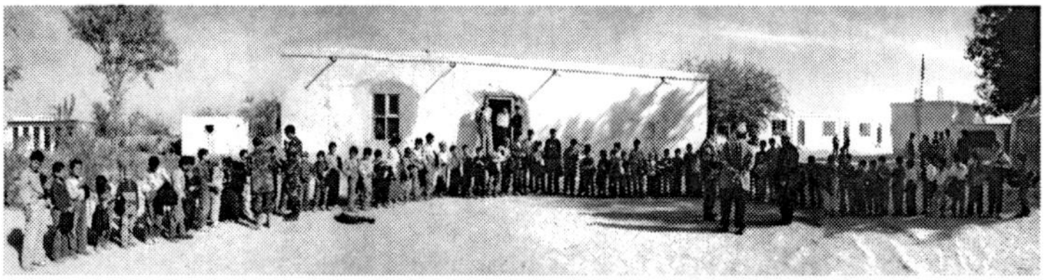

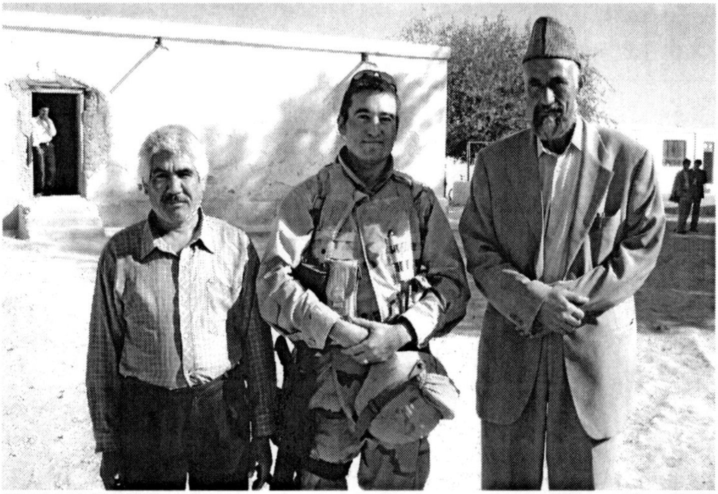

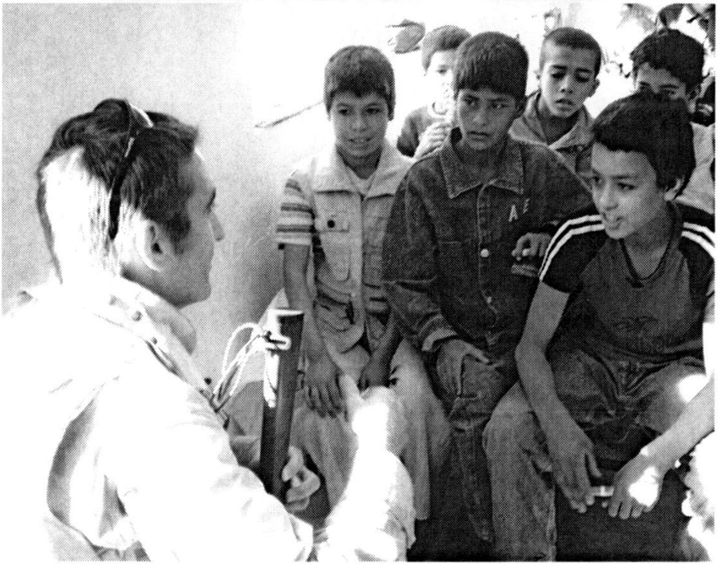

THE REPRIEVE, PART I

10 - 17 November

THE ESCAPE...

ᛉ

BAGRAM AIRFIELD, BAGRAM, AFGHANISTAN — As with most things governmental or military (or, God forbid, both), exiting the country for leave is far from simple. The constantly replicating reams of paperwork and the tribulations of scheduling aside, the act of traveling itself is beastly.

In order to be home for Thanksgiving with the family, I must attempt to leave Mazar-i Sharif in early November. Being a relatively small and unimportant outpost, our US air support is minimal. Instead, we generally rely on ISAF flights (Norwegian, German, etc.), which are notoriously finicky, canceling flights and bumping American passengers with little warning and less explanation. To get out normally requires a few attempts.

My first day's flight was unceremoniously cancelled, but on the second I took the hour-long convoy down to the International Airstrip. We waited on the tarmac for nearly five hours before the fashionably-late Norwegian charter arrived to whisk us down to Kabul Intl. Airport. There, I was very lucky to catch a ride on a C130 [a small military-spec cargo jet] operated by the Puerto Rican Air National Guard. An hour later, I was on the ground at Bagram Airfield, the administrative center of "Leave" operations. Here I would check my weapons, ammunition, and armor and wait for several days for a flight to Kuwait.

~

(Side note: Bagram seems to have tripled in size in the six months since we initially passed through. The circus tent that was our home for three days has been replaced by a massive Conex box apartment complex. Tens of thousands of personnel live and work at the air base, infesting the streets and public areas with unimaginable crowding [considering this is technically still a war zone]. I feel instantly out of place, like the farm hand visiting the big city for the first time. Transitioning from our little forgotten FOB to this burgeoning monstrosity is quite the culture shock.)

~

On the day of my escape flight, I am to be at the terminal at 0800 for a briefing (to supplement the four or five other briefings already suffered through at this point). There are several roll calls and several interminable periods of anticipation until my flight finally departs late in the afternoon. About one third of our waiting group does not get a seat on the plane. For them, the sojourn will be a day longer.

It is a five-hour flight on the larger C17 cargo jet, operated by the Air Force. It is marginally more comfortable than the C130, but just as loud, and I am still sitting sideways in a fabric jump seat. When we arrive in Kuwait, we are subjected to another bureaucratic wonder, with more paperwork, more briefings, extensive over-use of roll calls, and a roughly 28-hour layover. Part of this time includes an excruciating customs process involving the removal of every single item from one's luggage, carry-on baggage, and person for inspection. This can be particularly troublesome when you are carting a footlocker full of authentic Afghan gifts home for your family members. If one does manage to re-pack their things (there could very well be several unfortunate souls still there frantically re-stuffing luggage), the next step is a six- to twelve-hour lockdown. I do not, here, exaggerate. Once sanitized by customs, it is apparently imperative to prevent contamination. Thus, all passengers are shuttled into a fenced off area until it is time to leave for the flight.

It is then a two-hour bus trip to the Kuwait City airport to board the chartered military plane. It must be noted that the Kuwait freeway system is the nicest—if, perhaps, the only—one I've seen in this portion of the world. With the landscape outside, seen through slight curtain openings, it would take little imagination to believe the bus was crossing the American West, vice this Middle East.

We wait in the bus, on the airstrip, for the plane to be readied. Once aloft, it is another 13 to 15 hours flying back to the US, including a refueling stop in Germany. I have a middle seat.

A lifetime later in Atlanta, there is more processing (but thankfully no more briefings), and each go their separate ways on connecting flights. Mine took me to my parents' home in Columbia, SC. I arrived on a Thursday afternoon, roughly one week after leaving Mazar. The lady world arrive within an hour, and then we would join with the rest of the family for Thanksgiving.

I am severely jet-lagged, fatigued, and completely overwhelmed with the shock of returning to modern suburbia. But I will have to adjust quickly, as there are only 14 days to try and feel normal until I have to reverse this god-awful quest and return (eventually) to Afghanistan.

THE REPRIEVE, PART II

2 - 10 December

The Return...

It took several days to re-adjust. I was surely overwhelmed, and visibly so, by my sudden reinsertion into the regular American life. On some levels it was very difficult to relate to an environment that seemed so excessive and trivial after the perspective six months in the third-world brings. In other, very functional ways, I often felt lost in the swirling busyness. I needed to reacquaint myself with such simple things as privacy, freedom of movement, and, most of all, intimate contact.

After half a year apart from family and loved ones, I was surprisingly unprepared for the hugs and kisses greeting me upon my arrival. Relationships at this level were not something I could readily practice over the preceding months. A sudden reappearance into a loving environment is an entirely incapacitating experience. It is not something I can easily put into words.

Touch is a quite serious thing to have done without.

It takes time to reacquire one's humanity. And, as I am realizing, practice. Like a stroke victim relearns his left and right footed steps, so too must the separated relearn closeness with the ones he loves. But, only as I was beginning to again feel comfortable in normalcy, my reprieve was ending.

It is an altogether somber realization that you will soon forget how to walk.

An early morning flight brought me back to the Atlanta airport, where I would spend most of the day waiting for the follow-on flight to Kuwait. After the typically lovely tram ride from the outer reaches of the complex (where flights to premiere destinations like Raleigh, Boise, and Columbia, SC are generally beholden), I descended the escalator through the main terminal, towards baggage claim [switching from commercial to military travel always requires a rechecking of baggage]. At the terminus of my moving staircase, the local USO chapter had organized a waiting crowd, a crowd which burst into applause at my appearance. Lest I get an inflated ego about the whole thing, they proceeded to cheer for two more uniformed individuals arriving soon after myself and, presumably, for each of the several hundred more who would follow throughout the course of the day. Flush with celebrity, I decided to treat myself to a nice breakfast—figuring that quality meals would soon be in short supply, once again. I was thwarted in this last attempt to use US dollars, however, as no sooner had I begun my traditional last meal, it was paid for by a professional looking couple at a neighboring table.

In the eleven and some odd hours to follow, this scenario would repeat numerous times in various forms—though, unfortunately, not again involving food. Many offered their prayers and best wishes, emphasizing their appreciation and thanks.. No less than a half dozen initiated extensive conversations, more often than not centered on the question of just what on earth I was doing stuck in with all these Army fellows.

As the lone desert-camouflaged individual in an increasing sea of green Army digital, I guess the assumption of my ambassadorship was somewhat understandable.... and pause, as the older gentleman from the USO initiates another grand applause for our collected group of uniforms... The gratitude is overwhelming, especially as it comes so strongly from people who have no idea what I'm actually doing, or even what country I'm working in. It is sufficient that I'm wearing "Our Uniform" and I'm headed "Over There." "Thank you for protecting our nation." I can't say I understand their patriotic certainty, nor can I profess to truly share it. A country shrug and "I'm just doing my job, ma'am" is all I really know to respond.

When they thank me for my sacrifice, I flinch. That part of me is a little raw. I wonder if it is another kind word to them, or if they really understand that part of it. I know that two-time Vietnam vet could, sadness and pride balanced in his eyes as he wished me well. Who can say for the rest?

Two weeks home, with the lady at my side and our families surrounding us, are a sharp reminder of just how much we do give up. A half day's flight brings me back to Kuwait, and a half a world away from "my life." Stepping off the plane into the empty battlefield of an older war, I feel only one thing: isolation.

~

It is snowing in Bagram, no flights in or out. We'll have to hole up in Kuwait's transient village for a few days until the weather clears. I latch on with a pair of Army warrant officers, each having 26 years and several war efforts under their respective belts. I soak in their stories of combat from both Iraqs ('91 and today) and their recent adventures in southern Afghanistan. While intriguing to hear, thankfully its a far cry from my day-to-day reality.

When the Afghan blizzards pause, and everyone has had their fill of the Kuwaiti *Mak-Doenaldz* [per the Arabic phonetic spelling Ramin has taught me just enough to read], we board a C17 for Bagram. Midway through the flight, the cargo bay lights switch from green to red, signaling our transition into contested air-space.

We're back on.

~

Upon our 0430 arrival at Afghanistan's primary air base, we have several hours before the necessary administrative bodies open up shop. Over an extended breakfast, the Chief Warrant

Officers continue to regale me with their war stories. I, in turn, impress them with my fabulously pedestrian military service history misspent on construction sites. When the bureaucratic powers-that-be awaken, we retrieve our stored gear (weapons and such) and are informed of the plans for the next stage of travel. All those heading to (or through) Kabul are to pile in the back of a 5-ton (a canvas topped flat-bed truck) for a thoroughly unpleasant two-hour jaunt down to Camp Phoenix.

It is about 25 degrees outside.

In an effort for which I am truly grateful, one of the aforementioned storytellers, Chief Knepper, hits the phones and finds a more comfortable ride for me with one of his connections. Instead of the unprotected 5-ton, I'll have a seat in an armored—and heated—Humvee. In addition to comfort and security, I'll also have the ability to observe this entirely different Afghanistan — one that has dropped nearly 50 degrees in temperature since I left 3 weeks ago — clearly through windows, vice the blind ride of the 5-ton cargo bed.

~

Outside of the airfield's fence line, the accompanying village has taken on a new character. The former desert outpost now imitates a Mongolian hamlet, costumed as such with this dress of winter frosting. The surrounding fields of adobe ruins, before merely a raised texture on the desert surface, now cast dark brown lines across the basin. Their jagged profiles jut above the snow like the last remnants of a thousand gingerbread cottages, where all the candy bits have been picked off and only the broken foundations peek up between layers of vanilla icing.

Leaving the Bagram vicinity, these interruptions begin to fade into white. Roughly a foot of snow has covered the desert plain. The mountains and foothills are likewise powdered.

This austere landscape, clean of vegetation and human sprawl, seems cut from an Arctic photo spread in *National Geographic*; it is like nothing I've seen in the States. Where one would expect the crumpled edges of buried shrubs and trees, here the surface rolls smoothly, broken visually only by occasional strains and speckles of leather-hued rock faces.

~

The eventual arrival in Kabul means but one thing, an extended wait for the opportunity to leave. I am lucky to only pause a couple of days, many before me have waited over a week for their last flight. With this relatively quick final leg, I return to Mazar-e Sharif approximately one month after departing. By all accounts, I have spent as much time traveling as I have spent in relaxation, though the latter is actually the point of the trip.

But after six months away, such transience is
a small price for a touch of normality.

Even as that touch fades, and feeling again begins to recede.

WELCOME HOME (?)

12 December

FORWARD OPERATING BASE SPANN, MAZAR-I SHARIF, AFGHANISTAN — The bright-sider might opine that a man is blessed who experiences two homecomings, received when he arrives as well as after he leaves. Not possessing rose-tinted glasses precludes me from such romanticism at the moment.

Given my profound lack of a sunny disposition, it cannot be too surprising that I did not look upon my return to Afghanistan with much anticipation. Afghanistan, however, seemed to take her own perspective on matters. Within hours of my arrival to Mazar, Ramin was ringing my phone. "We missed you very much... The workers ask every day when you are coming back!"

The next morning, I see for myself. Huddled in the cold outside the complex gates, their faces light up when they realize it is me behind the wheel of the white Ranger, coming to pick them up. Each man gives me a strong hug and jabbers extended welcomes in Dari. Ramin narrates, "It is the culture of Afghani-people to kiss your cheeks in greeting—but we won't do that, in order that you won't be made to be uncomfortable... But everyone is excited to see you back safely here."

Needless to say, I am touched by the reception. It softens the blow, a bit, of leaving my family behind once again.

"Was Senior Chief really that bad to have in charge while I was gone?"

~

The next day, the workers arrange a luncheon of sorts. It is a show of gratitude for Senior's fill-in duty and a celebration of my return. They set up a table in the middle of the shop, right in between the tools and sawdust piles. Paper plates and Cokes are retrieved from the KBR cafeteria. From town, Ramin brings "burgers" [decidedly not hamburgers, instead an Afghani flat-bread wrap creation somewhat resembling the old Tucson standby, potato-egg-and-pico burritos]. Karim shows off his cooking mettle, serving up a slow-cooked red bean stew with fresh baked loaves of bread.

It's all very impromptu, and exquisitely so.

Senior Chief chuckles at the scene, before declaring, "Well, I'm hungrier than a hostage. What are we waiting for? Let's eat!"

It's rarely a good idea to ignore the orders of a salty old boatswain's mate, so eat we do. And the food is excellent. It is not long before I've decided this is the best meal I have eaten in Afghanistan (though KBR is hardly competition). Everyone present stuffs themselves on the bounty. Tea is, of course, served.

After no one can manage another serving, Ramin asks permission to pray a blessing. It is a short thanks to God for the meal. A little surprised, Senior and I explain that Christians tend to thank God before they've eaten the meal. Our Afghan friends are quite amused by this.

"How can you say thanks for something you haven't yet received? Before the meal, there is no guarantee from God that you will be allowed to finish it. Once the food is inside your belly, then you can thank God for blessing you with it."

We have no response for this logic.

A simple twist of custom, completely unanticipated by our trained graces but so entirely sensible. It is one of many slight paradigm shifts here, indicative of the inshallah° thought-culture in which no future minute's event can be taken for granted. I can't say whether this is merely an Afghan trait, or an overarching Muslim theme, but I find it particularly crucial to understanding this nation's burned in philosophy in the midst of assisted progression. This is a country of survivors, and even

in the most casual activities, this fact rises to the surface.
It may be my brief Western refresher that makes the
irregularity stand out, here and now. But, however
small such semantic distinctions, this is another one
of today's reminders of being a world away. The days
to come will assuredly be filled with many more.

~

Welcome home, they insist...

And while part of me recoils at the notion that I somehow
belong here, the other recognizes that even the most unlikely
locales grow into one's being, given enough time to seed. Such
is the nature of humanity. We were never built to hover.

** Inshallah: "if God is willing." Dari, though Persian in origin, is peppered
with this Arabic phrase whenever a future tense is used — including, but
not limited to: giving directions ("when you come to the signpost, inshallah,
make a left"), setting appointments ("the meeting will be tomorrow at noon,
inshallah"), and, of course, saying "See you in the morning.. inshallah!"*

STATUS CHECK

25 December

Didn't happen this year. Moving on...

1 January

The beginning of the year tends to cause one to reevaluate their station in life, find the "you are here" tag on the strip-mall map, come to grips with their place in the world, and so forth.

Okay...

I live in a small plywood box, with four other people, among a number of quite similar small plywood boxes at the base of the Hindu Kush mountains. Thick walls and concertina wire separate me from the country outside, much less separates me from the cold. Tonight, the temperatures will drop into the single digits. There are five blankets on my bed attempting to keep the warmth in. I will try in vain to resist the urge to make the hundred-some-odd meter walk to the restroom trailer. It is damn cold.

Cold is not something I'm used to. The farthest
north I've ever taken up residence? Los Angeles.
To me, snow is something you visit.

But then, there's plenty here I wasn't previously used to.

For the first 8 months of this deployment, the five core members of the Garrison staff were sitting on top of each other in a makeshift office crammed into half of a Conex-box. That's an O-5 Commander (The Boss), an O-4 Lt. Commander (The Coolman), a pair of Lieutenants (Johnny U and myself), and an E-8 NCO (Senior Chief Clark)[†] attempting to make a work area in a space roughly equivalent to a mini-van's interior dimensions.

We've gotten to know each other rather well.

For the new year, however, we've finally graduated to a usable office commensurate with our respective ranks. Given the situation, anyway.

The plywood B-hut we claimed needed a fair bit of work after being vacated by the Germans. Being a boatswain's mate, Senior Chief's first priority was a fresh coat of paint. Far from an ocean-going vessel as we are, junior paint chippers are at a bit of a shortage. But Senior Chief was not one to be stymied, and instead found a local contractor to do the work. This decision we would all soon regret.

The supplies attainable for a given Afghan contractor are limited. There is, for instance, only one readily-available solvent in the country: petrol. That being the case, diesel fuel is used to cut every oil-based substance from paint to varnish. The entire interior of our new office was thus coated in diesel-cut light brown paint. It was several days before anyone could enter the building, let alone move in. Even now, weeks later, the fumes are so pervasive they have saturated every item of clothing we have.

We can't breathe, but at least we have plenty of room.

~

Further displaying his sea-going roots, Senior Chief was compelled to stencil the letters "N," "W," "T," and "D" on the inside of our front door. For those who haven't lived their lives on ships, this is an acronym one would find regularly stamped about the inside of a naval vessel. It stands, appropriately, for "Non-Water-Tight-Door."

~

It would seem that Senior isn't the only one occasionally conflicted about our current station...

Being the test-case of the Navy's Army Assistance Program* has often put us at odds with the bureaucracy, which isn't yet built to properly support this brave new world of naval service. For all the eagerness in which we were volunteered for these positions within the Army ranks, the system wasn't prepared to manage Sailors embedded in a sister service for greater than a year. Problems range from minor administrative issues to major career-related ones—such as fitness reports, advancement exams, professional qualifications, and promotion credits—where the current system's rules are incompatible with the new situation. It is altogether likely that many Sailors, particularly the junior enlisted, will have their careers hindered by this volunteerism, rather than propelled. And that this will be due to simple lack of preparedness — and a senior class of bureaucrats more concerned with political realities than functional ones — is no less than criminal.

In light of the continual lack of recognition of our current effort by our parent service, Mark (The Caffeinated IT Guy)[††] had this to say:

"Obviously we have an entirely different view of what we're doing here than they do..."

(Turning to an Air Force captain and an Army sergeant, standing in the doorway)

"So, welcome to the Navy, gents, 'cause this isn't considered a Joint Tour."

(To the rest of us)

"And welcome aboard the ship, fellas, 'cause this doesn't qualify as 'Expeditionary.' Just ignore all that dirt out there."

(Face turning red)

"And somebody tell me who all these goddamn Europeans are walking around, 'cause this isn't a NATO tour either."

~

Even if we've figured out "where we're at," the Navy has yet to.

Under blind eyes we serve.

....

* *My own title, by no means an official one.*

† *Editor's note: Though the names of the ranks are different, all US Armed Forces use the same numerical designation and insignia for each equivalent officer rank. Thus, Commander Hassien as an O-5 was equivalent to an Army Lt. Colonel, two spots below an Admiral or General. An O-4 Lt. Commander is equivalent to an Army Major, and an O-3 Lieutenant equivalent to an Army Captain. The enlisted ranks get a bit murkier in translation, but Senior Chief Clark's E-8 rank is equivalent to an Army Master Sergeant, the second-highest enlisted rank.*

†† *Editor's note: As complement to The Coolman's acquired moniker, Mark was christened with the nickname "Left Full Rudder," for his comparable proclivity towards being spun up.*

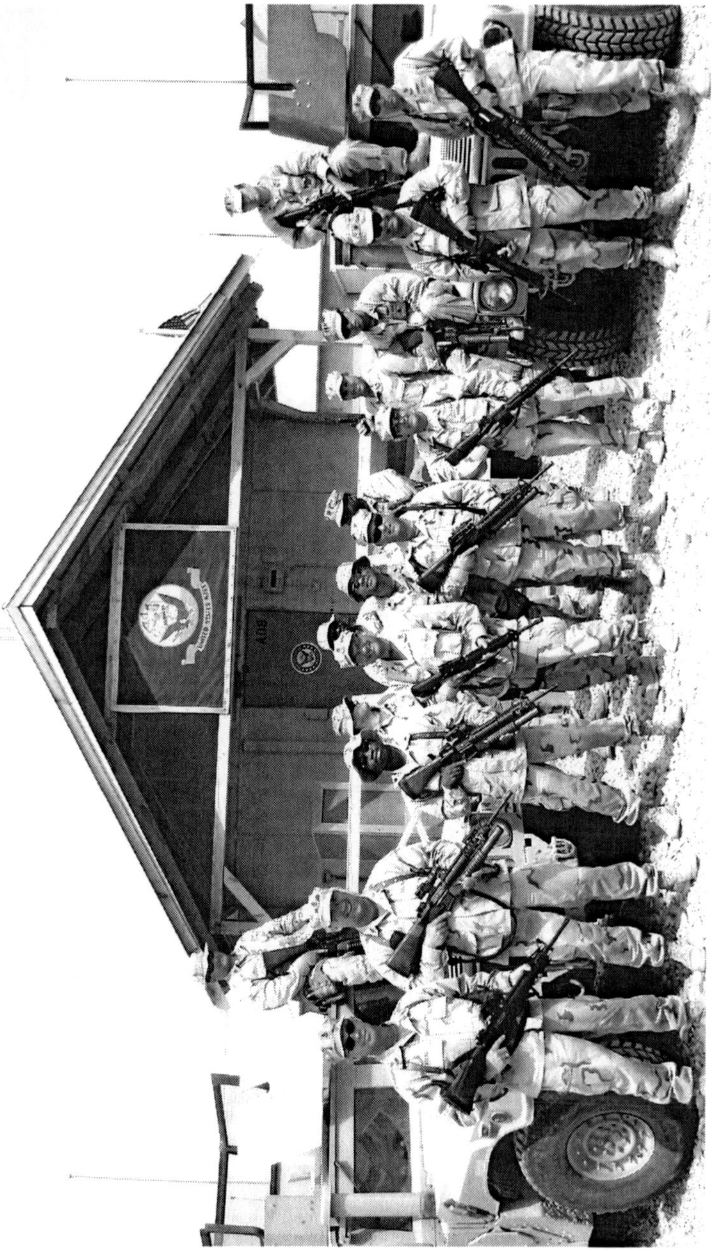

SOME IDEAS ARE BETTER THAN OTHERS

6 January

Either it didn't translate well or I was a little slow that morning; Ramin had to repeat the sentence a few different ways until I caught the request. The shop workers wanted to throw a Merry-Christmas-Happy-Eid party for us, only they had no idea what kind of things one did for a Christmas party. From my experience of the first (little) Eid, I responded that, in general, the celebrations seemed fairly similar—visiting family and friends, sharing big meals, exchanging small gifts. However they wanted to run the show, it would be fine, I assured them.

A few days later, Senior Chief Clark, Johnny U, The Boss, Mr. Beard (my civilian mentoring partner) and I wandered into the wood shop, per the invitation. Glittery ribbons and multicolored balloons hung from the rafters, gaudy plastic flowers were pinned up in strategic locations, and a wooden sign welcomed everyone with the words "Merry Christmas & Happy Eid, for Afghans & Americans, on behalf of the Wood Shop," written in English and Dari.

The center of the shop had been cleared; benches and chairs surrounded a plywood topped workbench serving as the banquet table. Paper plates, sodas, fresh fruit, and more imitation flowers were carefully arranged upon it. We obediently took our seats.

Ramin The Important Man stepped to the front of the shop and formally welcomed us. He explained, on behalf of the workers, that this was a party to celebrate not only the respective winter holidays, but the continued cooperation of Americans and Afghanis. The workers wanted to express their appreciation for our efforts in this small gesture of a Christmas/Eid party. They hoped we would enjoy it, etc. etc. etc.. Like any good keynote speaker, he waxed on while everyone sat hungrily contemplating their empty stomachs.

At some point, Ramin presumably realized his own hunger and wrapped up the speech so Karim could begin serving. First things generally being first, green tea with *naranj* [a local citrus fruit resembling an orange in appearance but tasting like a sweet lemon], Eid cookies, and Eid cakes were brought out to whet our appetites. When the cooking was finished, out came Karim's now-famous red bean stew and some roasted chicken. All was of course supplemented with warm, fresh flat bread.

Needless to say, it was a delicious meal.

After we had all successfully overeaten, Ramin again took center stage. The workers, he announced, had prepared a small program of comedy for our enjoyment. While we the audience sat attempting to imagine what sort of comedy show was about to begin, a small table with two chairs was set in front. Monan's younger brother, Qasim, gamely sat in one chair, Mohib (one of my apprentice soldiers) sat across from him. While Rahim set a large bowl of fresh yogurt between them and wrapped scarves over their eyes, Ramin continued his Bob Barker voice over. For this first act, he explained, the contestants would attempt to feed each other the yogurt while blindfolded.

Hmmm...

For the next ten minutes, the two young men proceeded to spill spoonfuls of yogurt anywhere but each other's mouths. The raucous laughter from everyone else in the room surely was no help to their concentration. Alas, the competition was for naught, as no consensus champion emerged. The audience could not agree whether the person covered with the most yogurt had won or lost.

For the next round of silliness, a single yellow apple was hung from the ceiling on string. The game was, in effect, a drier version of bobbing-for-apples. One at a time, each worker tried his best to bite into the elusive fruit. If he was lucky, no one pulled on the string as he lunged for the target. By all appearances, it was a nearly impossible task—albeit, an entirely entertaining one for the audience.

After the "comedy shows" had run their course, the workers presented us with Christmas/Eid gifts. We each received a framed picture of an Afghan monument or landscape, a bouquet of plastic roses, and a brightly-colored Christmas card that played music when it was opened. Loudly.

(I can't help but wonder where, in a country that is 99.9% Muslim, one goes to buy singing Christmas cards.)

The party now over, we gathered up our gifts and leftovers to stumble back to our day jobs. Each of us wore a face mixed with awe, slight confusion, and contented gratitude. Clearly it had been one of the oddest and most pleasant luncheons any of us had ever had.

~

Perhaps it was the afterglow of this well-conceived idea that warmed me to another much less intelligent one...

Since almost my first week with Ramin, he has been asking me to teach him to shoot. The convergence of my good mood with a range invitation overcame my better judgement, and somehow Ramin ended up out there with Johnny U, myself, and a small group of other Navy personnel.

Despite growing up in a country that's been at war since he was a child, Ramin had never held a weapon. This fact was rather apparent as he casually waved my 9mm around, scaring the bejezus out of me and several bystanders. I immediately recollected the firearm, and did my best to channel my father, carefully reviewing the rules he taught me as a boy (most notably, *"Don't point the goddamn thing at anything you're not planning to kill!"*).

Groundwork established, we went over some basic marksmanship techniques. Once Ramin demonstrated form close enough to correct that I didn't have to worry too much about being shot, I gave him bullets. We set him up on a 25 meter target and let him go. Three or four clips later, we're almost positive he may or may not have hit it with a bullet or two. Fortunately, there was a 10' berm behind the target to absorb any errant shots.

I soberly informed him that he could never be my bodyguard.

Apparently intent on encouraging my interpreter's delinquency, Mark (The Caffeinated IT Guy) and Johnny U called him over to try out a grenade launcher. Fortunately for Ramin, 203's don't require a whole lot of aim. Wearing a grin so wide you could see it from behind, he took the weapon and began launching the explosives in the general direction of the scattered Russian tank carcasses in the field. I thought his heart would surely stop, his excitement was such.

Dear Lord, what have we done? I said to myself.
And then: His wife is going to kill me.

~

Having narrowly survived Ramin's indoctrination to testosterone-fueled gunplay, I imagine Johnny U and I were flirting with feelings of invincibility. Or, at the very least, simultaneous adolescent regression.

Whatever the cause, at roughly the same moment in time, from behind the wheel of two roughly adjacent 4-wheel drive Rangers, we each realized that it was an absolutely perfect opportunity to race the two roughly-terrained miles back to camp.

At speeds well above proper operating parameters, we zigged and zagged across the desert, testing the limits of our respective wills... and of our suspensions. In and around the adobe ruins circling Camp Spann, we bounced and skidded towards the entry gate, neither gaining much ground on the other. By mere tenths of a second I finished ahead of my competition, who, to his credit, resisted a couple of fleeting openings that would have probably resulted in one (or both) of us flipping a vehicle. So there was some good judgement going on, there, at times. Sort of.

This experience taught us a valuable lesson: Johnny U and I were obviously meant to be Baja race drivers.

A little bit of research turned up an outfit in Mexico that provides a vehicle and support team (with helicopters, no less) for aspiring racers like ourselves to run the famous thousand mile course in Baja California. The cost is a piddling seven grand.

Recognizing that some ideas are better than others, we agreed to pass on this opportunity.

You see, for only $63,000 more, you get a grid position to run the course during the actual Baja 1000.

As luck would have it, Jon's got about $70K saved up that he and his wife were going to put towards a house. So we're going to split the cost; he's covering the fee and I'm going to buy all the beer.

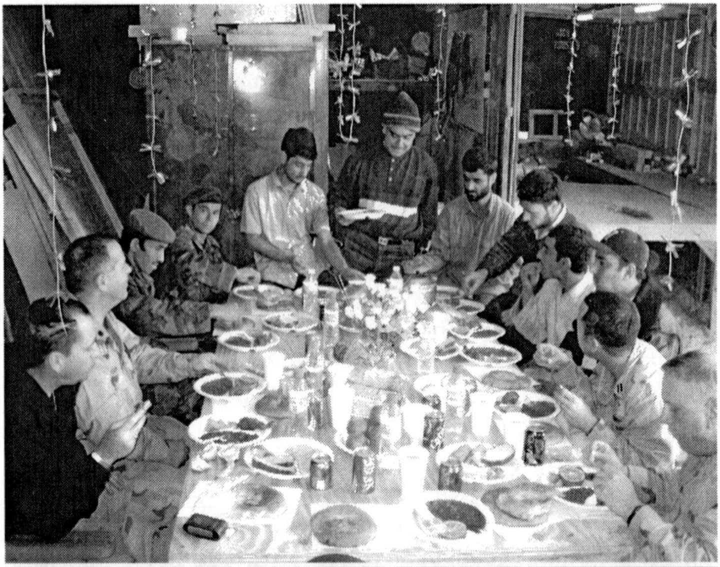

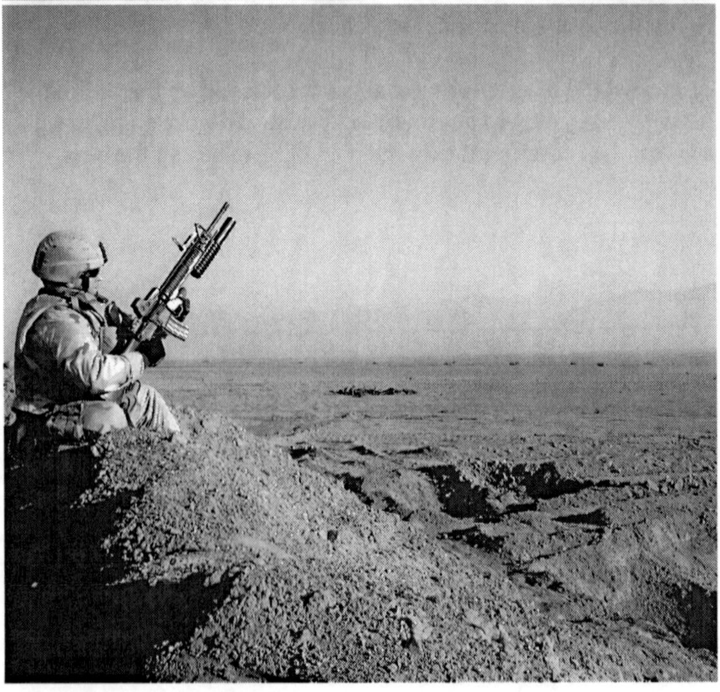

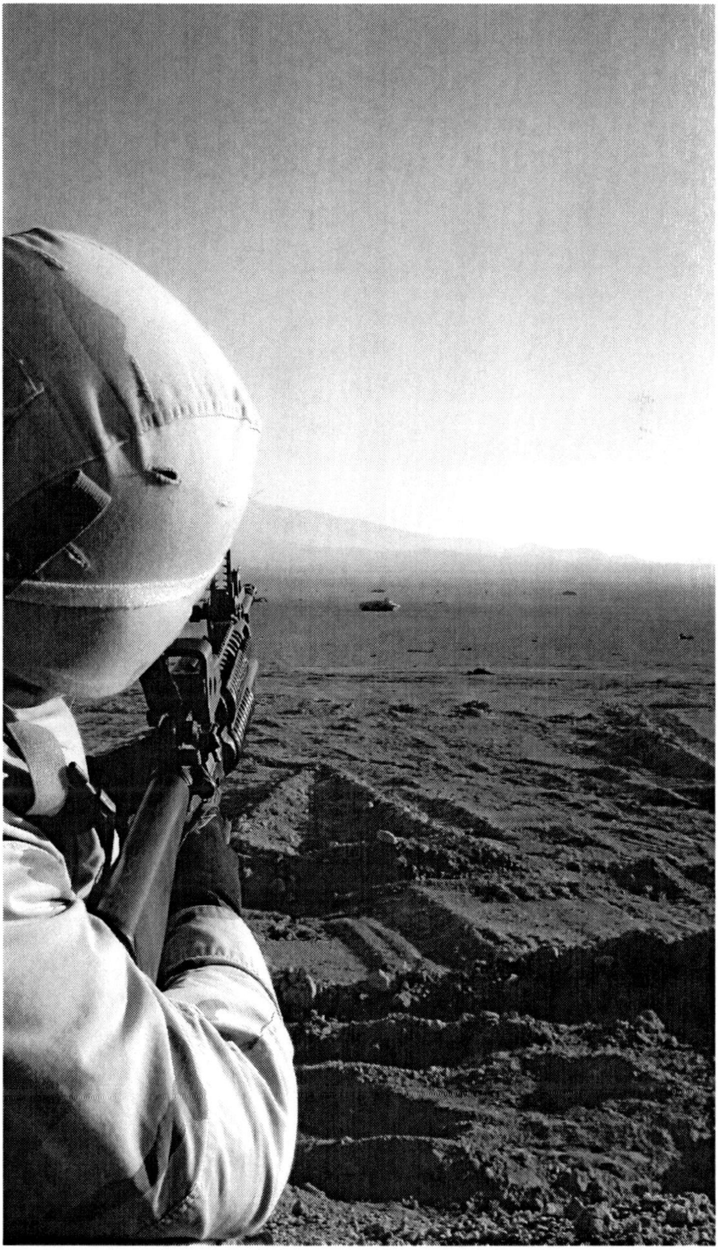

DIA DE LOS MUERTOS

9 January

Surely there have been better-themed days than this for our Johnny U...

Morning began with the unfortunate task of sorting the remaining belongings of a fallen soldier. Popular war films seldom show this part. When one contemplates what he might leave behind, doubtful he considers the half-empty toothpaste tube and the slightly used can of shaving cream. Not romanticized, perhaps, but such banality constitutes a sizeable portion of one's accoutrements nonetheless.

So here Jon kneeled, over a box bearing a dead man's name, sifting through what remained. Several times he raised his head to query us about one item or another, attempting to parse the possibly sentimental from the certainly mundane. A well-worn football and a leather bound bible are placed in the package headed to the family. A blank notebook and assorted supplies are set aside to be burned. Whatever is not sent home will be destroyed.

In the distance there is an explosion. We probably do not hear it, or have become too numb to such sounds to make note.

A quarter hour expires.

Jon's phone rings. The conversation is a short one. He drops the project at hand and rushes out the door. Something has happened at the firing range.

It is a scene, Jon will later say, he wishes
never to have walked in upon.

There is a small crater... and a small body. It is horribly
disfigured, but it is clearly that of a young boy. A man who
must be his father is wailing, restrained a short distance
from the blast point. A few other children, covered in
blood, are being rushed away for a medic's attention.

The world spins around Jon's head.

Someone breaks in to explain what appears to have taken place:

*A group of children, five, six maybe... well, they were combing the
range for expended shells. Collecting the brass for the pennies that
the scrap metal dealers will pay — they all know it's dangerous, but
they do it anyway — one of them saw a mortar half-ways sticking
out of the ground, and it looks like he tried to dig it up... Boom. The
kid never had a chance...the others...well, they're lucky we happened
to be here... we were pulling up right when that thing went off...*

The range is closed. An official investigation begins. A party goes
to the village elders, pleading with them to help keep children away.
Dehdadi is again reminded, with renewed emphasis, to warn its
sons and daughters to leave unexploded ordnance untouched.

For several weeks, the young boys will avoid the area. But
as their memories fade, the lure will regain strength.
Soon they will be back, silently picking the hills clean of
shiny brass bits, hoping to earn a little money for their
families. There is little that can be done to stop them.

Poverty is a relentless mistress.

A pallor hangs over Jon as he returns to his prior duty, one which
distinguishes a man who has seen what no one needs to see.
On two faces, today, he confronts the aftermath of mortality.

And Afghanistan reminds those of us who have
forgotten, death is more certain to her than life.

NAIBI AND THE MAGICAL CHAI BUTTON

14 January

AND IN THOSE DAYS IT CAME TO PASS THAT THE GENERAL OF ALL THE LAND BECAME UNHAPPY WITH THE LACK OF A PROPER DESK BEFORE HIS THRONE...

The Arabian Nights, which I recently re-read in context, has several recurrent cultural themes that stand out as prevalent even in the present day. Of these, the strongest seems to be the practice of hospitality as a moral duty. Whether descended of Arabic, Persian, or some other eclectic tribe, the people of southwestern Asia display an ingrained sense of responsibility for people in their care—be they friend or foe, kin or stranger. It must be stated that this underlying current is far beyond any traditional Western sense of hospitality, not only in its depth but also in comprehensiveness.

To the host's own detriment, even, will a guest be accommodated.

We see pieces of this displayed daily, from the interpreters who continually offer services far above and beyond their real responsibilities to the meagerly-paid workers who bring requested items but refuse reimbursement. On a lighter scale, the day-to-day business with Afghan officers will regularly show this propensity for hospitality. At times, it is more like being welcomed into one's home, than into their office—especially when it is the first meeting.

The other day, I received an invitation to visit General Naibi, the second-highest ranking Afghan in our northern region (and since the highest-ranking man is seldom around, he might as well be the first). Word of my carpenters' skills had reached him, information which brought him to realize his long-standing need for a new desk. Submitting a form was well below a man of his stature, so he summoned us with the intent to talk to the craftsman directly.

With The Boss as chaperone and Ramin (The Important
Man) and Monan (The Chief Carpenter) in tow, I set out to
meet the General. His cavernous office was empty when
we arrived, but for a few enlisted attendants milling about
the receiving area. The Boss, being a regular visitor of
Naibi's, led the way inside. We took our seats to wait.

Thirty minutes past our appointed meeting time, his car pulls up
in front of the building. The sizable, mustachioed officer promptly
quits the vehicle and lumbers past the doting soldiers into his
sanctum. He is a bear of a man, and though pleasant greetings and
contrite apologies for his lack of punctuality have already begun
streaming from his lips, I cannot help but be somewhat intimidated.

Halfway to his desk chair, he stops abruptly. "You do not
have chai?" he queries in Dari. "All this time you've been
waiting?" He chides The Boss, "This is your office if I am
not here; why have you not taken care of our guests?"

The General's face breaks into a grin as he takes
his chair. "Now we will have chai."

With the announcement, he raises his hand and pushes a roundish
button on top of the desk. Behind us, we hear a doorbell-like
buzzer. About fifteen seconds pass in silence. Three soldiers sprint
into the room. The first holds a tray of glass mugs. The second
carries a steaming teapot. The third follows with dishes of treats.

In Afghanistan, almost no meeting can take place before tea has
been served. The chai is almost unfailingly a weakly-brewed
green variety and generally accompanied with some combination
of candies, pistachios, unshelled almonds, golden raisins, and
a sort of dried yellow pea that is almost tasty but somehow not
quite so. This is common. A dedicated Chai Button is not.

To account for his tardiness, General Naibi tells us that he had been
attending a wedding ceremony. It began at six in the morning, on
the other side of Mazar-e Sharif. Seeing our surprise at this, he
nodded in agreement, explaining that this was a foreign concept

to him as well. In Kabul, he went on, a wedding is a cause for huge celebration. Everyone who knows the family joins in and the party can last for days. This morning's wedding was no such thing.

Two hours were set aside for the groom to receive guests. Later in the day, two hours would again be set aside for the bride to receive guests. Only men were permitted at the former, only women at the latter. There would be no mixing the two groups.

Naibi scoffed. "This must be a rural thing," he surmised. "In the city we expect a party, here it is like a funeral. These people think that is a proper Muslim ceremony..."

He paused. Then the corners of his mouth drew a mischievous smile. "...Or they are simply cheapskates!"

In the midst of the belly laugh that followed, he realized that our cups had been emptied. Without a word, he again tapped the magical button. Fifteen seconds passed. An attendant glided into the room, quickly refilled our mugs, and disappeared.

Another half hour was passed in jovial conversation before the General allowed business to be discussed. He described his desires to Monan, who obediently scratched them down into his notebook. A few measurements were taken, and the carpenter had acquired all the needed info.

To celebrate this accomplishment, we were again obliged to partake in a round of chai. Before the fourth fill, the General finally gave us the option to decline. We did so politely and made a gracious exit, leaving The Boss to discuss other important topics...and, presumably, drink another glass of tea.

In the end, the better part of two hours had been taken for approximately three minutes of actual business. Such is the nature of diplomacy, I mused, particularly in Afghanistan. As if to refute the second part of my conclusion, Monan muttered in wonderment as we walked outside. Ramin relayed, "He is asking how the people get anything done acting in this way..."

MAHI!

24 January

Colonel Ata's deputy, Major Salim (of fruit-bringing fame) was dead-set on providing me with an authentic Afghan meal that I had not yet tried. He ran through every non-meat item he could imagine...*Berger? Dal? Boloney?*

And to each I nodded, shaking my thumb towards Ramin (The Important Man), who has made sure I've been well fed from the Afghan markets. After a long, frustrated pause, an impish grin crept under The Major's moustache... "Mahi!" he erupted, jumping from his seat.

"He wants to bring you fish," Ramin relayed as The Major retook his chair, appearing altogether satisfied with himself. Fish, not surprisingly, was something I had yet to taste here in the middle of the desert. Seeing me somewhat incredulous, The Major jumped up again, pointing to the north and jabbering with gusto.

[Allow me a moment's digression to point out that The Major is the only Afghan who speaks directly at me as if I could understand every frenetic word. He will do this whether or not an interpreter happens to be in the vicinity. And, he will expect me to carry on my half of the conversation. I love him for this, if only because I find it endlessly amusing—and entirely incomprehensible.]

The Oxus River, which forms the border between Afghanistan and Russia, is apparently teeming with fish. Some of which, apparently, are brought to Mazar-e-Sharif, where they are indiscriminately chopped into variously sized chunks, tossed into boiling oil — skin, fins, and all — taken from the oil, wrapped in newspaper, brought into the office, and dropped triumphantly in the middle of Colonel Ata's desk by a smiling Afghan Major.

And they are remarkably delicious.

Four of us (Major, Ramin, Col. Ata, and myself) circled the mound of freshly fried fish, greedily pulling the white meat off the bones with greasy fingers. A rather impromptu picnic, it was, and soon we were all quite overstuffed. Seeing we could eat no more, The Major, offered up his second surprise of the day, handing me a towel wrapped package of sorts. Inside was hidden a clear bottle, chipped on the edges like a Mexican longneck Coke. He cast a sly smile and told me it was from his secret collection, smuggled into the country. I examined the labeling, which was a rather superfluous effort, as I can't read Cyrillic. The one word I could make out was printed in English letters on the seal: "Uzbekistan," a former USSR state due north of Afghanistan. Vodka. Apparently.

As we are strictly forbidden from consuming alcohol while in theater, officially I cannot tell you how the illegal elixir tasted.

Unofficially, it's not entirely unlike drinking hand sanitizer.

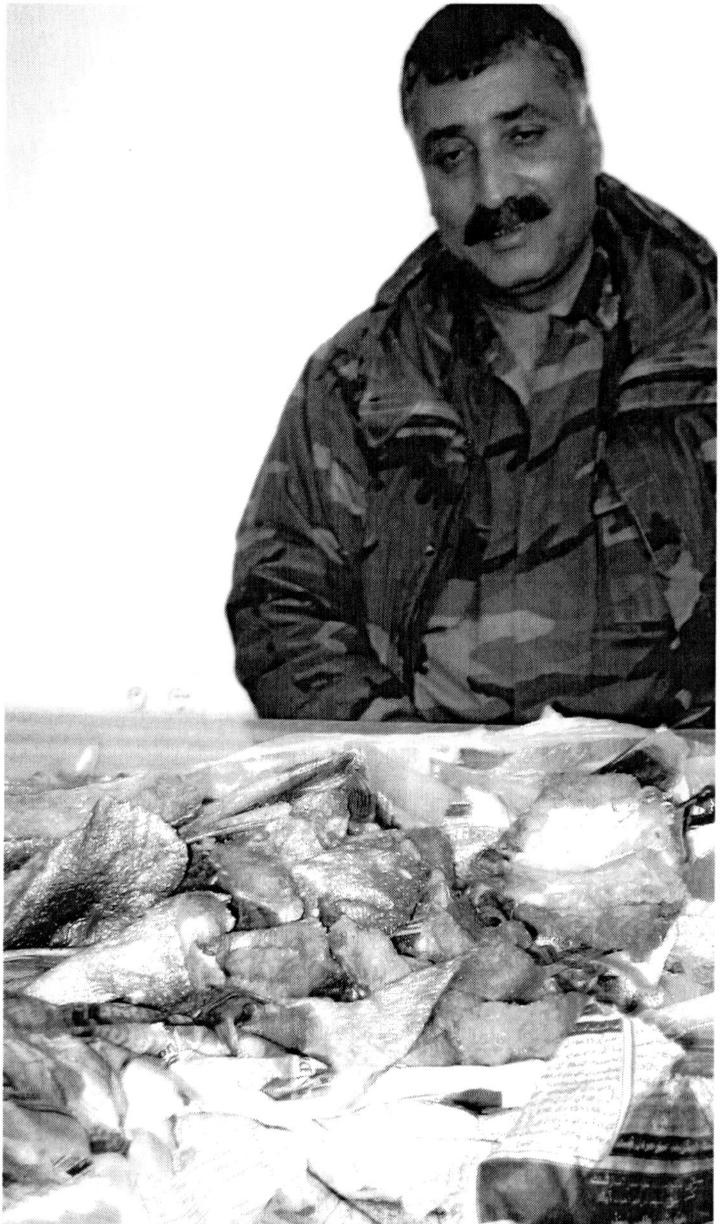

MORSELS OF UNDERSTANDING

27 January

There are a number of little things that make life here unique, many of which I've neglected to mention up to this point. Here's an attempt to rectify that:

FLESH-EATING BACTERIA...do not exist solely in the work of B-movie script writers. Northern Afghanistan is home to a scurrilous breed of sand fly that patrols the dawn and dusk hours of the warmer months, dutifully carrying the Lesch Moniasis plague. The insects cruise at low altitude, on the lookout for exposed skin. They are, quite literally, notorious ankle-biters. Unlike a mosquito-christened welt, the resulting bump does not itch, but develops a sore that gradually expands over the lower leg. After a time, the victim's skin will appear as if it's being taken over by "7-layer bean dip" [to borrow Senior Clark's apt description]. Left to its own devices, the bacteria will spread across the whole body, eventually compromising internal functions and killing its host.

Treatment is similar to chemotherapy, and is not available in this quadrant of the world. If an American or European soldier is so unlucky as to become infected, they are quickly shipped off to Germany or back to the States for the invasive procedure. Capable centers are few and far between for this otherwise rare ailment—only one U.S. military facility, Walter Reed in Maryland, is currently able to treat Lesch. If an Afghan contracts the disease, it is essentially a death sentence.

Despite the emphatic statements from the intelligentsia in Kabul, who categorically denied the possibility of Lesch Moniasis in our area for months (and refused to assist in preventative measures) even as confirmed cases piled up, every instance of the disease in Afghanistan came from our region [for 2006]. As it turned out, the powers that be were reading their map inversely. Mazar-e-Sharif was not the least likely area, but the most likely area to be afflicted. It only took a near-epidemic for this error to be realized.

THEN THERE'S THE MOSQUITOS... that may or may not carry the malaria virus. To the best of my knowledge, there have not been any cases of malaria, or mosquitoes that positively test for it, but the threat is apparently significant enough to require every service-member to take a daily dose of Dioxysomethingorother. These malaria pills wreak havoc on the stomach and cause the strangest dreams, so much so that many people regularly forget to take them—to the chagrin of the medical personnel.°

AND NOW A COMMERCIAL BREAK FROM AFN. Before any disparaging remarks are made of the medium, I must first give credit to Dwight and Mr. Boatright for undertaking the gargantuan satellite television project at Camp Spann. Due to their efforts and ingenuity, ten channels of the Armed Forces Network are now piped in to every residential B-Hut, along with two locally-controlled "MWR" [Morale Welfare Recreation] channels which loop various DVD movies. If you've never experienced the wonder of AFN, each station is dedicated to a particular category of television. There is a sports channel, a news channel, a "primetime" channel, and so on, each a collection of popular American broadcasts grouped by subject matter, irrespective of network affiliations [i.e., an ABC show might follow an NBC show and be followed by a FOX offering, all on the same channel]. The most interesting twist to AFN is the commercial breaks, which are entirely self-programmed by the U.S. military. The result is a series of public service type announcements strung end to end, filling the gaps between shows. Although the spots are poorly scripted, poorly shot, and poorly produced, there is nothing else remotely positive that can be said about them. More often than not, the commercials are decidedly annoying and probably in violation of numerous copyright laws—think cable access amateurism crossed with government warning labels. This is the twist part, certainly not the interesting part.

What is intriguing (to me anyway) is the sociological nature of the experiment—that is to say, observing what results when a bureaucracy is given unfettered control of the only microphone. The product shows us the priorities of the producer. If certain topics are repeatedly the subject of commercials, we should assume that these topics are what the government deems most important for us to know. On this logic, I offer the following list of the United States Military's greatest concerns:

1) Terrorists read my emails
2) Suicide is bad for unit readiness
3) Europe is very dangerous

After several months of AFN indoctrination, I finally have my facts straight. Terrorists can't read newspapers, so they will hack into my email account in order to learn sensitive information readily available from hundreds of popular news sources ... One should avoid suicide because it hurts the Army. Soldiers should never discard their lives as though they have no value—politicians and presidents will do that for them! ... People stationed in Europe should never leave the base because they will be attacked by people who hate Americans. If they do leave the base, they should travel in large groups of people with identical military haircuts and American clothes, but do their best not to appear military or American.

JUST LIKE THE CROATS, WHO ALWAYS TRAVEL IN PACKS... We don't know whether it's for protection, camaraderie, or because they all clump around the one Croatian soldier who speaks English,[†] but we never see a Croat flying solo. Like a jump-suited amoeba, the red-and-blue-clad blob floats about the camp, passing through the dining facility, hovering around the gym, and finally settling in the MWR internet room, leaving a trail of sweat and Slavic mutterings in its wake. It is quite a phenomenon.

EVEN MORE BIZARRE ARE THE BAZAARS... which happen on a bi-weekly basis on most every American camp in Afghanistan. Vendors from downtown (or other towns entirely) are brought on base and squeezed into some awkward, leftover realm of camp that offers some semblance of security. The merchants bring in loads and loads of whatever they can't sell in their stores, line them up in endless rows, and try to pawn them off on cash-laden Americans and Europeans for far more than they're worth. There are carpets, blankets and scarves, antique rifles and knives, jewelry and stoneware, reams of bootleg DVDs, and no small amount of junk.

Like at a good ol' country swap meet, each merchant sets up his booth of wares and makes his pitch to the passerbys. "Hey my friend! Come in look my store!" He will grab your hand with a hearty shake and pull you towards his most expensive items. "Look, high quality! I give you good price!"

Price, of course, is entirely relative.

First, there is the starting price. For a European, this is no less than ten times actual value (higher, depending on how ambitious the dealer). For an American relatively new to Afghanistan, five to eight times the real cost is standard. Those who've acquired a bit of a patina are offered a price only two to three times an item's value, perhaps as a sign of respect, for even the locals won't get much better than this first quote. General rule of thumb: the more Dari spoken by the customer, the lower the price.

[Ramin and I have discussed the merchant mentality at length. I regale him with stories of pre-printed price tags and haggle-free purchases. I try to explain the science behind pricing—attempting to predict the highest amount a storekeeper can charge without losing business to a competitor and balancing this against the minimum profit he needs to make. The result of this balancing act being the sticker price, and everyone will pay the same price. Duly impressed, he will shake his head and tell me "but in Afghanistan it is not this way!" In this country, the merchant judges his mark and throws out the highest, field-of-dreams, all-he-can-hope-for number he thinks he could ever possibly get from the customer and sequentially comes down from there, until he hits his minimum profit margin. The speed and depth to which he drops is a mixture of his evaluation of the buyer and the caliber of his competition.]

Once the merchant has announced the price, he awaits the response. The Europeans generally reach for their cash, disappointing the merchant who has obviously not been imaginative enough in his pricing. If the buyer does not immediately throw money at his feet, the merchant will bring the item closer, encouraging a tactile connection. "High quality! Very good!" he chants. Then it is the buyer's turn to name a price, "How much you want pay? I give good price." Back and forth it will go until the seller decides to close the deal. If he hasn't already done so, in go the things into a plastic bag. He pulls the buyer close, as if whispering a secret no one else should hear, and puts the bag in his hand. "Okay, my friend. I give you special price, no profit. No profit." [††]

The length of the haggle and the final price are wholly dependent on each player's respective stubbornness. If the buyer is sworn to secrecy about what he paid, he is probably justified in feeling a bit smug about his performance. If instead he receives an extra gift AFTER the deal has been made, the merchant is most likely trying to assuage his guilt.

Over time, we all accrete the trappings of the bazaar. Some pile up woodcrafts, for others it is a classical firearm affliction. The interiors of our B-huts become draped with pashmina scarves and our floors covered in cheap afghan rugs. Our mutual shelves, too, become filled with all manner of bootlegged DVDs.

THESE INFAMOUS "HAJI-MOVIES" …are a special breed of unauthorized copies. Named for the Army's current pet term for the locals (see: "Charlie," "Skinnies," et al), the "Haji" versions often feature several movies on a single disc. Some are compressed copies from original DVDs while others sport the classic camcorder-in-movie-theater look. Titles are misspelled on the covers and labels are generally missing from the discs. Movies imported from the Far East offer horrifically translated English subtitles, many of which overlay original Japanese or Chinese subtitles, making for a nearly illegible jumble of characters crowding the bottom of the screen. Many American TV-series are also available; some even advertise "Complete Season" for shows that have yet to air all of their episodes.

LOST...was a serial affliction begun by one of those box-sets. Given nothing more enticing to spend his money on, The Coolman purchased the first season of the popular drama on a whim, for our collective viewing pleasure. For those not familiar, the storyline involves a plane crashing on a tropical island and follows the collective existence of the survivors. The characters find themselves stranded indefinitely in an environment that seems to run on an entirely different set of rules than normal reality. We could relate.

Hooked ever deeper by each successive episode, we barreled through the first season. Until, that is, we reached disc 4 of the set. Disc 4 didn't progress the plot at all because, as it would turn out, disc 4 contained only reruns of the sitcom "Joey."

All of the Haji-version Season Ones, in fact, included this bonus disc in lieu of LOST episodes 13 through 17. Not much for quality control, these bootleggers. We were forced to buy the real thing. And again for the second season. Perhaps it is somewhat sadist to subject ourselves to images of paradise [the show is shot entirely on the Hawaiian island I left to come here], but the lure is unavoidable.[†††]

ROME... here refers not to another television show (though I've heard one now exists by this name), but to the moniker bestowed on our office by our Army brethren. Over the course of the last year, nearly every aspect of this base has come under the control of the Navy. The Boss has been elevated to Chief of Staff, second in authority only to the Army Colonel who presides over the entire region. All of the major functions are run by Navy staff:

Personnel Support? Navy. Communications? Navy. Supply Office? Navy. Network & IT? Navy. Base Ops? Navy. Engineering? Navy. Construction? Navy. Contracts? Navy.

When a new soldier arrives to the camp, he checks in with the Navy, is assigned his living quarters by the Navy, is tasked with his specific job by the Navy, gets his phone from the Navy, gets his internet account from the Navy, and eats his food under a KBR contract managed by the Navy. If he desires to build something for himself or have something built, he goes through the Navy. To shoot on the range, he schedules with the Navy. For this new soldier, every avenue he travels takes him back to the Navy.

If Mazar is the Empire, they say, our Navy office is surely Rome.

Whether this comprehensive takeover was truly intended by those who sent us here is debatable. However, it is in the true spirit of our mission. We, in part, came here to relieve the Army from the constant distraction of managing a base so that their efforts could be wholly focused on war-fighting and training. To this end, I believe we have been successful. While the additional responsibilities keep us far busier than our predecessors, we carry a sense that we have accomplished more than was ever expected of us, when the Army was forced to supplement its own forces with ours. It is with pride that we smile on hearing this Roman-themed banter.

Granted, that pride and humor can only cover exhaustion for so long. So it would seem necessary for further motivation to come from outside, but...

REMEMBER, YOU ARE THE LAST PRIORITY. Every month or so, General Platitude makes the arduous trek up here to deliver that message. By all appearances, this reminder is the only purpose of his visits. Surely history will draw him as The Great Motivator.

In practical terms, what this means is that our post is now last on the list for support, whether that be supplies, new construction, quality of life improvements, or, of course, funding. Ostensibly, we are drawing down in order to shift resources towards the south. In reality, our mission expands by the day, our numbers continually increase, and we are allowed ever less with which to accomplish and accommodate the ever-increasing tasks.

Being that this has become our Empire, it is the Navy—generally—and our office—specifically—that bears the brunt of this responsibility. Little we can do but hold course and push on.

"Strength and Honor."

....

* *I was one of them, lasting only a few days on the pills before permanently "misplacing" the bottle. The lucid dreaming and bouts of nausea trumped official orders.*

†*Editor's note: The aforementioned Croatian Linebacker. Unfortunately, Dreyzden himself came down with Lesch Moniasis a few weeks after this entry, and was rushed back to Europe for treatment. The remaining Croats (and their interpreters) were left in quite a bind, with only rudimentary English words and pantomine for daily communication. As you might imagine, this only isolated the group further... as did their unfortunate habit of regularly washing their feet in the sinks.*

††*Editor's note: Residents of (or travelers to) most any part of Asia will probably find the described schtick familiar. For them, I can offer the following rough ranking of aggressive salesmanship: If we place China as a low baseline and India somewhat in the middle, the Afghan peddler would rank above both, but still below the Indian hawker in China.*

†††*Editor's note: In the spirit of this entry's miscellaneous nature, a related aside... Hawaii being not such a large place to begin with, and the east side of Oahu (where LOST was filmed) a smattering of small beach towns and one big Marine outpost, the actors themselves became somewhat of a fixture in the lives of military men stationed on the Island. One of them was on my original flight returning to the Mainland (to start the whole adventure). Having not seen the show at that point, I wondered who the leathered-pants Iraqi Lenny Kravitz was to be garnering such attention. During our deployment, an actress was written out of the show after getting caught driving drunk through my Kailua neighborhood a few too many times (these were the types of updates from home I received). Finally, upon coming home, I was one of many servicemembers to share a drink and a smoke with the lead actor of the series, who made a point to wander down to the neighborhood Marine bar each week and chat up the returning warriors about their experiences. I think he got a kick out of finding out we were all watching his show on Haji bootleg DVDs.*

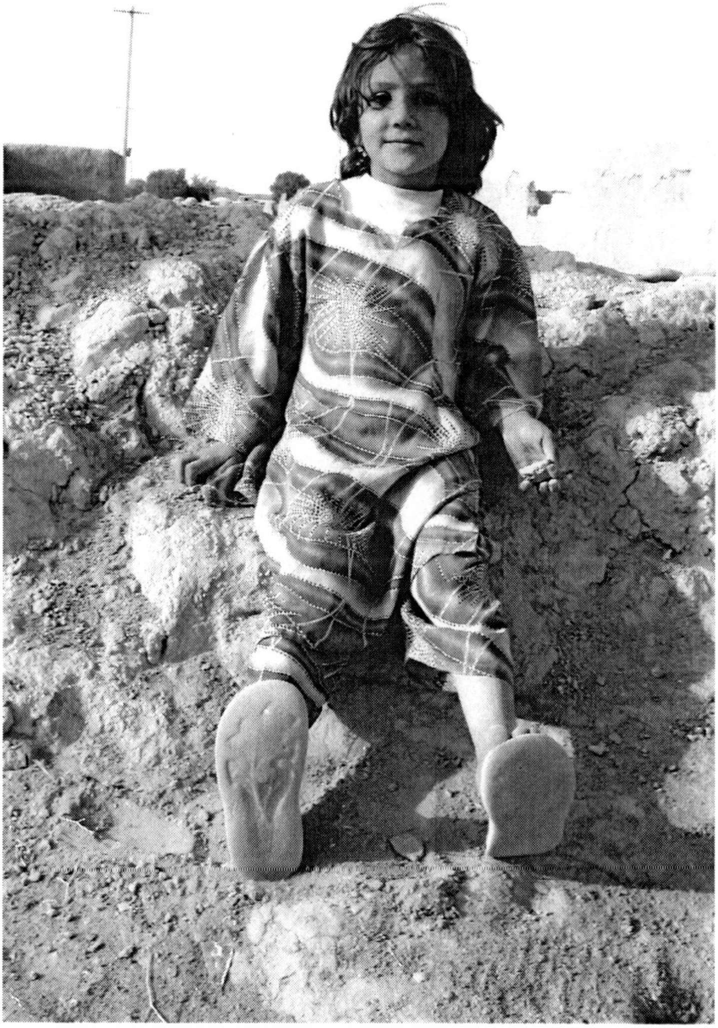

ASHURA

29 January

The 29th marks the observation of the Islamic holiday of Ashura. Centuries ago, it was a date mutually celebrated by Jews and Muslims to recognize Noah's preservation through the Great Flood. The joint nature was apparently lost long ago in the strain of the two groups' relationship. The day would later become, for the Islamic world, a commemoration of the martyrdom of Husayn—a grandson of Mohammad. For reasons far beyond my understanding of Moslem history, the day also signifies the schism of the Shi'a and Sunni sects.

With the arrival of the holiday to Afghanistan, I can for the first time mark a visible difference in behavior between the two divisions [in truth, before this week I never had any reason to contemplate Afghani Muslims as anything but a religiously unified group]. The Sunnis here have treated the day as any other religious holiday—that is, one of reflection and prayer. Shi'ites, however, have spent the entire week in mourning dress, every item of their clothing dyed black to demonstrate their loss. Today, the culmination of their observance, they will attempt to re-live the suffering of Husayn. For some this is a deep mental exercise, others will physically reenact the painful scenes in mass festivals reminiscent of some Catholic passion plays, ritually beating their bodies to spiritually connect with the martyr.

Unfortunately, being oft confined to the military grounds, I could not personally witness these scenes and rely on Ramin's explanations. My participation was limited to pointing at interpreters dressed in black suits and asking "why?" like a precocious child.

A little research gives me some revelatory light. Much like the schism of Christendom between the Italians and the Greeks [and into Catholicism and Orthodoxy], the dividing issue was over who was fit to head the religion.* After Mohammad's death, there was the question as to who his successor should be. It was proposed, and accepted, that the most capable man would be elected from the group of followers. However, a minority group believed that only a relative of the prophet could succeed him, choosing to support Mohammad's cousin, Ali, instead. This shia, or "supportive group," would continue [apparently with no sense of irony] not to recognize each successive leader of the faith, preferring instead to follow individual Imams, whom they believed ordained directly from God. The majority group of Islam does not support the idea of a hereditary chain of ordainment, believing that the community should decide on its own leadership—based on who is best fit to serve in the manner of Mohammad. The word Sunni, as they are called, denotes those who follow "the traditions of the Prophet."

This distinction helps somewhat to understand the markedly different attitudes towards the holiday. Without knowing all of the details, it is still logical to assume the genealogically focused Shia would be predisposed to amplifying the importance of the day (and the person for whom it represents). The more rational Sunnis, naturally, are a bit more reserved in their response.** Perhaps it is this pragmatism that prompted them to dispel notions of genetic sainthood in the first place.

....

*Although there were numerous disagreements between the two branches over the proper practice of Christianity, the final split can be chalked up to this organizational dispute. The West believed one man — the leader of the Roman church — to be in charge of all Christendom, whereas the East believed only God Himself to hold that title. Functionally speaking, the Greeks preferred a bunch of smaller quasi-independent demigods over a single autonomous demigod.

** Interestingly enough, there is a role reversal in one particular area. The Shia accept the practice of Taqiya (literally "concealment"), which allows one to hide his religion to preserve life. A Shi'ite is allowed to "deny his faith with his lips yet keep it in his heart," on the impressively rational logic that a dead martyr is less valuable than a live Muslim, as death significantly hampers one from continuing his worldly service to God. Additionally, viewing life as a special gift directly from God, the preservation of it is seen as one's premiere responsibility. The rise of Taqiya teachings among the Shia is generally attributed to their minority status among Muslims and persecutions associated with that position. Ironically, the application of Taqiya appears to have been used more often to hide one's Shia affiliation from other Muslims, rather than hiding the Muslim religion from oppressive non-believers.

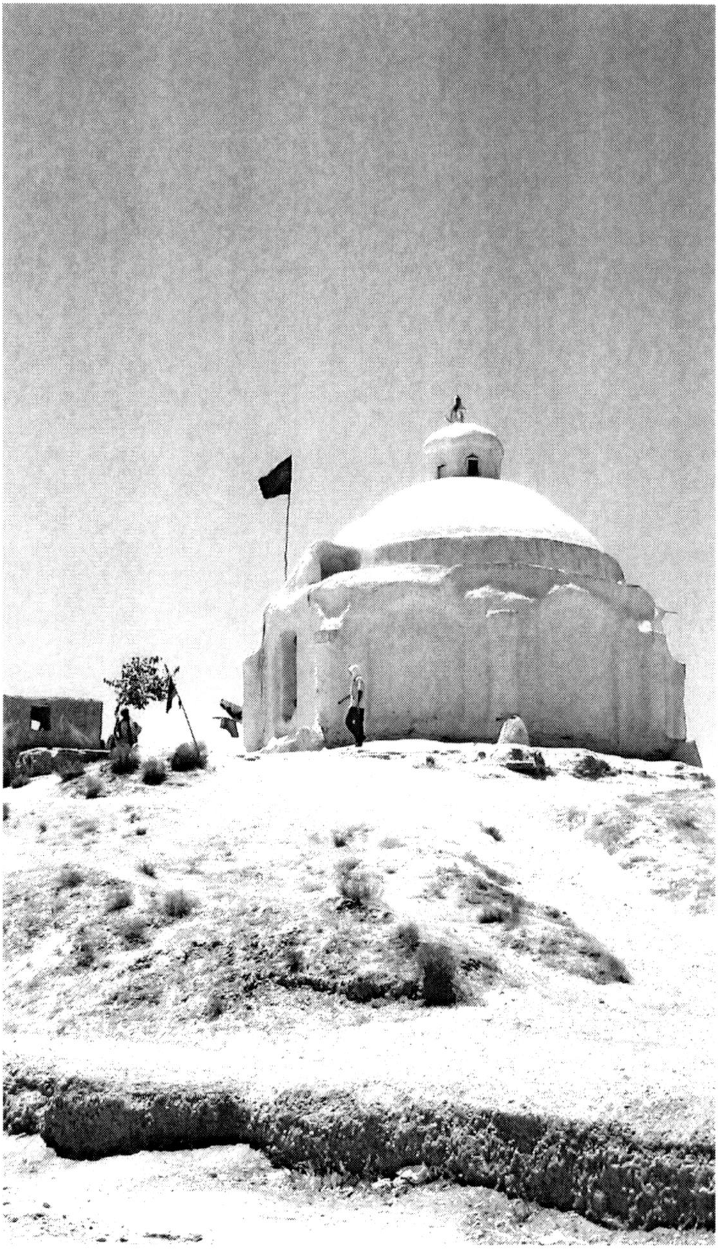

CONSIDERING MORTALITY

10 February

One of the first things I ever told the lady was that I was going to live forever. Clever woman that she is, she did not dismiss my claim outright, but questioned how exactly I planned to accomplish this feat. It was simple, I responded, I've decided not ever to die.

Certainly some tragedy could befall me and interrupt my plan, but I figure it is the best mindset with which to approach the situation. Whether one believes in an afterlife or nothingness at the end of their days, the time spent on earth is a one-shot opportunity (unless reincarnation is your bag of tea). It seems only logical to seek to extend that experience.

Recent scientific studies show substantial portions of the aging process to be initiated by [apparently arbitrary] biological tags that tell the body, "Ok, it's time to start getting old." Experience further tells us the physical impact one's mental state has on the timeline. A person psychologically reserved to approaching death—"made his peace," et al—hastens his demise, where the man with unfinished business often seems to stave off the reaper long enough to accomplish his necessary acts.

It seems the rush to one's end is, in large part, artificially imposed. And since I believe Life to be the most valuable commodity on earth, the proper course of action is to decide not to give it up. Emphatically.

All this is to say that I am thoroughly unprepared to comprehend a situation in which Life has no value.

~

A crowd of senior personnel were gathered on the steps of the Garrison office late this morning as I returned from the ANA camp. They were wearing odd expressions and speaking in hushed tones. Something was most certainly out of sorts.

A soldier who had been missing for several hours has been found, dead.

The somber conference was attempting to figure out what exactly to do next. An investigation would begin immediately, appropriate areas cordoned off, appropriate officials notified... but with all evidence tell-tale'ing suicide, the unanswerable question on each man's mind was "Why?"

Off to the side stood Big Minnesota, idly thumbing the corners of his uniform. All the color had drained from his face. It was his misfortune to discover the deceased's body slumped lifeless in the corner of a storage room; a pool of blood and a discharged 9mm round laying claim to the unspeakable story. He hadn't yet come to terms with the facts so displayed. Presumably it will be some time before he can.

Like a black cloud slowly overtaking prairie skies, the dark news gradually spreads throughout the soldiers. A ghoulish slow motion pervades our outpost, as no one is quite prepared to process this unsavory event.

~

Hours later we sit, still dumbfounded, attempting to work through the shock. Johnny U is again inventorying the former possessions of a deceased American, and we all hope it is the last time such a duty falls to him. Memorials and procedures are discussed, and we wonder how such things should be approached.

Does this person deserve the same formality and reverence for one who died in combat, in service of his country? Such is a difficult line to mark, without disrespecting the dead...

Procedural concerns can only mask the underlying issues for so long. After some period of silence, Senior Clark mutters some rhetorical questions on self-preservation. In concurrence I note that no one drowns with dry lungs. The body forces the fatal breath of water in a final attempt to survive. We are wired not to give up, he and I agree; a serious reshuffling of priority has to take place to overcome that.

For the better part of the afternoon, we trade queries of the "what could possibly cause" form, making no headway in understanding the unfathomable.

I just can't wrap my head around it. Perhaps that is to be expected.

ANNIVERSARIES

16 February

KAILUA, HAWAII, USA — One year ago, this morning, I wake up to a quite different future than today. Beside me the lady is quietly snoozing, barely a day removed from her Hawaiian arrival. The trials of a post-Katrina New Orleans are more or less behind us, several thousand miles away.

The sun breaks through the trees and into our new bedroom, painting shining streaks over the covers and my beloved's closed eyelids. The warmth nudges her awake with a yawn. Her eyes slowly open, find mine, and she smiles as someone freshly contented. Reburying herself in my arms, she finds occasion to continue lying comfortably careless, breathing in the still morning.

There was no work today to rush to, as I had taken leave to welcome her. The only pressing task before us was breakfast, and a decision as to where we would play tourist. For now, though, we were happy to simply rest in each other's good graces, contemplating the new future before us.

Somewhere between brewing morning tea and frying up some fresh eggs, my phone rang to spite me for not leaving it off. It was my Ops Officer, apologizing for his interruption, but it was important that I come in and talk with him today. I tell the lady it was nothing, and she nods agreement, though we both silently feel an impending damnation. No one ever calls you in from leave to relay good news.

That in mind, I push the meeting towards the afternoon, so that we can enjoy today before bad news can taint it. Resolute, we walk the two blocks down to the beach and set up camp. The work day has left it rather empty, making the tropical vista more or less ours alone to share. We snap pictures and dance in the surf, celebrating the beach that would be ours, so close to home.

An afternoon is planned, a short trip over to Waikiki so she can see the soccer fields where all the world seems to come and play. Most of the last month's evenings I have spent there, working my way on to a Brazilian squad, one of the premiere teams on the island. I've beat my body through endless tryouts and practices trying to make the roster, and just days before was informed that I had. This too, we have to look forward to, weekends of soccer matches—the camaraderie on the field and the family built on the sidelines of wives and girlfriends. All these pieces of a new life together comfortably falling into place...

We push the visit to work later and later, perhaps by deeming it an afterthought, its content will be no more important than such. Late in the afternoon, we casually arrive and make our way to the Commander's office. His face confirms my fear; there will be no good news.

He attempts some convoluted reasoning as to why it must be me, but abandons it. Ultimately, it is what it is. Two weeks. Two weeks until this Hawaiian future is put on hold. Two weeks to prepare to leave my life behind for a year and a half. Two weeks.

She's crying uncontrollably.

This isn't what she had planned, this isn't how things were supposed to be. Her whole life was set aside to come here to start anew with me, and now I wouldn't be there. It isn't fair. It isn't right, she gasps between sobs.

Two weeks. Figure it out.

It's a long drive home. In the bed where hours before we laid in happy contemplation we now hold tight, attempting to console one another. We fail.

Two weeks.

Two weeks to try and squeeze in a past future, two weeks to attempt to ready ourselves for a new future.

Phone calls are made; friends and family weep and curse the government. They pledge support. One of my closest friends vows to enlist just so that he can accompany me and thwart whatever danger may befall my path.* This brings a small smile. Most everyone is shocked, bewildered, and ultimately sympathetic. It's a raw deal, a rough hand, and any number of equivalent clichés.

It is two weeks.

~

One year to the day, I sit on a porch that I have built, in a camp I have shaped, in an Afghanistan I hope to have affected, and listen to her cry.

She isn't crying because I am gone at this moment, I realize. She cries for a year of me being gone, she cries for a future that was put on hold, she cries for a life together that was ripped from her without warning or remorse, on the sixteenth of February, one year ago.

....

* *God bless the Horstman.*

ATTACK OF THE 50 FOOT KARZAI

22 February

FORWARD OPERATING BASE SPANN, MAZAR-I SHARIF, AFGHANISTAN — Ramin (The Important Man)'s phone rang just minutes after we pulled up to the shop this morning.

"It is Colonel Ata...he is over at the Training Building. They are requesting from him a carpenter."

"For what? He knows better..."

My general policy in managing the woodshop has been to not, as I like to say, "rent out" my carpenters. We fill project requests, not labor requests. There are a few reasons for my stance; I can quote the noble goal of forcing the ANA officers to quantify their respective needs ahead of time, but mostly I have tired of projects spiraling into massive requests once work has begun. Unlike the private contractor who would love to come over to fix a doorbell and end up renovating your entire house, I derive no benefit from scope escalation.

As such, it was with considerable trepidation that I listened to my obviously-harried Colonel's request.

"The officers in charge of President Karzai's visit need help setting up the meeting room. They are asking for one carpenter to come with trim and some nails to frame a poster."

One carpenter. A little trim. Some nails.
And presumably a hammer.

Thinking myself presumptively clever, I instead brought two carpenters and what I thought was an ample array of tools and supplies for whatever "trimming" job might meet us at the Training Building. When we arrived, a gaggle of senior

Afghan officers were hurriedly buzzing about the hall, arranging seating, hanging nationalistic slogans, and engaging in whatever other preparations people find necessary for presidential arrivals. A pair of Colonels whisked away my carpenters into the cacophony. Ata limped to our company, explaining wearily through Ramin how the various bigwigs had been harassing him with a litany of demands since their arrival.

As if to underscore the point, one such requestor spun up to us at that moment. "He is asking for the woodshop to build 60 small flag stands to put on the tables for tomorrow." Before I could summon the proper emphatic words to point out the impossibility of such a request, Ramin interrupted me. "I am sorry sir, now he is asking for 80."

"80 flag stands? Today? Does he expect me to shit them out right here?"

"No sir...actually, I believe he expects you to shit out 80 after you have shitted the first 60."

There did not yet exist adequate words in my vocabulary to describe the no-ness of my answer. Incredulous vulgarity was instead pressed into service. Experienced enough not to translate, Ramin patiently explained to the uniformed gentleman about our shop's limited capacity, and that such a project would have required much more lead time than...an hour. There was some protestation. We were, of course, reminded that his minutes-old idea was extremely urgent and very necessary to the success of the endeavor. This part did not, in fact, require interpretation; I've seen the movie enough times not to need the subtitles.

Leaving Ramin to further discuss the no-ness of my decision with our interloper, I waded through the official mess after my disappeared carpenters. I found Karim studying a 10-foot tall canvas poster of His Eminence. Karim's right hand dangled a hammer, the left propped up his quizzical expression. He looked at me, then at the obviously inadequate trim in his cousin's hands, before raising his arms in exasperation.

One carpenter. A little trim. Some nails. And presumably a hammer.

When Ramin had extricated himself and Ata from the preceding lecherous conversation, he queried the pair of Colonels overseeing this "trimming" project. "They want for a frame around the picture and to have it mounted on the concrete wall. Also the same for the other picture."

Other picture? I was led out to the entrance hall. On the floor lay what appeared to be a rolled-up white tarp, about 15' wide. One of the Colonels waved his hand over the bundle and exclaimed something proudly in Dari.

"This is the other picture? Dear Lord..."

"Yes," Ramin confirmed, "This one also, they need mounted."

One carpenter. A little trim. Some nails. And presumably a hammer.

Clearly overmatched, the trim, nails, hammer, and carpenters went back into the truck. Along with them went an oversized canvas poster and a rolled up print the size of a Revival Tent. Back we went to the shop, where the full capacity of my small woodworking establishment could be devoted towards the endeavor.

The simple request of earlier proved increasingly absurd as we unrolled the President's plastic portrait. At nearly fifty feet in length, the printed image area easily exceeded the square footage of my entire shop. It was difficult enough to find unobstructed ground space outside, not to mention keeping vehicles from accidentally running it over (as one particular US Colonel nearly did) and inadvertently causing an international incident.

Several hours later, once the carpenters had rigged a proper framework, we returned to the scene. Now properly equipped with hammer drills and associated paraphernalia, the first graven image was installed rather seamlessly. Meanwhile, I argued with several ANA officers about the placement of the massive tarp. They were adamant that the monstrous visage be installed inside the meeting hall. I suggested we try putting the image somewhere it would actually fit. This was apparently out of the question.

After the smaller poster had successfully been implemented, my carpenters returned their efforts to its slightly more grandiose sibling. As they finished the frame on the unfurled Karzai, reality overcame the dissident officers and they abandoned their inside demands. They summoned a work group of soldiers who tilted the finished uber-poster into place against the outside of the Training Building. After several abortive attempts at properly situating the image, the group eventually realized that their Karzai was twice the height of the selected building.

This was, of course, a problem. A new building was sought out. Only one structure on base, a maintenance garage, had a wall large enough to frame the portrait. Looking for all the world like cartoon ants carrying off stolen picnic goods, the mob of soldiers hoisted their President and transported him to the newly christened site.

For the next two hours I observed Afghan ingenuity at work, as the soldiers and my carpenters worked the massive frame into place using a small table, an entirely too short ladder, and a couple of long 2x4's. I cringed like a worried parent as first Manan, then Rahim, perched himself at the top of the precariously improvised summit to drill through the frame into the concrete wall. The holes were filled with a pair of concrete nails apiece, as my mind's eye watched each hammer swing's momentum threaten my carpenter's balance atop the makeshift pinnacle. I reflexively prayed the Lord's hand hold Rahim against the wall. Fortunately, He complied.

Despite every appearance it wouldn't be, the installation was successful. As the sun set over the Afghan President's gaze, hours later than our days normally end, I lit a celebratory cigarette and examined our offering. I shook my head, then chuckled a bit as I repeated our early morning request to no one in particular.

One carpenter. A little trim. Some nails.

And presumably a hammer.

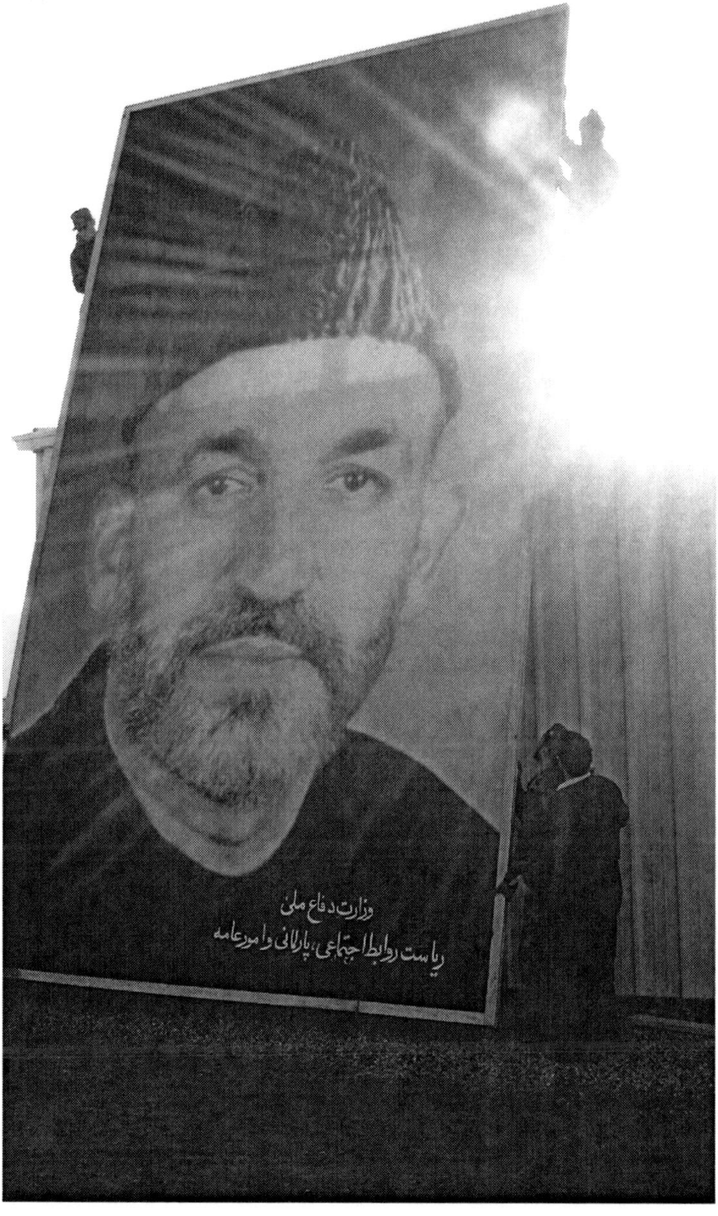
وزارت دفاع ملی
ریاست روابط اجتماعی، پارلمانی و امور عامه

SNOW DAYS

28 February

"Paka wa pustin"

"I have no trust for Afghani weather…"

Such is Ramin (The Important Man)'s stock answer for my repeated pesterings about whether winter is over yet.

The Dari colloquialism above sums up Afghan attitudes towards weather. Literally, it means "bring a fan and a coat!" In spirit, it means "don't waste your time forecasting." I can't speak for the rest of the country, but in these northern provinces, the weather shifts more often than General Platitude's ideas about what our mission is.

In 36 hours, we transitioned from a balmy and clear 70 degrees, to a monsoon-caliber rainstorm, to, finally, a full-on blizzard. Nearly two feet of snow dropped on Mazar within the span of just a few hours. The next afternoon, it had all melted away, and the sun was again shining brightly.

Barely two days had passed, and we'd cycled through all of the seasons. Quite a change for someone as myself, whose primary residences have rarely exhibited seasons at all, let alone winter.

TEMPORARY CELEBRITY

15 March

Being that Afghan schools, particularly in the Northern provinces, take several months of winter break, it had been some time since we had been able to schedule a school supplies drop. Senior Volkl's H.A. [Humanitarian Assistance] storage Conex was crammed full of donations. The shelves and a significant portion of the floor in our B-hut were covered with white flat-rate shipping boxes. Next door, a stack of nearly 300 such cardboard vessels threatened to capsize and crush our Johnny U. Even the deck in front of the Navy Garrison office was succumbing to the school supply overflow. With the base perhaps one more mail call away from bursting into a crayon and pencil mushroom cloud, it was with no small amount of relief that Senior V noted the reopening of classes in March. He wasted no time scheduling a "Back To School" drop for a nearby girl's school.

A seven-ton supply truck was filled to its canvas limits with a myriad of scholastic goodies. Joined in convoy by several Humvees, a full complement of charitable sailors, and the requisite Afghan escort, the cargo headed out towards the destination.

Like many of its contemporaries, the school sat inside a medium-sized courtyard buried within a tightly walled neighborhood. Despite being less than a few kilometers from our gates, it was nearly an hour before our belated arrival. As one might imagine, squeezing a seven-ton rig through a maze of donkey trails and under webs of low-hanging bootleg power lines is a process anything but smooth.

To her credit, the rig driver only got it stuck once.

~

Like many of the schools we'd seen, this one had also overflowed into tents. Outside of the main building, three classes were in session under the white canvas shelters as we arrived. It was all their poor teachers could do to keep them seated while we set up.

Under the watchful eye of a village elder and a pack of humorless older women (representing the Principal and some senior faculty), we began laying out the donated goods. At one end, boxes of clothing and shoes were piled for later distribution by the elder. Next to it, colorful stacks of toys for all ages. Then there was Johnny U's 300 boxes, each packed especially for a single child by church groups back in the States. Beside him, bulk school supplies were readied. On the end, I prepared to begin Backpack Operation II, armed with dozens of brightly painted backpacks (each uniquely created by Walla Walla, Washington schoolchildren for their Afghan counterparts).

As the principal brought out her best students to receive these first gifts, Ramin (The Important Man) explained how American children—all the way on the other side of the world—had painted and prepared the tote bags especially for them.

The custom packs were quickly exhausted by the appreciative audience, so the Afghan soldiers and I switched to bulk supplies—bags, notebooks, pens, and the like— as each class was paraded out to receive their share.

Over in the opposite end of the courtyard, I noticed Johnny U among a sea of tiny white headwraps. Upon further investigation, I found him cutting open up the aforementioned 300 boxes, one by one, for each little girl who had received one. In his wake, a sea of giggles as gleeful girls dug into their special presents, pulling out toys and trinkets, crayons and coloring books. In front of him, little scrunched faces trying so hard to sit patiently until he could release their treasures. This was all spread before me like some bizarro-Christmas morning. I laughed a little louder than I should have at my friend's predicament. He was feeling a bit self-conscious, I think, as he looked up and stretched out his shoulder, "Man, my arm's really starting to hurt!"

"Ah, but look at you," I replied, "You're their hero."

~

Back in the main courtyard, the girls had discovered our female soldier. They jockeyed for position close to her, stretching out their little arms to shake her hand. A uniformed lady sergeant was like nothing they'd ever imagined, and certainly had never seen. She was a celebrity for the moment, posing for pictures and sharing smiles, as the crowd of girls looked on with starry-eyed disbelief.

Though underspoken, perhaps, compared to the rest of us, the sergeant's presence in front of these girls imparted more than a hundred male officers could have. Whether they received something so complex as the seeds of societal reorganization, or simply saw reason to hope for their own futures, I am certain that moment will remain in their memories long after their new pencils and crayons have been used up.

~

As my attention refocused on the whole scene, it became clear that order was quickly deteriorating. Hundreds of kids were packing the courtyard, hoping for some share of the donations. Inside the main school building, young girls were yelling from their classrooms, begging their teachers to let them out. A mob of children was swarming a pair of Navy gents with a garbage bag full of candy. A village elder was sprinting about, swinging a brand-new red nerf softball bat over his head, attempting to herd the children into manageable groups.

Madness.

Amazingly, the 80-something-year-old matador eventually succeeded in reestablishing some semblance of order. As he held the kids at bay, we were able to distribute the rest of the school supplies.

Meanwhile, a significant crowd of local families had gathered outside the courtyard gates, awaiting their turn. As we were already past our scheduled mission time, we said our goodbyes and remounted the convoy, leaving the elders and faculty to spread the general clothing and goods among the waiting families.

Exiting the village maze, Ramin turned from his passenger seat and remarked, "These are my favorite days…"

"Mine too," I replied, "Mine too."

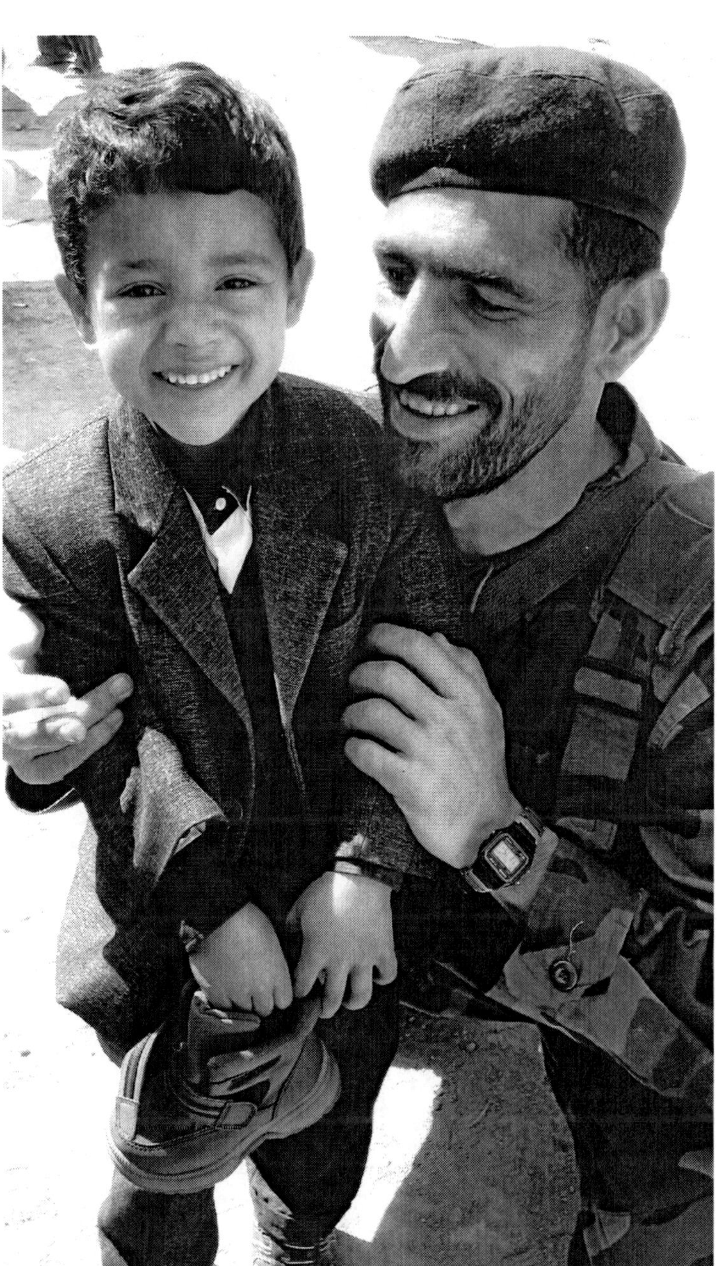

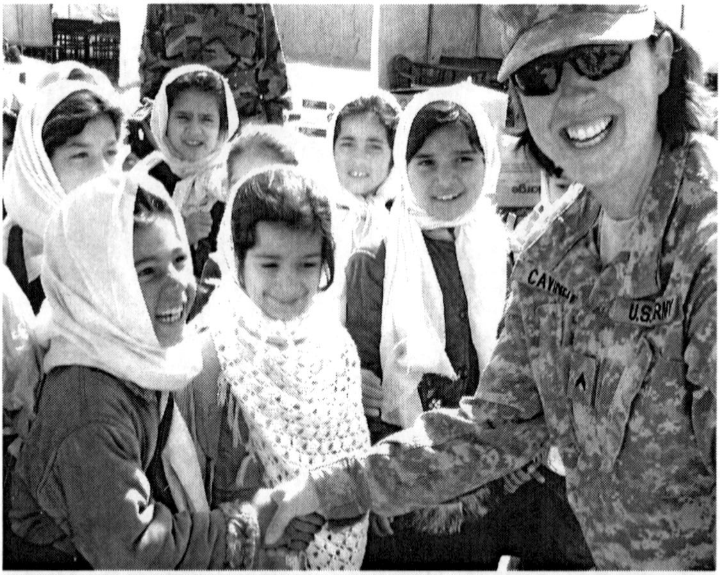

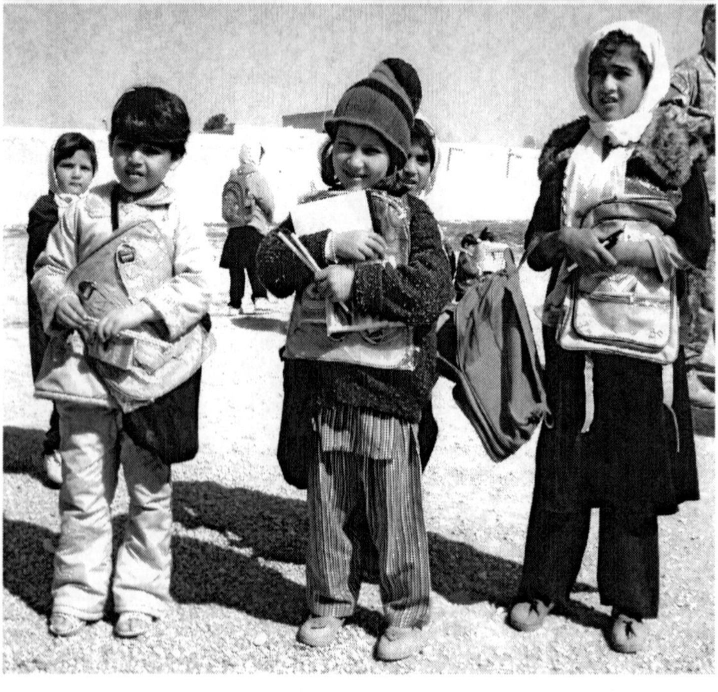

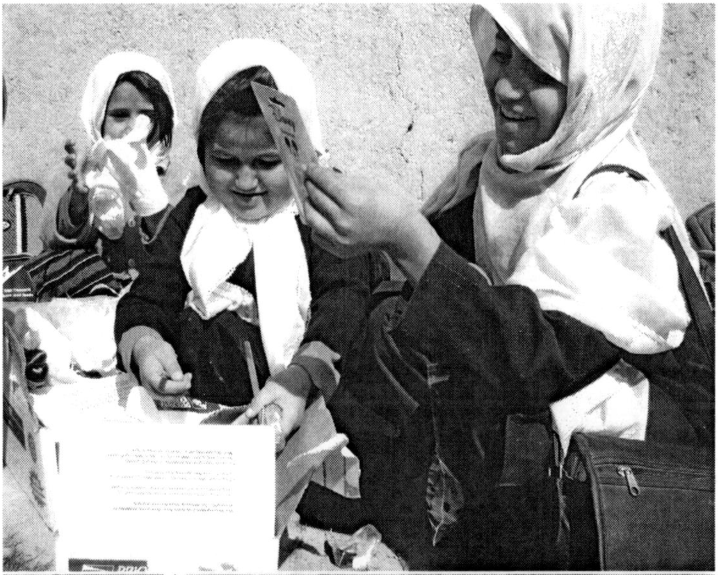

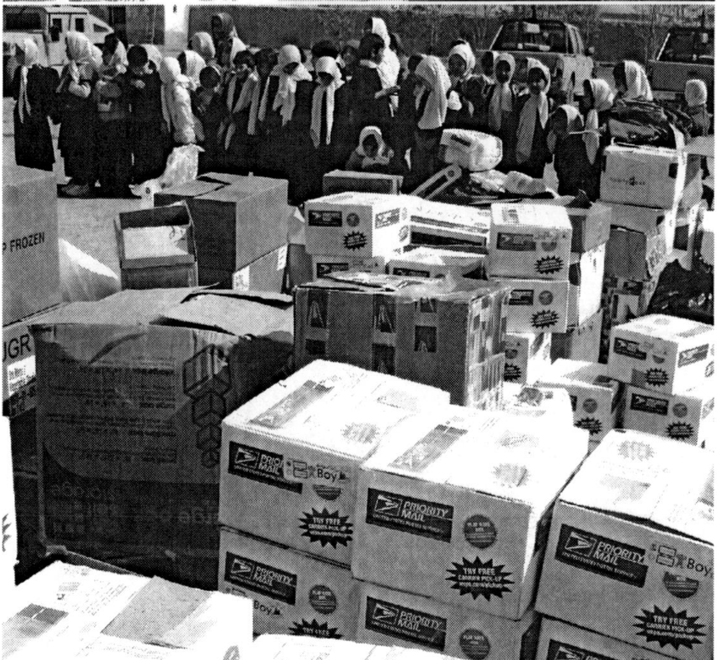
PRIORITY MAIL

WHO IS TYLER DURDEN / FROM KOREA WITH LOVE

21 March

It should be self-evident that different people idolize different aspects of humanity, particularly those embodied in our favorite actors, sports legends, and characters. That said, there is a certain type-cast that draws the greatest attraction; that is the leader, the king, the boss—particularly in the ambition-driven professional circles I've run, first in Architecture and now in the military. Everyone wants to be the number one, the cat in control of the empire (or leading the revolution against it). This isn't simply manifested in vicarious starry-eyed fantasies, but prevalent in even the simpler desires. I regularly hear my colleagues pine to own their own businesses (or their own firms), with their name on the door and the masthead.

Such has never been my ambition. I've never cared about being king. Having freedom to move, act, and create— that is my dream position, regardless of the title.

While the rest watch with rapt attention as Clooney's [or Sinatra's, before him] Mr. Ocean oversees the greatest Vegas heist in movie history, with ten of the slickest fictitious thieves under his command, I have always been fascinated by his number two. Uninterested with nominal leadership positions, the right hand man holds the operation together and pushes it through to its climax. He simply acts, with smoothness and uninhibited freedom, making what needs to happen, happen. This is what catches my attention as entertained observer; this is the part that tickles my ambitions.

The phenomenon is not limited to this story, of course. Most every tale includes a kingmaker, though he is seldom the target of any prolonged focus. In the one tale that comes to mind where the kingmaker overshadows the king, he, in fact, does not exist. All the same, this quality of effectiveness and connectedness, seamless operation behind the scenes, has always appealed to me. Others can chase thrones, I'd prefer being the man who can deliver them. But, such is all merely fantasy's confession. The reality of this sort of position I've found to be considerably less ideal.

Over the course of this year, I've mimicked many of the traits of a man of effectiveness. In order to keep my own projects afloat—and my carpentry shop, for that matter—I've had to figure out how to acquire for our needs, and how to make the necessary things continue to happen. I built networks of local contacts, discovered and tapped into various wide-spread pools of resources, and found shortcuts through bureaucracy. When international contractors finished projects and vacated the area, I caught the fire-sales, loading up on all sorts of equipment and materials impossible to find in Afghan stores. With cash and local connections, I developed enviable flexibility. I embraced the part of the guy who could get things, and who could get things done. Though, it is not nearly as enviable a role as I imagined.

~

The other day, driving around with Ramin, he looked at me with concern. He asked if I was okay, had I not slept well?

I told him I wasn't sick or sleepy, just tired. Very, very tired.

While he was trying to ask why, my phone rang. It was a short conversation; after some negotiation, I made a mental note of the caller's need and returned to our discussion on fatigue. Ramin continued, asking what it was that was tiring me. The phone rang again, and there proceeded another conversation like the first, with a different individual. Before Ramin could again renew our discussion, we were stopped at the base entrance gate. A guard rattled off some project proposal to me. Moments after I finished with him, Ramin's phone rang. Colonel Ata was relaying a construction request from some ANA Kandak Commander. At this I laughed and looked over to my passenger, "Do you see why I'm tired?"

Ramin chuckled.

"You know, damn near every ANA officer and NCO on that base knows who I am. And they all need something from me—something very necessary and very important that they have it right away. The Americans too, constantly needing something. The terps, of course, even the Germans and the Croatians hit me up. It used to be, people would come into the office and I could direct them to Mr. Coolman. Now? Everyone's looking for me... Everybody wants something from me.

"I mean, really, do you see why I'm tired?"

It is one thing to be the man of effectiveness within a partnership or collective, quite another to be such for everyone. Being the latter has absolutely exhausted me.

~

Meanwhile, with the ever-increasing role of the Navy here, The Coolman's slate of Army meetings has been expanding exponentially—and with it, the number of things to spin him up. It was well past time for both of us to take a break, once we could pry him out of the rafters.

Technically, we are allotted two four-day "R & R" (Rest and Recuperation) during our year in country, to be taken in the resort-like city of Doha, Qatar. This promise is an exceptionally cruel bait and switch, as the realities of travel and percentage based quotas make it mathematically impossible for people to take two [some are unable to take any]. The Coolman and I were fortunate to get a pair of slots at the end of March, even though the dates fell outside the official window in which we were allowed to take them.

Before we could legally leave Afghanistan, we had to trek down to Camp Phoenix so I could relinquish my suitcase of cash. For me, vacation could not begin until I was relieved of its contents and associated responsibilities. We hopped a C-130 flight south to Kabul International, caught a convoy over to Phoenix, and cleared finance just in time to catch another convoy back to the airport. All before lunch, unbelievably. With a few flights scheduled for the afternoon to Bagram, we were set to do the impossible, making it through Kabul — including Phoenix — without getting caught in the flag pole's black hole. Most importantly, the biggest portion of my go-to-guy role was out of my hands for good. I was infinitely more relaxed with that knowledge.

A few hours later, The Coolman and I were sitting on the runway in a small "Blackwater" craft [one of several contract planes that circle the country in service of the military]. The other eight seats were filled with South Korean Army officers (gallivanting around Afghanistan produces interesting combinations of travel partners). Sitting just behind the pilots, we watched them go through their pre-flight checks, flipping on switches, firing up the engines...and then cutting the engines and flipping off the switches. One of the pilots pulled himself out of the left seat, turned to the cabin with a bewildered look on his face and explained that the airstrip in Bagram had been shut down. "Birds!"

Birds?

"Yeah, apparently... the tower says they have a black cloud of birds—thousands of 'em—hovering over the strip. We won't be able to land. We can't leave here until the birds clear out there."

One of the Korean officers translated for the rest, all of whom immediately doubted his skills as an interpreter. At his request, our pilot confirmed that it was indeed a flock of birds preventing our departure. While the Koreans discussed this turn of events incredulously amongst themselves, the pilot introduced himself to The Coolman and I. He was a retired Marine Gunnery Sergeant, and had been flying soldiers around Afghanistan and Iraq for several years now, landing on little dirt strips just south of nowhere and dodging RPGs here and there. Noticing the other conversation dissipating, he offered a simple Korean greeting to the delegation, thoroughly surprising The Coolman and I—not to mention the Koreans!

Though he was apparently already at his limits of Korean linguistics, he proceeded to rattle off the names of various villages he knew in the country instead. Like a gospel preacher's call and response, the officers cheerfully repeated the village names they recognized. The pilot explained to the English speaking officer that he had been stationed in Korea for 10 years, and had lived or passed through many of the cities and towns. The delegation broke into smiles and nods at this information.

After a bit of a question and answer session, he received word that the bird pandemic had subsided. The start-up processes were repeated, and the plane pulled down the runway, headed for Bagram. Our front row seats gave us a clear view of the cockpit activities, and we were, admittedly, somewhat mesmerized by the complicated process of maneuvering the small craft. The pilots sat left and right of the multiple directional controls, deftly reaching over and around each other's arms in perfectly choreographed actions. This they did without so much as a glance, as practiced in their complementary movements as fraternity Step Show participants*, never once disrupting each other or breaking form. It was a hypnotic performance to behold.

~

Safe from the bird cloud and on the ground in Bagram, our most pressing concern was dinner. There had been one private restaurant on the sprawling air base, though we'd heard news of its unfortunate demise by fire. Undaunted, we headed towards its former location, hoping it had been rebuilt.

It had not. A charred carcass of a building remained where the restaurant once stood. With a sigh of disappointment, we turned to walk away, but were interrupted by the call of an older fellow, pushing a debris-filled wheelbarrow. He pointed at us and made an eating motion with his hand. Nodding his head happily, he ushered us around the corner and into a side building. The building, it would turn out, was the Korean Army's Bagram cafeteria. Not ones to argue fate, we proceeded to the serving line. Adjacent to the silverware buckets, a logbook beckoned for signatures. One of the blocks asked, "Invited By?" There wasn't quite enough room to write "old man with the wheelbarrow," so we left it blank. A tempting spread buffet of rice, greens, kim-chi, chicken, and bananas was ahead of us. I grabbed a pair of metal chopsticks (a first for me—metal chopsticks) and a steel tray. I couldn't help but laugh at the tray in my hands, with eight or nine small bowl-like depressions formed into it. Years ago, I would playfully tease my dear friend Lily about her Korean serving habits, as she carefully separated each item into a dozen small bowls. A little tofu here, a little cucumber in another, a little broccoli in yet another, and so on, delicately prepared. Her efforts were all for naught, though, when I would liberate the ingredients and toss them together on my plate.

A quick private smile crossed my face, then, as I complied with the divisions, in honor of the memory (or, perhaps because I really had no other options with the separatist-designed tray). Needless to say, the meal itself was a wonderful change from our daily KBR cuisine.

~

Certainly, it was a perfectly surreal Korean-themed
day in the middle of Afghanistan...

....

* *For those unfamiliar, Step Shows are a long-standing tradition at Black fraternities in the U.S. The competitive performances are a bit of a hybrid between dance and drill, and generally more complex than either. The movements are often so tightly choreographed that the slightest timing mistake would cause fast-moving bodies to collide. My memories of such shows came instantly to mind as I watched these two pilots manipulate the complicated controls.*

†*Editor's note: The mathematics are fairly straightforward. No more than 15% of the force can be off-post at one time. Leave and R+R cannot be taken in the first three or last three months of deployment. Practically speaking, Leave takes up nearly a month of time and R+R two weeks, including travel. If you have 100 soldiers, the numbers work out such that only 90 of them will get to take leave (6 months x 15 pax), with no slots left over for R+R. It is only in fudging numbers that many soldiers at distant outposts are able to get time off at all. Of course, those officers stationed at major hubs such as Kabul or Bagram have no such issues with travel times (being able to fly directly out of the country) and are able to use all of their allotted vacation — while drafting and enforcing the rules that prevent soldiers downrange from using theirs.*

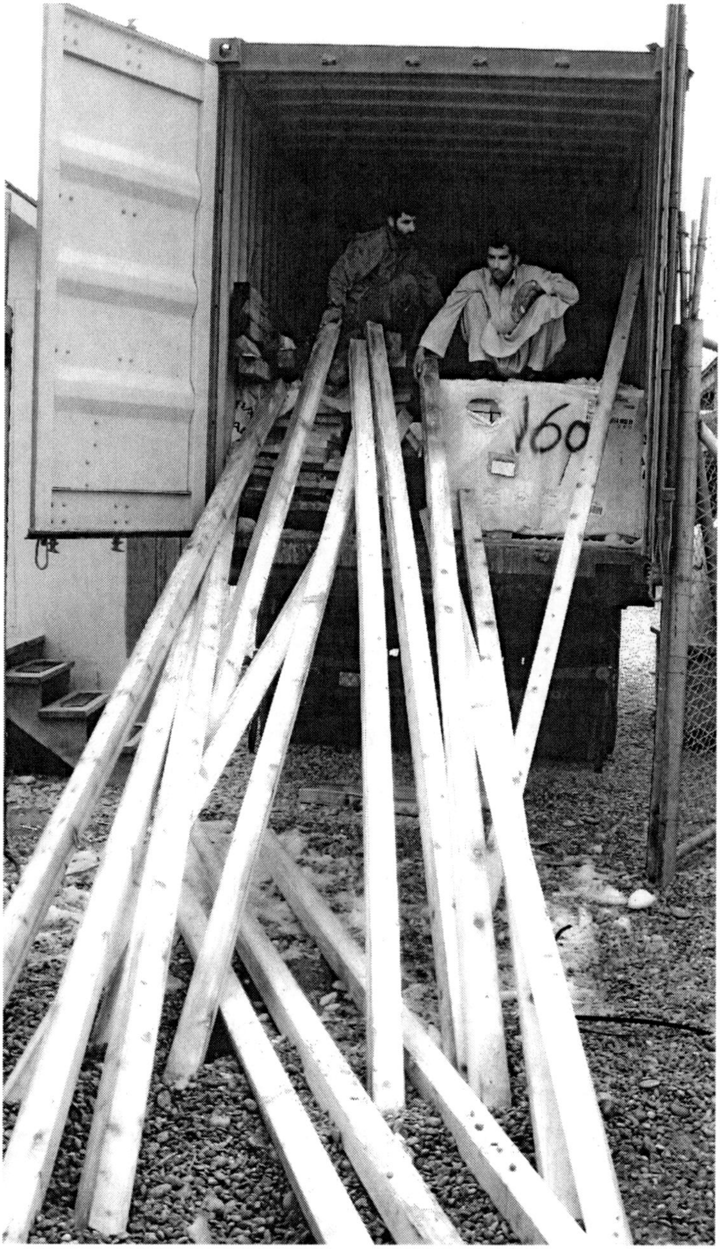
160

TOURISTS OF ARABIA, PART I

25 - 30 March

DOHA, QATAR —

DAY 0 ... It's quite late in the evening when our plane lands in Qatar, and our bus of Afghan refugees is getting antsy. Word is that last call is a quarter to midnight. It is already past ten and our handlers are ushering us into a random non-descript warehouse for a litany of briefs. We've been treading through lowest-common-denominator instructions from lowest-common-denominator personnel for nearly an hour when I lean over to The Coolman to mutter, "Only the Army could manage to take all the fun out of drinking!"

We fill out all sorts of meaningless paperwork and sign our names to various promises we don't read as the clock looks on, callously continuing to tick down despite our impassioned pleas otherwise. Sometime after the hand sweeps past eleven, our tormenters begrudgingly allow our release. They do make an attempt at redemption, however, calling out after our quickly disappearing throng that tonight will not count against our allotted R&R time. Our "Day Zero," or arrival day, will officially stretch through tomorrow. It's a welcome concession, but there still remains the matter of making tonight count for something.

30 minutes until last call.

We ignore such frivolities as unpacking or changing out of our uniforms, heading instead for the crowd of people outside yet another non-descript warehouse building, figuring that this must be where they're hiding the beer.

Were we not on such an imperative mission, I would certainly have paused at the absurdity that presented us inside the warehouse. For the R&R soldier, our government has generously prepared a row of stage-set pseudo-bars—complete with "outdoor seating," glassless windows, and perfectly harmless fake names—in which they can taste a bit of pseudo-freedom in an entirely controlled environment. At the moment unconcerned with savage irony, we make a beeline for the doorway beneath a neon leprechaun. 25 minutes.

Under the "pub's" unnaturally bright lights, a diminutive Filipina named Gladys reaches over a green Formica plank to take our enthusiastic Guinness orders and our military IDs. The IDs are swiped and on some hidden daily database a single check goes by each of our government names. Only three checks are allowed each night (again we are convinced that the Army is most concerned with preventing any real Rest and Recuperation from occurring).

A lanky Asiatic gentleman carefully prepares our pints—correctly, to our surprise, right down to the shamrock in the foam. In any other circumstance, chugging such a perfectly poured pint of Guinness would be nothing short of criminal. But, considering we had but twenty minutes to consume our official three drink ration, I do believe God and the Leprechauns will forgive us our transgression.

I offer this philosophical query to our drinking companion Patrick, an appropriately red-faced Irish hooligan (up from Big John's Khost tribe), but he's too busy rushing through his allotments to answer. I consider this acceptable confirmation of the theory from a man who should know, and continue in kind...

~

The next morning, we are fortunate enough to snag spots on a tour. Although locally-stationed personnel are free to come and go as they please, we, the R&R'ers, can only venture into civilization under the careful structure of arranged tours and watchful chaperones. Our government entrusts us with the controls of multi-million dollar technologies, with ungodly amounts of firepower and ammunition, with the decisions under which men live or die, but apparently not enough to walk the streets of a friendly host country unsupervised. Ah, but of what value, consistency?

Today's trip is a short open boat cruise into the Persian Gulf. The harbor from which we will depart is some thirty minutes away from base, in the heart of Doha, Qatar's capital city. As our bus takes us away from the scorched earth nothingness of inland Qatar, I notice the gradual appearance of development approaching, like the fingers of southwestern sprawl that slowly overtake the American desert. Before long we are firmly in the midst of Doha suburbia, with rows of Arabic McMansions filling the horizon. Stuccoed two and three story boxes form perfect ranks alongside us, their EIFS[†] accoutrements mimicking a full range of inspirations—from Turkish Mosques and rugged castles to Babylonian splendor and Victorian flair. It is pure Vegas pastiche, only less restrained.

Entering the business district of the city, we are greeted by a 60-story visage of the king of Qatar, waving from the façade of a corner office building. I swear he's beckoning, "Hey my friend!"

Further on is the newly-constructed harbor front, with beds of tropical flowers, monumental public art, and tiled walkways. Bobbing in the water are rows and rows of long wooden dhows (traditional fishing boats). The dhows thoroughly outnumber the docks, so they are instead roped to each other in chains, side by side, with only the innermost boat tied to the dock. Our boat was the fourth in such a chain, requiring us to board and cross three consecutive decks, jumping between vessels to reach our assigned craft.

We settle in atop the traditional flat pillows on the roof deck as the dhow is released and edges out of the harbor. The city skyline wraps around to our left, displaying dozens of waterfront skyscrapers under construction. Nearly every building is topped with a crane, neatly silhouetted by the morning sun.

The dhow continues its cruise away from the city to relatively open waters and sets anchor. We are offered the chance to swim. We do. Neither one of us can pass up the opportunity to have gone swimming in the Persian Gulf. Much like Salt Lake in Utah, the Gulf's high saline mixture allows one to float with minimal effort. 18- and 19-year old kids on break from Iraq throw each other from the bow and do cannonballs. Others are content to lay out on the deck for a little tanning. After we are sufficiently engaged in relaxation, a Middle-Eastern lunch is unveiled, with hummus, tzatziki, saffron rice, pita, grilled meats, and various delectables. For many of our group, it is strange and foreign. For me, admittedly, it is welcome comfort food.

We work off lunch by napping heartily in the sun, crisply burning our winterized skins.

Nonetheless, we finally begin to feel relaxed...especially on the realization that three more pints of Guinness await our return.

DAY 1 ... Although we do manage to sign up for another tour for today, it is a short one, and not until the evening. We're left to wander our bleak surroundings in search of something to occupy the meantime. As far as we can see, the camp is nothing but an endless grid of nameless warehouses. We hear rumors of a Chili's restaurant hiding somewhere within the fabric and head out in search of it.

Our "map," courtesy of the handlers, hardly deserves the title. It displays none of the base's physical features, nor does it show any of the buildings. Listed only are the handful of destinations intended for R&R personnel, with general cardinal directions between them. We can only assume Super Extremely Important Things happen within the 90% of the structures shrouded from our knowledge, but with just a bare tenth of the campus deemed suitable for reference, the map offers us the navigational equivalent of an unconcerned shrug.

After a time we come to an area set apart from the rest of the base by high fences and guards. Somewhere inside this Fort Knox lies the Chili's. Miraculously, our IDs allow us passage through the controlled entry...

...And we have been transported, it seems, to some sterile luxury apartment complex in Mesa, Arizona. Dozens of sprinklers lavish green grass islands with irrigated water, under the watch of balconied stucco façades. There's a sand volleyball court to the left, beside a shaded ramada. In the center, a massive pool reflects the desert blue sky as it laps against brand new cool-deck.

"Hey Russ," I query The Coolman, "do you remember that scene from LOST where the camera pans in on the random picket fence subdivision hiding on the back side of the island?" *

"Yeah...and meanwhile everyone else on the island is living off fruit and sleeping under palm frond tents?"

"I think we're there."

~

After taking a moment to bask in the surreality, we head past the pool to the oddly prominent Chili's restaurant flanking it. A pleasant young Filipino lady seats us. Another takes our orders. In short order it becomes apparent that every one of the green-poloed staff is Filipino, from the waitresses to the short-order cooks. Odd.

As we devour our first taste of semi-well-prepared American food in six months (from Saudi Arabian ingredients, put together by Filipino cooks and served by Filipino waitresses, in the middle of Qatar), we ponder the details of our host's employment.

"Must be strange to have to get a security clearance just to work at Chili's...."

~

A few hours later, we are again on a tour bus heading for the Gulf. Our destination tonight is an Iranian restaurant overlooking the harbor. It is a sprawling castle of a building, with different themed dining rooms splayed about, and multiple terraces of outdoor seating. The Coolman, our new Irish friend, and I find a table by the water and begin perusing the menu. There are several dozen cocktails to choose from, but as we soon discover, nary a one contains a hint of alcohol. We settle on the house's special, "Al Raasara Cocktail," a swirl of tropical juices (mango, guava, pomegranate, and several others) and absolutely no vodka, despite Patrick's most persistent efforts to woo our waiter.**

The sun begins to set over the harbor as we sip our fruity drinks and nibble on Middle-Eastern fare, and it is abundantly clear that the picturebook romantic scene is missing an important element. Instead of our respective ladies, we have only each other's company for these moments of relaxation. It is a momentarily sad thought, but even missing a piece, the picture is a far cry better than the last year of dust and stress. With each bite of our first-class seafood dinners and each breath of fresh gulf air, Afghanistan slips further and further away...

....

[†] *Editor's note: EIFS, Exterior Insulation Finishing System. Pronounced colloquially as "ee-fizz," it is a spray-on foamy stucco-approximate applied to the surface of otherwise perfectly good buildings. A college professor of mine likened its use to covering your house with kitchen sponges and relayed tales of Chicago kids launching their skateboards into EIFS facades, competing on who could get theirs stuck in the wall at the highest point.*

[*] *After two season's worth of watching survivors of a plane crash eek out a primitive existence on a desolate South Pacific island, the opening sequence of the third season begins—to the certain shock of all viewers—inside a perfectly normal looking stucco suburb, panning back to reveal its location tucked away on the back side of the same island as the castaways. Perhaps not the most readily-accessible reference, but certainly the most apt for this surreal discovery of a southwestern-style apartment village inside a military warehouse grid inside a Middle-Eastern desert.*

[**] *"This one comes with vodka, right? ... How 'bout this one? ... Hey, if I get this cocktail, can you put some vodka in it? ... Don't forget to sneak the vodka into mine. ... Okay, so mine's the one with the vodka, right?"*

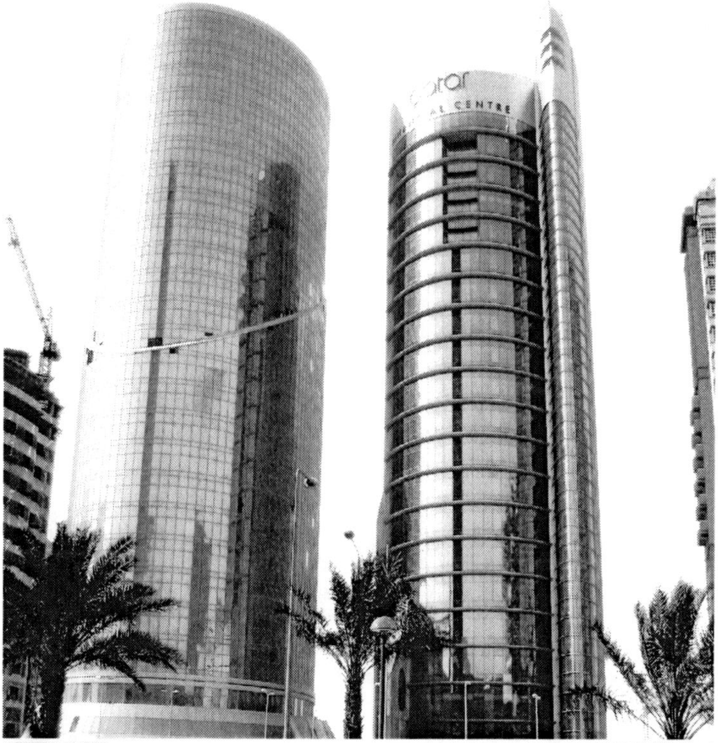
CENTRE

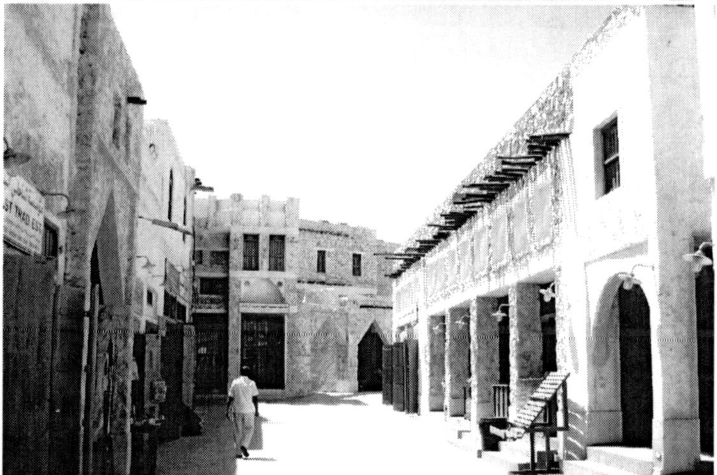

TOURISTS OF ARABIA, PART II

25 - 30 March

"Kumar, Take Us To Whitecastle"

DAY 2 ... We snag a trio of slots on yet another tour but—*HOSTILE FIRE DRILL! ALL PERSONNEL TO PROTECTED COVER! LOCK DOWN! LOCK DOWN!* ...And so on and so forth. All the trips are cancelled and we're holed up in a brown warehouse looking at each other incredulously while they pretend they're in a war zone outside.

The three of us attempt to shift to another brown warehouse where we would at least have an internet connection to occupy the interim, but we're spotted. Some Air Force kid, thoroughly overestimating his position in life, yells a command in our direction and, no shit, draws down on us. More than a little surprised to have a weapon pointed in our faces on Vacation Base, we retreat numbly, too shocked by the turn of events to offer much in the way of response.

This is but an inkling of the positively absurd focus on security permeating the rarefied Qatari air.

It isn't until afternoon on this "Day 2" that we manage to find the troop Dining Facility, as it hides within yet another identically nondescript brown warehouse and isn't on any map. A hunch pushes me to walk the perimeter of the building before entering...and I am validated. This secret squirrel DFAC has not a single sign designating its function. It is apparently such a strategically important dining facility that it cannot be labeled, lest the terrorists find the source of our nourishment.

Aside from the clearance-required Scottsdale condominium square (with dedicated Chili's), Vacation Base is an endless grid of nameless indistinguishable rectangles, unmapped and unlabeled — a Cold War strategist's wet dream.

I tell my luncheon mates that I, for one, am grateful to know that had Al-Qaeda developed themselves a sophisticated network of satellites last night—from which they could very well now be studying detailed hi-resolution satellite imagery of this base—I can rest assured that they will have no way of knowing which building we're munching french fries inside. Unless of course the locally-sourced fry-cook happens to mention anything about his job to those in his migrant community who watch him get on and off a USAF-painted shuttle every morning and evening.

The overemphasis on hi-tech, ostentatious, and obtrusive security measures pervades every thread of Vacation Base's fabric while low-tech, no-shit, common-sense, gaping holes abound. I wish every voting American could see the outright stupidity of expenditure their taxes support far and away from their fields of vision.

Our collective mood slips further and further down with each example, slamming into the bottom with a profound thud, when we actually meet and talk with a locally-based Airman. His job is to "escort" official convoys around town with his late-model Ford Expedition. He wears civilian clothes and can come and go from the base as he pleases. He and his fellows are free to live off base — drink, eat, and play on the town — and generally conduct themselves as permanent tourists.

This is all well and good, except for the fact that he and his fellows draw all of the same special pays as servicemembers in Afghanistan or Iraq in honest-to-goodness capital-W Wars. Like us, they draw combat pay, hazardous duty pay, and all the rest while cavorting around Qatar as welcomed guests inside an entirely safe and modern US-friendly nation. Let it not be missed that this is the place where we are sent to relax away from the respective Wars.

To reiterate, this uber-casual chauffeur in Vacation City receives the exact same bonuses intended to compensate soldiers in Afghanistan and Iraq for putting their lives on the line every day in service of their country. I am livid just to recount this fact. There has never, ever, been a terrorist attack in contemporary Doha, Qatar. Westerners live, work, and tourist there in droves. There is no insurgency, no war, no revolution, no fighting, no threat of any kind. But your tax dollars pay him as if there was. And for good measure they surround him and his fellows with excessive equipment, technology, and security while servicemembers down range in Afghanistan and Iraq go without.

I guess it's no small wonder why they persist in pretending this is a war zone. It's apparently rather lucrative.

It's a good thing Gladys will have three pints of Guinness to distract me.

DAY 3 ... Today we will get to see just how dangerous Doha is for ourselves, on a day-long guided "Cultural Tour." An exceedingly friendly Desi-looking man introduces himself from the front of the bus, as our guide. Kumar is his name. He waits for the vehicle to leave the base before turning to again face his audience. The early, determinedly non-scenic part of our drive is overdubbed by Kumar's spirited exposition on Qatari history.

For many years the state had been a minor kingdom, dependent chattel of neighboring Saudi Arabia with little resources and widespread poverty. All of this changed less than a decade ago when the king managed to wrest the local oil rights away from Saudi control. Billions of dollars suddenly flowed into the economy, spurring all sorts of construction and major business development.

Overnight, government intake was outpacing public outlay by leaps and bounds. The monarchy was in the rather unique position of having far more money than they could figure out how to spend. Social programs were vigorously financed and education was made free for all citizens—from grade school through university. Lucrative trust funds were even set aside for every native-born Qatari [28% of the population]. Millions were pumped into urban renewal—actually, urban creation—and into tourism stimulation. In a scant six years, the tiny after-thought of a nation had recreated itself as *The Pearl of the Middle East*.

Our tour sought to follow this developmental trajectory, beginning in the traditional markets of Doha's rural outskirts. Kumar could find no better place to start than at the spiritual ancestor of our modern car dealership, the Camel Market. Acres of pens hold camels of all ages as discriminating buyers in traditional robes walk up and down the rows, dutifully examining potential steeds. Just past them I can see new stucco boxes under construction, edging suburbia closer and closer to this last bastion of the old silk roads. My wistful philosophy is interrupted by the more pressing question of just what it would be like to have the shrill sounds and scents of ten thousand camels in your new backyard.

The next stop is an expansive courtyard fruit and vegetable market. Kumar explains that all of the grocery items are imported, primarily from Saudi Arabia and Dubai (UAE). Oil is Qatar's only natural resource, and it's rather difficult to make a meal of. After a brief walk around the stacks of colorful foreign bounty, we head off again.

Our third destination is the "Old Souk" [Souk is the Arabic equivalent of "Bazaar"]. The souk is several hundred years old, its complex network of rough-hewn stone walls criss-crossing over the equivalent of several city blocks. There are countless narrow passageways penetrating through the veritable fortress, with hundreds of small shops lining their flanks. Their enthusiastic vendors offer a multitude of wares, from silk dresses to curry powders to trained hunting falcons. One could easily spend days exploring the alleyways and courtyards, and the shops that face them. We see several European tourists that appear to be doing just that.

Moving closer into the new downtown, we next arrive at the "Gold Souk," where a new collective of merchants offer all sorts of jewelry and precious stones for our perusal. We gape at perfect black diamonds and reams of gleaming pearls. From these shops we head for the Gulf harbor, to break for lunch at the now familiar Al Raasara restaurant. Instead of sitting harborside, as before, our group is treated to a plush, private room. The three of us invite Kumar to join us at our table, interested to hear, perhaps, the stories not suitable for group consumption.

The Kumar Story is more interesting than we'd bargained for... A marketing executive in Sri Lanka, he came to Doha on a friend's invite for a short vacation. He instantly fell in love with the city and decided to extend his vacation, calling back to his company and requesting a two month leave of absence. His friend suggested that while he was on his "sabbatical," he could make easy money working part-time as a tour guide. Kumar's personality was a perfect match for the job [as we can attest], and the management was overwhelmed with positive feedback from the customers.

When the two months were up, Kumar packed up his things and prepared to go home to Sri Lanka. He dressed for his last day of work, led his farewell tour, and returned to the company office to say goodbye to his hosts and retrieve his work visa. Oddly, the boss didn't acknowledge the scheduled resignation and instead casually informed Kumar that he was being promoted due to his excellent work. A raise and more responsibility were in order. The company had just signed a contract with the U.S. military, and the next few months were going to be very important. Once things were settled out, they would send Kumar home as he wished.

Every few months, the exchange would repeat itself. Kumar's request to leave Qatar was ignored, and he was given a big raise.

Now, fully two years later, he sits at our table with three new friends, explaining how he just wants to go home. But, the touring company holds his visa, and until they release it, he can't leave.

"I can't talk to my mother anymore on the phone..."
he says so softly. "She just cries..."

The sadness only holds in his eyes for a second, and he is smiling again, asking if we're going to get a huka pipe to share. We do. For the next half hour we drink tea and smoke apple flavored tobacco from a large glass water pipe, squeezing every bit of enjoyment out of our brief reprieve—and out of the huka.

After our thoroughly relaxing post-lunch festivities, we cruise by the freshly finished seaside skyscrapers. A bridge takes us to what Kumar calls "The New Downtown," a manmade island string, where no less than two dozen opulent resorts are under construction. Like the Miami he undoubtedly aspires for it to be, the King has built a new city on trucked-in dirt, raising a phenomenal commercial center upon what was once open water. The architecture runs the full gamut of imitation, po-mo abuts neo-islamic classicism, reflecting in the glass and stainless steel of slick ultra-modern towers. A film of expectancy and glitz hovers over the prenatal strip. Promotional billboards at every corner sing of Doha's new "Pearl."

In the midst of this rampant excess, we find our last stop, an eight-storey, multi-winged monument to consumerism. This "City Center Mall" is like nothing I've ever seen, with a full-size ice-skating rink on floor one, and an amusement park on floor seven. Rolex and Montblanc have dedicated stores on level three. Acres of glass front the multiple foyers, under humongous tensile fabric fins and peaks. Lamborghini and Porsche drivers valet their cars out front. A number of pearlescent H2 Humvees are parked prominently to the side, vividly and distinctly removed from the function of their armored namesakes we were driving less than a week ago.

Only days removed from comparatively prehistoric rural Afghanistan, I am almost too overwhelmed to be disgusted.

DAY 4 ... Having exhausted our tour allotment, there is little to do on our final day but relax and wait for our government-sanctioned pseudo-pub to open in the evening. The three beer limit is taking its toll on many. I hear that 4th beers are going for $20, plus the cost of the pint, as entrepreneurial types market usage of their IDs. Though these individuals certainly have their priorities out of order (as Patrick puts it, "money is replaceable"), I can't bring myself to pay such a surcharge.

Having been outbid, Patrick tries a new tack—flirting with the bartender. I tell him not to waste his time, that Gladys is smart to his ways by now. "Besides," I remind him, "she'd lose her job if she gave you an extra beer."

"Not to worry, my friend," he counseled, "I'd fly her back to the States and marry her, so it would be okay."

"Just to have one extra beer?"

"Absolutely," my thirsty Irish friend responded. "It'd be worth it."

SHORT-TIMERS SYNDROME

20 April

FORWARD OPERATING BASE SPANN, MAZAR-I SHARIF, AFGHANISTAN — Way back in '98, my best friend Phyl and I were closing out our senior year of high school. Most of the real work was done, SATs and college admissions were behind us, and our next few years were clearly mapped out ahead. We were left with little to do but bide our time.

Having over-packed our schedules in the prior semesters, we had the luxury of two free periods in the middle of the day, flanking the lunch break. This we supplemented liberally, staging elaborate escapes from classrooms after attendance had been taken, creating sophisticated excuses ahead of time for absences, or just simply not going. We criss-crossed Southern California on invented missions, caught matinee movies, and took leisurely brunches at distant dining establishments. Other days, we'd stick closer to home, crate-digging at local music stores (for our impromptu afternoon and weekend parking lot deejaying sessions) or shooting pool at the nearby "Billiard & Spa" store, where the bored day-shift salesman would let us test out the tables for hours (so long as his manager wasn't around).

In sum, we did everything but schoolwork, as we waited while the clock ticked down to our freedom. As much as we may have indulged and enjoyed our social situation, all of our professional focus had shifted to the next stage, leaving us thoroughly unmotivated.

So, that's about where we all are right now. Only without all the post-adolescent adventure. Mostly.

Whatever goals we set out to reach here have either been met or necessarily abandoned. Our messages to our respective "mentees" have surely grown stale. Our patience with the ANA, secondarily, and the US Army, primarily, has waned. It has been nearly a year away from our lives, and all anyone wants to do anymore is just to go home.

Finally, our reliefs are on their way, our time is wrapping up, and we can begin the process of extricating ourselves from this job and this temporarily permanent life.

~

As part of the process, we've instituted "The Navy Reintegration Plan," to ensure proper reassimilation into the Navy and/or civilian life—without the corrupting effects of Army speak. You've perhaps heard of a "Swear Jar," where those attempting to clean up their speech pay fines for uttering curse words. In the same spirit, Senior Clark installed the "Army Wurdz Can."

Posted below it is a list of the unfortunate Army jargon that has seeped into the vocabulary of our otherwise intelligent group. Uttering the disgustingly ignorant catchall "Huah" costs a sailor a quick dollar. A quarter goes in the emblazoned ammunition can for such beauts as "latrine," "full-battle-rattle," "higher," "high-speed," "tracking!" and a whole list of other silly concoctions. Also outlawed are the Army's pseudo acronyms (as in DFAC, which intends to stand for Dining Facility) and misused phrases (like "At Ease" when one means "Attention").

No one wants to go home sounding like Army.

~

On other fronts, we rush to complete various important efforts. Like finishing the sixth and seventh seasons of MacGyver, so that we will have watched every episode and learned everything there possibly is to know. Or combing the bazaars and creating

shopping lists for our interpreters to make sure our families will
have every Afghan souvenir they could possibly want—because
none of us are planning on coming back anytime soon.

Job-related concerns are rapidly diminishing in importance.
More and more often, heated discussions suddenly stall
as their participants realize that in just a few weeks,
they won't care at all about the issue at hand.

It is a rather liberating acknowledgement.

Our focus has shifted to the next stage. Like the college fantasies
of high school seniors, this rapidly approaching future is hard
to truly grasp at the moment. It is murky, new, and vastly
different from today. It will take considerable readjustment,
to be sure. But it is all we can really think about anymore.

On a whiteboard in the office, a counter is updated daily with
decreasing digits towards the day of our departure, and the day
of our arrival home. Beside it, one of our less restrained has
scribbled a quote from the esteemed philosopher, H. J. Simpson:

"Awwwww.....The Waiting Game sucks...
Let's play Hungry Hungry Hippos instead!"

NO WOMEN NO CRY

15 May

Ramin cried when I left. I don't mean sniffles, either.

(It's quite a co-dependent relationship one develops with their interpreter, working together every day, all day, for a year)

The workers, too, are "very sad," I am told. They bear far more stoic faces than The Important Man. He tells me "they must look like men, and not appear sad…"

"…but I, I do not care. I will cry like women… You are my best friend."

He nearly breaks my spine, hugging me goodbye.

Behind him, my guys stand aligned at the door of what was my carpentry shop, quietly watching me leave. We are all reserved to the knowledge that, barring some spectacular change in fortunes, we will never see each other again.

I don't believe I have ever beheld a scene with such inherent finality. Many people and places have I left behind, but never without at least some illusion that return was possible.

Far too many events, requiring far too many players, and far too many years, must transpire before I could even conceive of standing again in this place.

The best my imagination can render is a return somewhat like those who pilgrimage to the overgrown killing fields of Vietnam, decades later. But that would necessarily be a far different world than this. And in a country so rent by poverty and war, I can't convince Hope that these men would live long enough for such a reunion.

It is an altogether chilling summation, and it brings emotions entirely foreign to my psyche.

But I promise a return anyway, and we all make an unspoken agreement to ignore the impossibility.

337

EXHALE

18 June

NAVAL BASE PEARL HARBOR, HAWAII, USA
— The long diversion has come to an end.

Today I put on a decidedly non-camouflaged uniform
and reported back to work in Pearl Harbor...

...and attempted to restart my Hawaiian chapter
so abruptly set aside 16 months ago.

Thanks to all for your prayers, well-wishes, care-packages,
donations, emails, and thoughtful readership over the last
year-plus. I plan on writing a "ps" or two over the next few
weeks to kind of sum up and reflect — and answer the types
of questions everyone seems to be asking since I got home.

So please forgive me a few more interruptions
to your regularly scheduled mail.

POSTSCRIPT

29 August

(My last Afghan entry to take up valuable space in your inbox. Thank you all for kindly receiving my miscellaneous ramblings over the last year and a half. In truth, the original purpose of all this has been to have an outlet through this turbulence. I guess that makes you all phenomenally affordable therapists, just for listening. Thank you for that. Please don't send me a bill.)

I've now several weeks to reflect on this alternate life I once led... to digest. I seem to have spent much of the time since answering questions from curious friends, colleagues, acquaintances, and (quite often) complete strangers. I've developed several versions of summary, in various abbreviations, dependent on the time permitted (and often, the alcohol consumed).

From that now-practiced rhetoric I can tell you all, in semi-short version:

Working every day with the local people of Afghanistan and developing those relationships was, without any doubt, the most important and fulfilling part of my experience — and what made it bearable.

Working every day with, and within, the bureaucratic apparatus of the United States Army was one of the most frustrating and life-sucking trials of my professional career. Everything that ever made me chafe about the Navy was peanuts compared to the grand scale of organizational ineptitude that is the Army. The Navy is a well-oiled machine of free-thinkers and can-do'ers by comparison.

If perhaps only by comparison.

Even that difficulty, however, pales in comparison with the reality of being separated from your life, your family and loved ones, for such a very long time.

People of Afghanistan, great. Army Leviathan, not so much. Separation is tough. Such are the main points, from which we'll usually diverge into whatever details of the three my questioner is most concerned with.

But naturally there is so much more than this, much that's difficult to talk about, much that doesn't even seem that it could be explained. Such is why I am compelled to write this and why it has taken me so very long to do so.

There exists such a chasm in understanding between the deployed and the "regular" people back home that the impediment to honest speech is severe.   Some things just can't be discussed.

~

Two days after we returned home, I found myself on an Air Force C130, gripping the mesh nets as we wove through the air. The pilot is attempting a diving turn to avoid fire. The grey-bellied beast groans and bores hard into it. But the nose never lifts. More than a free-fall, we are driving straight toward the ground. I feel the bottom drop out and brace my legs as we crash mercilessly through the desert floor. I blink. The cargo bay flickers in silence. I think my eardrums are blown. I wait. Either for pain or the hereafter. Neither comes. The lights in the cabin short, and go out. Blackness. I'm sitting, locked straight, in a guest bedroom in Norfolk. The lady is asleep beside. I'm sweating hard. I don't go back to sleep.

They told us we might be more comfortable calling our comrades
long distance than talking with the people we'd known our
entire (previous) lives. It seems absurd, but there is much truth
there. For 15 months these men have been my family. Every
moment of significance, and many of no particular significance
at all, was accompanied by my compatriots — Russ, Jon, Carlton
(alternatively, The Coolman, Johnny U, and Mr. Boatright)
and the others. Highs, lows, successes, struggles, triumphs,
frustrations. There is built such a level of trust and mutual
understanding, a reflexive dependence on each other is cemented.

And then it's gone.

We suddenly reappear alone in a world that's become quite
foreign. It is awash in trivialities, Walmarts, and *People* magazines.
"Everybody knows" about things we've never heard of. Trends
and fads have come and gone without our ever being aware. The
whole apparatus spins and rolls on sets of culturally agreed upon
tracks and mechanisms, the map of which we've mostly forgotten.

Instead, we've lived this entirely separate, parallel
life, with its own rules and realities, one that bears no
resemblance to the brightly-lit existence we return to.

Sociologists can tell you that communal conversation requires
a certain level of shared experience, underlying foundations
that are assumed and understood by both parties (even if
they don't consciously realize it). Inescapably, we return
sitting atop an entirely different base of understanding.
Readjustment to normal life is a slow process of reverting
that foundation, stone by stone, to one like the original.

But how many stones can really be discarded and replaced?
Certainly some elements will always remain, some new
understandings and perspectives have taken root.

One of my closest friends, when given a campfire and a few beers, is inclined to describe his approach to life as (I will attempt to summarize) a constant process of picking up new and interesting pieces of knowledge and trying to fit them inside with the structure of understanding he's already built for himself. Sometimes the new pieces don't fit nicely, and he is forced to either discard that new piece as untruth or rebuild his structure such that it will fit.

I've been given a whole mess of new pieces, and it's taking some time to sort them out.

As such, even now I still feel a certain disconnect.

I'm disillusioned by an American military force that purports to be the strongest in the world, yet seems ready to collapse under its own bureaucratic weight. I'm saddened by a political machine that has taken the nation hostage, and ignored necessary work in Afghanistan (and at home) in favor of throwing lives and resources away in Iraq. I'm disgusted with the glorification of an American lifestyle focused on superfluity and consumerism; fatigued with the willful ignorance of reality outside this comfortable existence and haunted by the depths of poverty and sickness I've beheld.

There's anger too, though its source and target aren't entirely clear. Perhaps much of it is a feeling of being betrayed, though not in the way you might expect. Country, society, and religion have sought since birth to ensure I understood certain truths about life, certain ways of thinking, certain understandings. A year in the desert stripped these preconceptions bare and revealed the rickety legs that prop them up. My eyes have been opened to an immensely greater swath of human experience and fallibility, and my patience thinned towards the institutions that encourage blindness.

Returning home, all I can see is rickety legs...

...And droves of smiling military officers, politicians, and religious leaders scrambling to cover them with shiny, silky pastiche.

Such thoughts banging around in one's head are sure to hamper proper reassimilation.

~

Even were I to regain exactly the mindset I had before leaving, the world here has changed much while I was gone. Nearly everyone I knew at work has left for another station, even the senior people who conspired to send me off are not here to receive my return. Friends and family members lead entirely different lives then I remember, and no one is sure quite where I should fit into them. Like a modern-day Van Winkle, I've awakened to find everything has moved on without me.

It's been two full years now since a hurricane blew through my adopted New Orleans home, setting off the chain of events that sent me around the world and back. And somehow, I still feel displaced. It is as if I shifted off-track somewhere back there and instead of merely becoming lost, I found myself in an entirely separate existence. A rather amorphous one, at that.

An entire lifetime I've lived in these two years, and though I would never have proposed this path to walk — and certainly never would have chosen it of my own volition — I wouldn't trade these experiences for the world. I've been privileged to engage with exquisitely varied people, organizations, and cultures, and to imbibe formerly exotic thoughts, ideas, and beliefs at a level of intimacy and depth I could never have imagined. I witnessed the rebirth of a people and walked in the footprints of history at the crossroads of the world. I could never give up these waypoints I've traversed, whatever the tribulation.

As a young child, I once infamously proclaimed my desire to "know everything there is to know." Perhaps, I am a step or two closer today then I was a life ago.

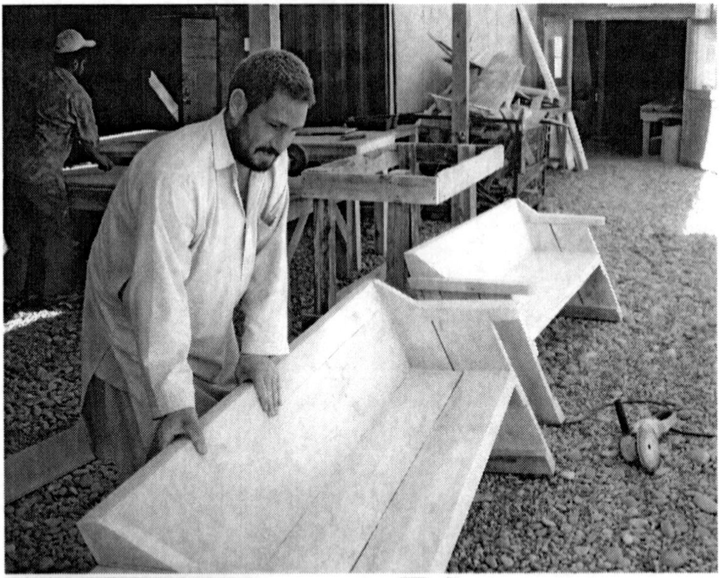

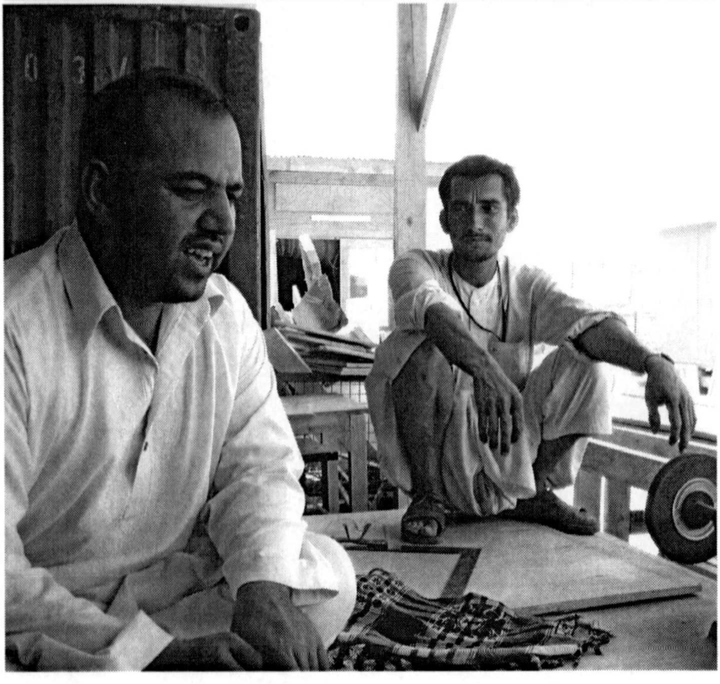

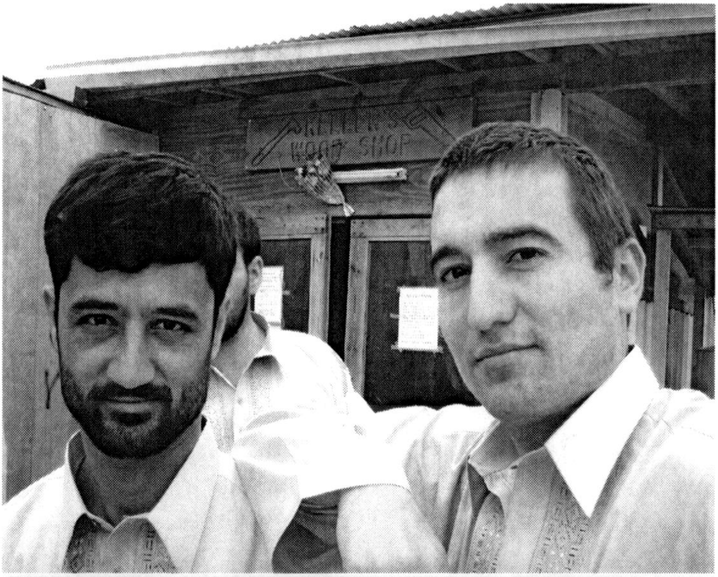

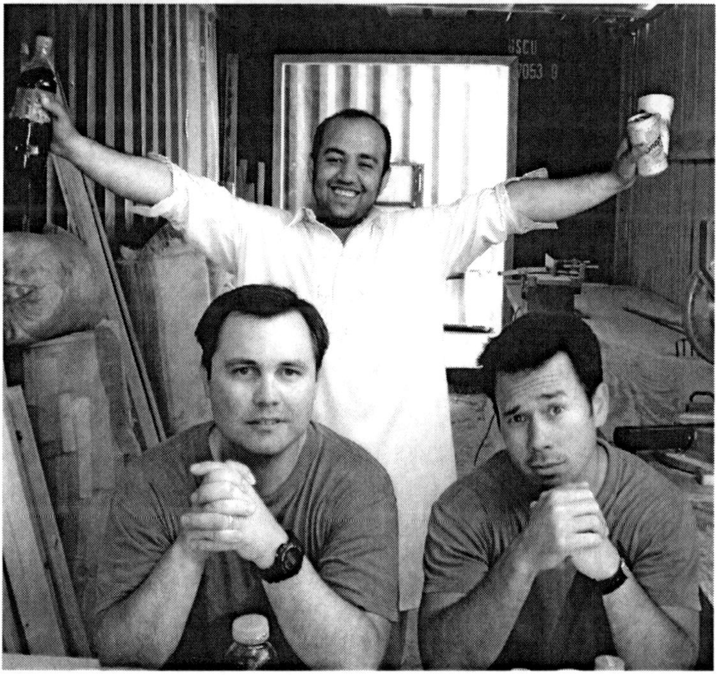

BOOK III

Requiem for Innocence

It is incredibly tough to reopen a series of chapters
that, in your own mind, end with a close friend's death
— or underscore the dissolution of a marriage.

But, whether mundane, ironic, naively prescient, or otherwise,
these daily musings recount the re-orienting of a life's
trajectory. My life's trajectory. They can't be forever ignored.

The space of time perhaps offers new perspective on exhumed
tales, or enough numb distance to engage epiphanal ones.
In re-reading these nearly decade-old words, it is not how
much I may have forgotten of those days that strikes me,
but of how much is unrecorded. The stories and lessons
that have stuck with me, the go-to memories I can relate
on request, some of the most clearly remembered moments
are somehow not documented in the original texts.

In a heavy cherry-wood chest I brought back from Afghanistan,
there is a stack of folded, inked-up papers with notes of essays
I meant to write years ago. A matching set of other, more
profoundly difficult unfinished tomes has likewise sat neatly
untouched in the back of my head. The following is an attempt
to unravel the old scribblings and complete both sets — a bit
belatedly, to be sure. They are by no means chronological,
moreso a semi-topically-organized spilling out of thoughts,
as the years have resettled them in my own mind.

This third book is then, in a sense, a collection of unwritten letters.

STATUES (OF LIMITATIONS) [†]

As much as I would want to consider old writings dateless, in some sense the original letters are frozen in the past, memorials not only to what life was like in those moments, but also to the limitations imposed by time, medium, and, of course, security in describing the daily events in a war zone.

There are a mix of miscellaneous notes, details, and stories that informed and colored that "life away" that for various reasons I wasn't at liberty to divulge in the original letters. In fact, unbeknownst to most of the readers, my essays themselves were held and sent out several weeks after being written, simply to comply with both the letter and spirit of security restrictions.

The old phrase "loose lips sink ships" is no cute aphorism, but a serious mantra drilled into the heads of all who serve in dangerous places. While soldiers and sailors regularly chafe under what seems a too widely applied directive, the truth is that one can seldom anticipate what bit of innocuous current information might be relevant to some ill-wisher somewhere, particularly if combined with several other innocuous bits of information. So, my own thoughts too went into a semi-artificial queue such that nothing would be current by the time it was read. It is a special challenge to attempt to be both timely and sufficiently non-specific while trying to still tell a good story (and keep the folks back home reasonably updated).

Naturally, some otherwise interesting details had to be left out entirely — like the base within a base within a base that held a secret special forces team that wore no nametags, but rumbled in and out every so often on souped up Mad Max dune buggies. Instead of a gunner atop the vehicle, as in the typical Humvee, one scraggled soul with a SAW strapped himself into a hammock slung between the rear wheels, covering the six from six inches off the ground as it bounced underneath him in a blur. *"The Bearded Ones are coming!"* the Taliban were known to screech over franctic radio communications, as these elite warriors wiped whole provinces clean of the enemy scourge.

One of The Coolman's most interesting projects as Ops Officer was in rehabilitating an old dirt air strip, just outside of Camp Spann, so the bearded offensive could fly in and out at a moment's notice. There's a fantastic semi-classified photo of Russ and the burly spec ops Major puffing cigars on the muddy strip as a C130 drops in behind them — the first successful landing there in decades. I've little doubt it's his most treasured souvenir of the whole adventure, even if he couldn't show it to anyone for years.

~

The string of fascinating things I couldn't yet share really began on our first day in country, as the Mazar team was surreptitiously ushered into an unmarked hut on Camp Phoenix for our in-briefing. This being an Army-hosted event, of course, there was a powerpoint presentation waiting. For the next hour, a somber and incredibly articulate Intel officer lectured the group on the uncensored version of recent Afghan history. Rather than the ubiquitous ANA map of the country outlining the seven Corps jurisdictions, the map we spoke over split the country up according to warlords. Many commanded only small slivers of territory, others large swaths of the rebuilding nation. Nearly all had been on the CIA's payroll during the Soviet wars. The Colonel flipped through a series of slides showing the corresponding posts in the new Afghan Central Government now held by these would-be shahs.

He stopped on one massively mustachioed mugshot.

"This is General Abdul Rashid Dostum."

He flipped a slide to an organizational chart. "As you can see here, he's just a few steps down from the President.. and probably still moving up. Even though, technically speaking, in order to accept his current post General Dostum has relinquished all claim to his former territories and disbanded his militia... in practice, he controls most of Northern Afghanistan."

The Colonel's eyes grazed our circle of Naval officers. Our historical and geographical knowledge of the area was thin. Two weeks prior, we had been assigned to Herat, in the far east.

"His center of power, still, is in Mazar-i Sharif, where you all are headed." He pointed to the city, circling his hand around it over the map.

"Now, what that really means is.. you gents shouldn't have much to worry about. The Taliban no longer have any real foothold up there. Dostum has a standing order protecting Americans in the North. Long as he's happy down here, we expect that to continue."

The physical center of Dostum's power was, in fact, a few miles outside of Mazar-i Sharif. Astride the smallish adobe village of Dehdadi sits a 19th century fortress called Qala-i-Jangi. It is a behemoth structure, tall, scalloped fringed walls encasing a raised grassy plain several football fields long. A few buildings pop above the surface here and there, belying the massive labyrinth below.

At the outbreak of the US-Afghan war in 2001, it was serving as a prison for captured Taliban. Their subsequent uprising in November of that year was one of the first major flashpoints of the conflict, coming to be known as The Battle of Qala-i-Jangi. Though a quick youtube search will now bring up several documentaries, at the time, the event was invisible to those in the United States. Several hundred Taliban prisoners were killed along with dozens of Afghan fighters. The lone American casualty, "Mike" Spann, was an agent for a CIA sub-organization that doesn't technically exist. Indeed, four years later, on the outpost now memorializing him, our group knew nothing of the massacre just outside our gates until we unearthed video clips buried in the base's servers. The images are bloody and terrible, in stark contrast with the silent ruins, crumbling stoically in my own photos.

Today, or in 2006 for that matter, a passerby would be forgiven for thinking the fortress deserted, but within and beneath its thick walls, Dostum's machine still hums. Every so often, Colonel Ata would be summoned to oversee some emergency repair or improvement — off the record. We did not create forms or track the work, and at a time when we couldn't get proper funding for critical ANA projects, I always wondered where Ata found the cash to pay for bathroom remodels at the semi-hidden living quarters embedded within Qala-i-Jangi.

~

As the reader has no doubt surmised by this point, operational and political realities on the ground often strayed far from the anticipations and the regulations set forth by the governing bodies in Kabul. We could hardly point fingers at Ata for having an emergency slush fund.

In quiet recognition of the ill-functioning system (and the logistical impossibilities of centrally supplying dozens of far-spread outposts without any real infrastructure) many of us downrange carried suitcases of cash. The cash, of course, came with numerous restrictions, many arbitrary, that piled up as the war progressed. Some were intended to prevent abuse and fraud, others, like the late 2006 stipulation against "regular or repeated services" came from attempts to force at least some types of contracts onto a centrally-controlled system.* Eventually, the nausea-inducing scroll of regulation became so onerous that even obviously legitimate acquisitions would be rebranded in the records as one of several common items that wouldn't be questioned — just to avoid the monday morning quarterbacking from the Chair Force in Kabul. (*chairs*, by the way, were off limits, but *chair parts* could be requisitioned at will.)

By the time we had arrived in Mez, the most common listed purchase was for gravel.

In addition to being an important construction component, as the go-to paving material for just about all surfaces in and around military outposts (and continually being washed away by the extreme winds and rains of the high desert), gravel was ubiquitous, and always on order. If you need anything to do your job, we were told, just have the vendor write it up as gravel. I have no doubt, according to official records, US soldiers bought enough aggregate to bury Afghanistan several times over.

In short, consumables were safe purchases, and running a wood shop meant I was ordering materials and consumables continuously — including the human consumables that staffed the shop. When the restrictions on "services" came out, the entire venture was threatened on a technicality. At that point, we sat down with Rahim and Monan and did a different type of mentoring; we showed them how to start a construction materials company. Rather than pay the carpenters directly out of the cash bucket (as had been done originally), and order materials separately, we would order some of the materials from the new company and the company would pay the salaries of the carpenters out of the overhead. What would have been profit for the company was to be saved in a business fund, such that when the day came that American money stopped flowing into Afghanistan, they would have sufficient capital to open up a proper workshop in town.

Most of the material and tool purchases made under this arrangement were fairly mundane, simply saving me the effort of arranging convoys into town to buy them myself — which was itself becoming more difficult as the overall situation in Afghanistan began to deteriorate and security fears ratcheted up. However, there was one morning when, upon opening the shop, I was informed by Rahim that all of our saw blades were incorrigibly dull and productivity was being correspondingly slowed. He asked if he could leave to go acquire whetstones to sharpen them, I obliged. As he packed his things, Ramin explained, "Ok, so now Rahim will be gone for two or three days."

Come again?

"You told him to go and get the stones..."

Where is the store? Iran?

"Oh, no, Sir. You cannot buy these sharpening stones in stores. He must climb the mountain to get them. It will take several days' time."

Sure enough, a few days later, Rahim returned to the shop with a backpack full of slate gray rock shards. From the side of a mountain.

~

Fortunately, I wasn't completely beholden to what was available in the Afghan shops (or on the sides of mountains), there was one place much closer that I was able to consistently find exotic tools and materials. A Turkish construction company had the contract to build Phase I of Camp Shaheen, the last building of which was a regional military hospital that was nearing completion in late 2006.

I was initially on a mini-quest for The Boss, who was trying to find some copper tubing in order to construct a homemade still.** In my rounds I had noticed a spool in the Turks' laydown yard. On a whim, Ramin and I knocked on the door of the foreman's trailer. A few moments passed, and we were beginning to think better of the whole idea when the aluminum door rattled open, revealing a giant black mustache. Before we could stammer out our reason for disturbing, the mustache was inviting us in for tea.

We took our seats in worn padded chairs next to a parakeet cage. Orkun, to whom the mustache and the birds belonged, noted that he picked up his new feathered friends on a whim, as they were outside the market where he went each week to get tea. He made the best tea in Afghanistan, we were duly informed, because he would buy several varieties and carefully blend them.

It was true, about the tea. It was certainly the best I'd had in months, though some of that might have been due to the copious amounts of sugar our Turkish friend dumped in the cups.

Such began a beautiful friendship, and a regular weekly stop for the Important Man and I. Tea, and relaxed perusement of yards and yards of tools and materials. With the hospital almost complete, Orkun was happy to sell off most anything we were interested to acquire.

Out in the warehouses though, we were often left to deal with our Turkish friend's less linguistically savvy assistants. On several occasions, I found myself on end of a long translation string, as Ramin spoke Dari to the company's interpreter, who turned and translated for the Turkish site manager.*** The manager would respond in kind, and then the process would reverse. It took devilishly long to get any queries resolved. Eventually, I took to simply preparing a list with Ramin, so that the two interpreters could hash things out amongst themselves.

As we walked the rows of half-used boxes of screws and bolts, Ramin taught me another Afghan proverb: *Don't throw anything away; even if it is snake's poison you may find use for it.*

....

† *Spelling intentional.*

* *The recipient of one such centrally-sourced service contract was known to pester Ramin with late night phone calls, offering my interpreter bribes if he would vouch for outrageously marked-up quotes for certain work items. I reported him to Kabul and initiated procedures to terminate his contract for cause, which they blocked.*

** *Yes, even the highest ranking officer at our post was scheming to break General Order #1.*

*** *Among the myriad ethnic groups in Northern Afghanistan, there is a race known as the Turkmen who, presumably through influences left over from the Ottoman Empire and previous incursions, speak a mutually intelligible dialect of Turkish. Turkish contractors working in Central Asia have, not too surprisingly, made good use of their assistance.*

LESSONS LEARNED

The original version of my closing letter from Afghanistan was appended with this footnote:

"Let it be noted that I have learned far more about the Navy, and what it means to be a Naval officer, in the desert with a handful of displaced sailors, than I had in the previous three years of wearing the uniform. I mean this with full respect and gratitude towards the seasoned officers and, especially, the chiefs I had the luxury of serving with there. It has spoiled me. Especially as I return to a primarily civilian-staffed pseudo-military command trying to overcompensate with continual NAVY functions and regalia. It all rings rather hollow, if not completely absurd, as if the folks running the amusement park bumper cars installed stoplights and traffic cops, expecting licensed drivers to take the proceedings seriously."

As if to drive home the impact of the culture shock of returning, even the gap between stateside and deployed service felt severe. In retrospect, this doesn't seem so surprising. The related observation of the exponential educational value of that deployment does still ring very true, dramatically affecting the remainder of my Naval service as well as my approach to the post-military career to follow — especially climbing the rungs of leadership.

The constant juxtaposition between Army and Navy ways of doing things (not to mention the pepperings in of other services, other NATO militaries, and civilian contractors) offered a continual thesis study on management practices.

~

The recounting and evaluation of "Lessons Learned" is an integral component of the AAR (alternatively After-Action Review or After-Action Report). I was first introduced to this debriefing structure in

Camp Shelby, where it followed each field exercise. The post-event sister of Operational Orders (which are given prior to the exercise) the AAR begins with a review of the original plan of action. What was supposed to happen is compared with what did, and then the unit outlines the *Lessons Learned* from those discrepancies, targeting areas that should be improved, refined, or rethought.

Near the end of our Infantry indoctrination in Mississippi, the team undertook the week-long final field exercise, combining all the previous training elements into one continuous operation. There would be convoying between bases, platoon movements on foot, responding to ambushes, urban warfare, room clearances, and so forth, filling long hours under the Mississippi summer sun with non-stop activity. The action would break late each afternoon for daily AAR sessions with the NCO's running the training. In a large forest clearing somewhere deep in the wilds of Camp Shelby, a circle of logs and stump stools made for an outdoor conference room of sorts. The Navy men, up since the break of dawn and exhausted from the weight of their armor in the stifling heat, slumped around the makeshift meeting area. Before the first such session could begin, a senior officer or two pointed out to the sergeant an unused temporary classroom not 20 meters away from the log circle. A spacious reinforced-tent structure, it had more than enough room for the group and could get everyone out of the sun. It had actual chairs.

The sergeant looked immediately uneased, glancing back and forth between his sweat-drenched seniors and the shiny white tent. "I'm not sure that is authorized for us, Sir..." he stammered.

The gaggle of Captains and Commanders murmured incredulously for a moment, amplifying their disbelief ever louder amongst themselves before throwing the collected challenges back at the shrinking sergeant. After a few minutes within the swirling tempest, and realizing it was unlikely to subside on its own, he announced that he would call his Lieutenant and find out about the tent for tomorrow, but could we please get on with the AAR?

~

The concept of pre-authorization seems unshakable from the Army ranks, reflecting an institutional ethos towards stasis over movement. Whereas I can remember from my earliest days of OCS [Office Candidate School, Navy's boot camp for commissioning], we cadets being not-so-subtly encouraged by our Marine Corps drill instructors to stop asking questions and act quickly, logically, according to our training. Indecision gets people killed more assuredly than less-than-perfect actions made decisively. Naval officers are trained from inception to be proactive and situationally aware — always evaluating the environment and the options it allows.

At another Shelby training course, weeks earlier, hundreds of sweaty, over-heated soldiers were strewn about in the heat, awaiting their next turn on the live-fire range. Off to the side of the clearing, unmolested and ignored, sat a 20' refrigerated Conex box with "ICE" emblazoned on its side in red letters five feet tall. Dying from the heat, The Coolman and I approached the box and peeked inside. Sure enough, it was stacked to the ceiling with 5 lb bags of ice. Tossing a couple on our shoulders, we returned to our compatriots and broke them open. The grunts went silent, staring on wide-eyed as though Hendrix himself had walked out of the icebox, strumming. *Is that authorized?*

Through a simple act of common sense the sailors gained instant fame. A few days later, the soldiers were helping themselves to bags as well. An Army Lieutenant waved me down to tell me he'd researched the matter and the ice was, in fact, intended to be used by the training companies. The command was worried about overheating. *How did we know?*

Returning to our initial tale, out on the comprehensive final training course, four more days would pass, and each AAR would start in the same manner, with the Navy brass querying about a location change and the sergeant assuring them he had sent the matter up the chain.

On the final day of field training, the beginning of the AAR was interrupted by the sergeant's Lieutenant. "I've got great news," he beamed. "The General has approved a location change to that tent for this AAR." He and the sergeant puffed up with pride. *The system worked.*

The system, such as it was, mandated that even the smallest change of plans be sent up to the top of the command structure, lest the General wander by one day and see things proceeding at all differently than he expected. Deciding where variance is or is not acceptable is something to be determined at the highest possible paygrade.

~

It's not to say that the Navy doesn't also revere the chain of command, but its use and purpose differs much from the one of its sister service. In simple terms, the Navy is built to resolve problems on the lowest possible rung of the hierarchy, thereby freeing up its brass to focus on (ostensibly) more important concerns. In the Army, the grunts in the field are neither trusted nor empowered to make decisions, regardless how trivial.

There is a reason to the rhyme, of course, and it comes down to the purpose and operation of the two services. The Army is fundamentally a force of occupation, they are built, first and foremost, to hold ground.* Rapid decisions are far less critical than discipline. The geography of the system is also unique. In all but the most extreme of circumstances, the primary chain of command is co-located with the foot soldiers. Its been so structured for a millennia, from Agamemnon to the smoky tents of Ulysses S. Grant. The Army moves as one methodical giant, controlled by a single brain.
The Navy is a far different beast. With operational units ranging in size from a single littoral attack boat with a couple dozen men aboard to the floating cities of the Nimitz carrier class, and a significant portion of the fleet spread about under the ocean's surface in isolated tin cans, a run-everything-up-the-chain approach is untenable. Every ship an island, its captain is expected to internalize the requirements of the broader mission and act in support of that duty. Given both the complexity of

the systems and the shifting nature of the watery battlefield, subordinates are themselves empowered to make appropriate decisions for their purview. The buck doesn't stop at the top, it stops at every floor. Flexibility and responsibility are inherent in the system and the culture. The most simultaneously chilling and ecstatic moment for a young ensign, fresh from the Academy, is the first time he must bellow to the boat, "I have the con," and the entire hulking ship comes under control of a 22-year old kid for eight overnight hours.**

~

This flexibility seems to translate, unsurprisingly, to notions of hierarchy. In the Army, the rigidity of the chain amplifies the slightest difference in adjacent links. A freshly-promoted Army O-3 may begin demanding his rightful salutes and Sirs from those O-2 Lieutenants that were yesterday his peers. A Navy Officer's Mess would find this absurd (and probably castigate the boor). Where all two dozen or so Army pay grades are of supreme relative importance, the whole of the Navy's ranking structure (though nominally identical), in practice, seems to fall roughly as: Junior Enlisted, Chiefs, Junior Officers, Senior Officers, Flag Officers. Further formal distinctions are precisely that, only a formality. Within these groupings, it is not uncommon for members to be on a first-name basis with their counterparts (or a call-sign basis, for the pilots), a concept apparently abhorrent to the Army, who seldom seem even familiar with their compatriots' given names.

Getting caught up in this specific culture clash led
to one of the most important lessons I learned on
that deployment, the value of diplomacy.
I still have, filed away somewhere, a massive spreadsheet and multi-page report tallying the use and state of every room on Camp Shaheen — the ANA base under my supervision. It exists because I once told off an Army Major back in Kabul, not so politely explaining all the different ways he had no idea what was going on, on the ground, in Mazar-i Sharif.

It all started over toilets.

On one otherwise unnoteworthy Saturday morning, we received a message from the south to expect several thousand new Afghan Army enlistees at our doorstep the following Tuesday. The ANA, apparently, had been airing recruitment advertisements on radio stations across the country for the past two weeks. The ads instructed interested young men to report to Camp Shaheen, en masse, on the aforementioned Tuesday.

Eventually, someone in Kabul realized it might be sporting to inform the folks in Mazar-i Sharif about the incoming flood. As part of a series of frantic messages between our team and the flagpole, I had requested of the recently-promoted Major at Central Engineering emergency authorization to contract for additional port-o-johns to accommodate the influx (in addition to the tents and beds we were scrambling to acquire). Unlike "hard" goods, which we had reasonable latitude to appropriate, the toilets were part of a service contract administered out of Kabul, and out of our control. The Major curtly replied that his records showed we had, in fact, more toilets than authorized. Further, by his count, more than 50% of Camp Shaheen was available for berthing — we should be taking no special measures to accommodate the new recruits.

My extended response was a superbly-constructed defense of our original request that made not the slightest attempt at diplomatic wording, and clearly inferred my opinion of the new Major's intellectual capacity. He did not answer. A couple hours later, I was called into The Boss' quarters.

I closed the door as asked, his demeanor communicating all I needed to know about the direction this talk would take. I'd heard tell of the man's Come To Jesus Meetings, and it was clear I was about to be the recipient of the latest edition.

He was stone-faced as he recounted taking calls throughout the afternoon about my insubordination, and the punishments he'd promised to get the offended off the line. With the words of those senior men atop those I had supplied in dismantling the Major, he indicted my behavior. "Lieutenant...*Junior Grade*..." He stretched out the full formal rank for emphasis of its posteriority.

"This breach of military discipline will not be tolerated,"
he paused, slate eyes searing into mine.

"...Again."

He softened, glare turning to fatherly sigh.

"Travis. It doesn't matter if everything you said was true."

He chuckled a bit at the thought of the red-faced Army engineer, and gracefully allowed me to exhale. He continued the lecture. It doesn't matter how right you are if you can't deign the slightest to protocol. In the military, as in life, being the smartest isn't good enough to get things done or to get people to listen to you. Diplomacy isn't just for international treaties, it is how you get people to treat your ideas as their own and to be just as passionate about them as you are. In other words, be careful how you present things. Make sure you are giving them facts to act on — not something that can be construed as unsupported opinion.

"Now, I don't want to ever talk about this sort of
thing again. Get out of here and, LT— "
A slight smile creased his lips as I paused in the doorway.

"If anyone asks, tell them I beat you mercilessly."
The next few days, Ramin and I canvassed every square meter of Camp Shaheen, interviewing soldiers and documenting the actual usage and condition of each interior building space on the Afghan base. What we found, and recorded, was of far greater interest and value than the spoutings of a pissed-off Lieutenant.

While it should have been obvious that Kabul's context-free approach was inadequate — a simple allocation calculation for an entire base at once, dividing square feet by heads — what we actually found within that context shed considerable light on the ultimate needs of the ANA, and where current planning was failing them.

Quoting from the original report:

> The 209th Garrison is an incomplete organism, attempting to fulfill all of its assigned missions without having all of the proper pieces. Numerous major facilities are, as yet, unbuilt. Buildings ostensibly categorized for housing soldiers have been reallocated to house these otherwise unsupported functions.
>
> In addition to missions that were either unplanned for or not yet supported, there also exist primary functions that have inadequate support. The most notable deficiencies are in office space and training space. The first is evidenced by the numerous ANA officers and NCOs who have turned their living spaces into dual purpose rooms, bringing desks into their sleeping spaces (or beds into their offices). Additionally, a lack of adequate conference space has prompted some Kandaks to subdivide Barracks areas to create meeting rooms, briefing rooms, and—in one instance—a makeshift TOC. This is presumably the result of a minor disconnect between planned needs and resultant needs. The latter deficiency above, however, is more puzzling. Despite the fact that the primary mission at the 209th is training, and despite the substantial international manpower devoted to that training, only one building on the master plan is actually intended for training. Dozens of classes and workshops take place every day on this base; one dedicated building is clearly inadequate to house each of these efforts... As a result, the most common adaptation of nominal barracks spaces is into classrooms.

In short, the phased construction of Camp Shaheen prioritized housing troops — to the extent that virtually nothing but barracks had yet been built. The Major in Kabul was looking at numbers that told him there was a veritable glut of space for beds, not realizing that all of this space has been taken up by the other functions that hadn't been built for.

Assigned a certain amount of space per unit, the Afghan commanders did as should have been expected of them, they carved it up to utilize every foot to fit their needs at the time, irrespective of titles on a base map in Kabul or posted above room numbers. Oversize barracks were sliced up (in many cases with the help of the previously discussed Walls Project) and became libraries, class rooms, and offices. Offices became sleeping spaces because Afghan officers don't bunk with their conscript foot soldiers. Utility rooms became makeshift kitchens and chai-making stations. The adaptability of an Afghan knows few bounds and seldom follows the expectations of foreign advisors.

After days of traipsing throughout Camp Shaheen's innards, I worked through the night to prepare the report (a bit of self-imposed penance, to be sure), and submitted the carefully-worded results to Kabul in lieu of a grovelling apology. I can only assume it accompanied smart diplomacy from The Boss on other channels.

In the end, we got the toilets.

~

Afghan toilets, in fact, endeavored to supply me more than one lifelong lesson. In the years since, teaching urban design courses to aspiring young architects who have been cultivated to believe their superior talents will prevail over the public's base tendencies, I return again and again to Colonel Ata's office and the endless frustrations of idealistic planning for the unwashed masses.

It was late autumn in Mazar. The burly Australian PM of the facilities services company huffed over lukewarm chai. Our annual budget for his work was blown. Two innocuous-seeming culprits lurked in the stack of work order requests: toilet repairs and doorknobs. He'd exhausted all local suppliers for parts, and was now forced to import at ever-increasing cost. Counting off the replacement knobs he'd installed, one hundred...two hundred... over three hundred since last year! *That's more'un a knob a day mate!*

A determined Ata grabbed the most recent work orders and marched off to investigate, Ramin and myself in tow. Upon interrogation, all three of the day's requestors ultimately confessed the same story: *locked door, no key, broke it open, submitted request.*

The toilet situation was worse. The septic systems, built to handle months of use between pumpings, were being overloaded in mere days. The pipes were continually blocked or broken. Ata had an inkling of what might be going on, and we hiked over to where a new unit of trainee soldiers were bunked. He called the sergeant over and traded a few words, nodding as the man gestured.

Turning back to me, he shuffled his boots in the
dust, pantomiming as he picked up a flat rock so
unearthed. Ramin translated as he explains.

Back in the mountains and the villages where most of these
young soldiers come from, it is a very ancient and rough way of
life. They've never seen bathroom tissue or had plumbing, much
less a bidet. Out in the hills, when a man needs to relieve himself,
he'll kick around for a bit and find a nice, flat, smooth stone.
(Turning the rock over in his left hand) *this* is his toilet paper.

We walked inside to the rows of eastern-style commodes,
the bowls embedded into the raised floor and thick
porcelain treads ringing the basin. He points downward.
They're tossing the used ones down the hole, filling
up the tanks below and blocking the plumbing.

Heading back to the truck, Ata sighs, muttering
about creating signage and training plans to teach
soldiers not to flush rocks down toilets.

Undoubtedly, it will eventually get added to the indoctrination
guides that already implore new soldiers not to report to training
bare-footed, because they've just sold off their freshly issued boots.

....

** In the most general terms, the Marines invade and take ground while the Army holds
and defends it. The Air Force and Navy provide air and sea support, respectively, for both.*

*** I only relay the experiences of ship-driving brethren, I was
a seabee, my job was to build things not pilot them.*

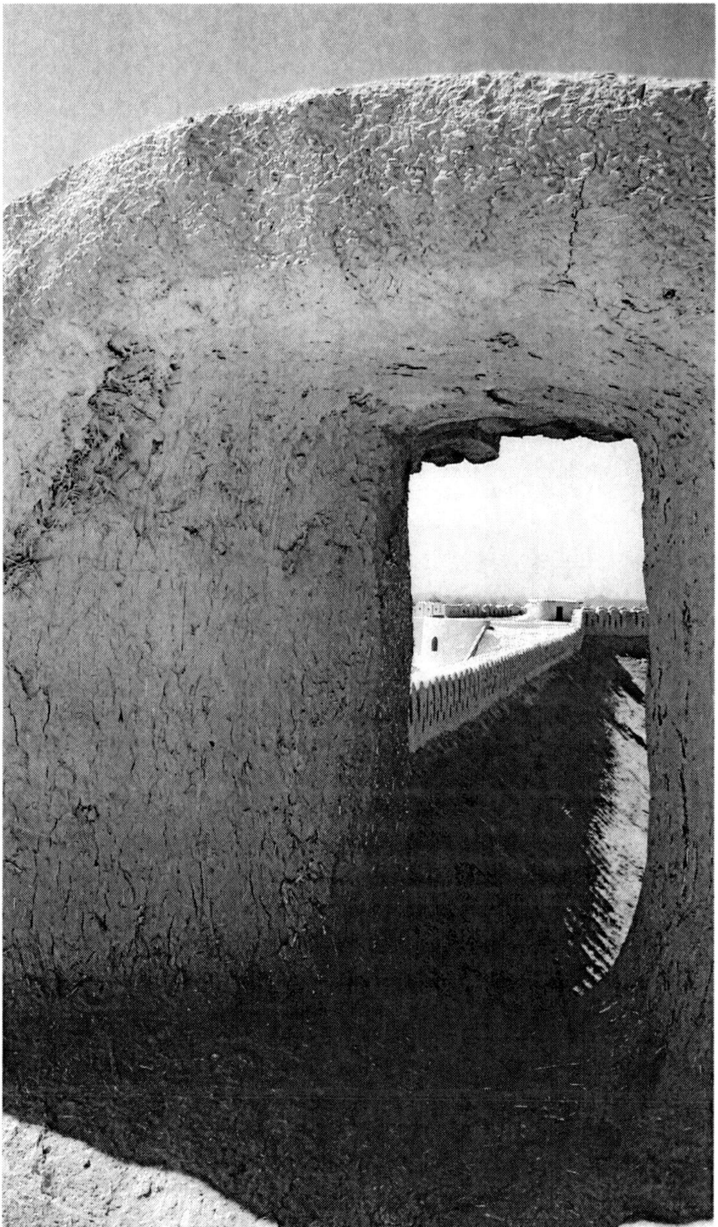

ATA ON ATA

As I dig through old notes, I come across a worksheet of sorts. It is an interview form produced by the Army, to be used by mentors to evaluate their "mentees." There are entries for "personality/disposition," "hobbies/interests," "tactical competence," "apparent ambitions," and so forth. Scant room is given on the form for elaboration beyond a few key words. The sheet is dominated by a "Leader Evaluation" block, where the interviewer is to rank their Afghan counterpart in various technical and tactical capacities as "Competent," "Requires Training," or "Incompetent." Curiously, these three ratings are also to be used to evaluate "Leadership Potential" in the same areas — it is unclear how one demonstrates competency in potential.

There is a matrix of little round bubbles where the interviewer is to mark his judgement of his charge's competency. The handy instructions outline a color-coded legend for which to fill the bubbles. It is a black and white print-out, so the bubbles for the range of responses all appear an identical gray.

At some point during the interview, it is apparent that the utility of the given sheet was exhausted. On the unformatted reverse, the life of one Mohammod Ata Rasoli is freely outlined instead.

~

Ata was born in 1965 in the village of Do Abi Yaftal in the mountains of Badakshan. The region sits at the crux of east and west, where Russia, China, and the central Asian republics meet. Its current boundary, which forms the distinctive northeastern finger of Afghanistan, is the result of a series of agreements between then Czarist Russia, Great Britain, and British-influenced Afghanistan to create a buffer-zone of non-engagement between Russia and the eastern British empire (i.e., India).

As mentioned previously in these texts, the decades preceding Ata's birth were ones of stability, prosperity, and modernization. By Ata's 13th birthday, however, the communist People's Democratic Party of Afghanistan had seized control of the country from Mohammed Daoud Khan — who had himself overthrown the reformist King Zahir Shah, just five years prior.

Within two years' time, agents of the USSR would be invited in to prop up the flailing communist experiment. Ata, now in high school, would be forcibly enlisted by the Soviet-run infantry. Refusing conscription, he fled into the mountains of Badakshan where resistive forces were coalescing around a charismatic leader who would later earn the moniker *The Lion of Panjshir*. Throughout the 1980's Ahmad Shah Masoud's northern militias grew in numbers and prowess, developing into an incredible opposition to the Soviet occupation.

After Ata captured a Russian field officer and, not sure exactly what to do with him, brought him to the rebel leader's feet, Masoud promoted the young soldier to the officer ranks. Ata would continue to serve under Masoud for the next two years as the Mujahadeen drove the Soviets out of Afghanistan.

For a brief period, Masoud's own forces became state security for the reborn nation and re-centered their base of operations at Kabul, Ata included. History well knows the new governing structure was short-lived, doomed to infighting among the previously aligned resistance forces.

As is well-documented, the resultant vacuum following the Soviet retreat and the struggle for power among the victorious commanders plunged the country into civil war. The Taliban invasion would follow. Ata and countless others fled to Pakistan. Nearly uncontested in their drive northward, the Taliban would soon control most of the nation.

As Masoud tried to re-consolidate his power in the north during the mid-1990's, Ata was called back to Badakshan to help lead the newly-formed 29th Infantry Division as a Battalion Commander.

This Tajik regiment was later combined with other units as the *Jabha Moqawomat* (meaning, Against Taliban), and then with the Uzbek militias of Abdul Rashid Dostum* as part of a larger collective known to the West as the Northern Alliance. This "United Front" continued to absorb smaller militias from around the country, representing a complex patchwork of ethnic and tribal identities. At the time of Masoud's assassination, two days before the terrorist attacks on New York City, the United Front had retaken 1/3 of the country from the Taliban, which maintained another third of the geography (centered around Kabul), with the remaining third of Afghanistan, to the south, fractured between countless other factions.

After the attacks of 9/11, the United Front retook Kabul with American air support and expelled the Taliban forces from the country (temporarily, it would turn out). An interim Afghan government was again installed, led by Hamid Karzai, and the United Front nominally disbanded. Ata was installed as the Head of Security for the Presidential Guard. In the weeks and months to follow, the reclaimed nation underwent a grand reorganization of its very structure, with a contentious process of sorting out emolument for the leading actors in the liberation. Leading Generals of the resistance were rewarded with cabinet positions and other key roles within the government. Dostum, for his part, negotiated a seat at the head of the revived Ministry of Defense, as the Deputy Defense Minister under Mohammad Fahim.

Under the new organization, Ata was reassigned to the 7th Corps, Balkh province, in the far north of Afghanistan. The post would be short-lived, as within a year, the entire system would be scrapped in favor of the newly christened Afghan National Army.

Reminiscent of the gentlemen Colonels of the rebel American South, an honorarium given any man of reasonable accomplishment, transitional Afghanistan had no shortage of nominal Generals — far more, in fact, than appropriate posts in which to install them. Now mimicking international standards and nomenclature, the ranks and hierarchies of the ANA were re-made from the ground up.

In practice, this meant a whole class of titled and decorated men being re-ranked to fit the new structure. Once a Field General, Ata was made a Lieutenant Colonel and put in charge of military facilities in the newly christened 209th Corps, one of six regional divisions, centered on Mazar-i Sharif. His right-hand, Major Salim, had been a General under Dostum in one of the Uzbek militias.

The billets' official descriptions call for trained, professional engineers. Neither qualify.

....

* *Dostum's stronghold and base of operations was Mazar-i Sharif. The city only briefly fell to Taliban control before reverting to Dostum and the United Front. Even after his move to Kabul and promotion within the Central Government, as well as through the subsequent military re-organizations that ensued, Dostum continued (and continues to this day) to hold underlying control of the region.*

As previously described, in a 2006 intelligence briefing, we were informed in no uncertain terms of such "facts on the ground." US operations in the North were under protection of Dostum's standing order — any Afghan to harm an American in Mazar would be executed.

The order seemed excessive in an area that was already otherwise friendly to US forces, but as the European ISAF troops began undertaking operations in the north in early 2007, we were shown quite clearly the distinction. The German and (various) Scandinavian convoys were regularly attacked in areas considered safe to our trucks.

Granted, these nominal Provincial Reconstruction Teams were doing nothing of the sort, instead roaming the countrysides burning down poppy fields, while American PRTs pumped millions of dollars into physical infrastructure. The word of Dostum surely loomed large, though I'd like to think the disparity between actors (and their motives) contributed as well.

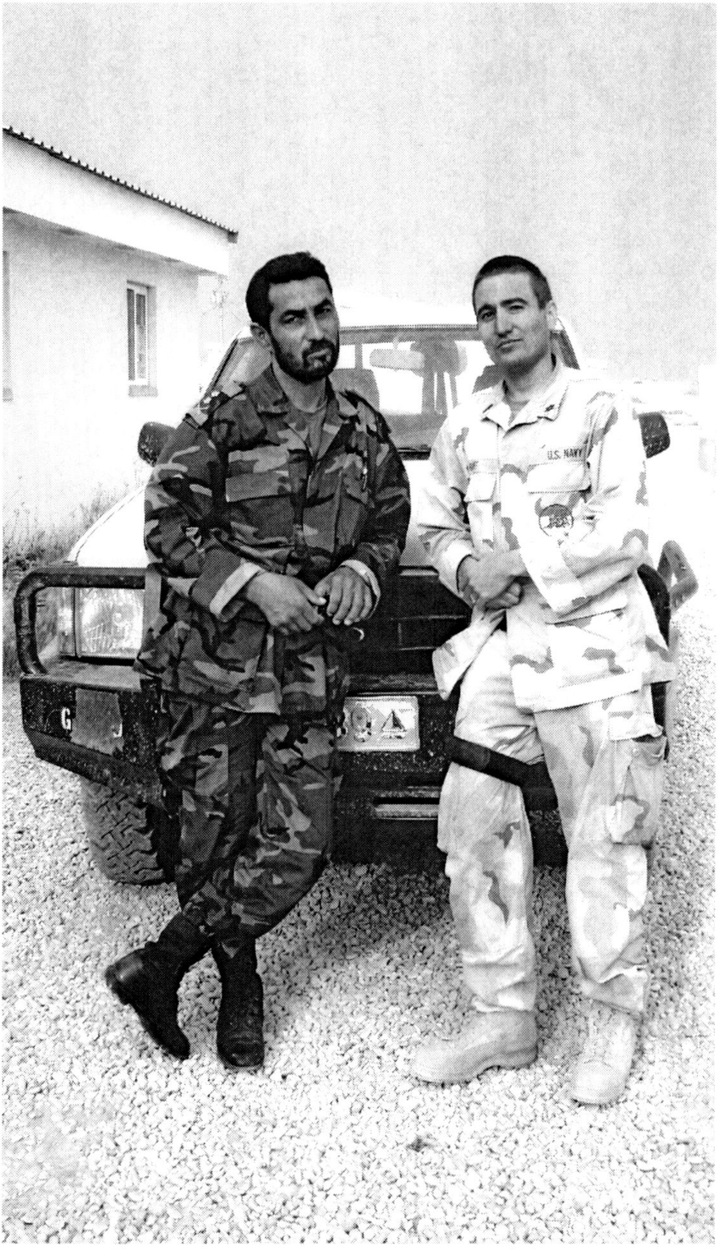
U.S. NAVY

MALIQA NAHID

Years before he became so very Important, Ramin Amiry was a young man who had his whole life figured out. He has quit his university studies to follow his nose for business, first setting up shop on a busy Mazar street, selling assorted goods to neighborhood families. He is so successful at this venture, that he saves enough Afghani to buy a taxi, which he rents out to a cousin to drive. Soon enough, he has bought two taxis, with accordant drivers, and his own array of tools in which to keep them running. His store, too, is doing brisk business.

With his highschool sweetheart, Ramin begins making plans for marriage. Young, fit, and successful, he is a sterling catch for any prospective bride. Not unaware of his nephew's growing wealth, a distant uncle graciously offers his own daughter to Ramin's family as an enthusiastic bride. Ramin, well-focused on his life's plan, pretends to know nothing of the offer and politely ignores the overtures.

Unbeknownst to them all, the safe haven of the north, so meticulously guarded by Dostum and Masoud's alliance, was about to be overrun. Bitter fighting erupts in Mazar-i Sharif. What started as a Dostum-directed retribution by a rival devolves and outright war engulfs the whole region. Defenses undermined, the Taliban move on Mazar and take the city.

Ramin's sweetheart, and her whole family, are killed in the crossfire.

The rest of his carefully-orchestrated life is quick to follow. The Taliban raid his store, shuttering it and confiscating his first taxi. The second taxi, out in service under another driver, is totalled in a collision with a truck.

It has all come apart.

In desperation, Ramin's father travels to visit the distant uncle. Over cigarettes and cups of chai, he tells the uncle that his nephew has dutifully reconsidered and will accept the marriage proposal, please forgive the young man's prior impetuousness. The boy has nothing to offer his daughter now, the uncle retorts, angrily refusing the entreaty.

Ramin, in respect of his father's humility,
pretends to be devastated at the news.

In truth, he is not so easily discouraged and unwilling to settle, regardless of the turn of events. Unlike his father, Ramin is not despaired by the change in fortune.

"Actually, I was glad, but I want him to think I am sad.." he would later explain to me. He did not want to marry the girl.

    "Was she not pretty enough, Ramin?"

"Well, she was not ugly..." he paused,
"actually, Sir, she was fat! Too fat!"

~

Ramin returns then to university, where he meets the woman who will become his wife. His father-in-law-to-be must recognize some potential in the penniless suitor, deciding to finance the young man's continued studies.

The wedding is an uncharacteristically bland affair by traditional Afghan standards. Under Taliban occupation, there can be no wine, no dancing, no photography, no mingling of the sexes — including the husband and wife. In short, there can be no celebration.

I have seen the one photo that exists of the ceremony, surreptitiously taken of the groom. He is cloaked in traditional garb, as are his father and uncles standing beside him. Wreaths of plastic pink and white flowers and silvery blue streamers hang around his neck, nearly covering him in artificially-colored accoutrement. There is a lifelessness to the image, all the joy that should have accompanied it drained out by the invaders outside. Ramin's face shows only incredible boredom. The bride, of course, is nowhere to be seen, cordoned off with the other women. There are no smiles, forced or otherwise. This is Taliban Afghanistan, in all its somber surreality.

~

Five days later, the Taliban invaders are routed and finally, resolutely, ejected from Mazar-i Sharif. The city has been at war for nearly a year and a half. Its sighs and groans of relief soon turn to celebration. There are smiles, there is dancing, there is joy.

Except on one new husband's face. "One more week!" he growls.

"If we had waited just one more week, we could have had a real wedding!"

SHOTGUN WEDDINGS

Inferred, but never directly described in the original letters, my own nuptials were likewise a rushed affair. Throughout the training period in Mississippi, there was reasonable doubt as to whether there would be any time at all. In the end, a few days leave were given between the final training day and the flight out. It was a full day's drive down to Port Charlotte to catch a boat out to Little Gasparilla, a wispy spit of an island off of Florida's southern gulf coast. My mother had gathered our handful of close family members, but there was no time for invitations or bridesmaids or best men or any other normal accoutrements.

I wore a cuban wedding shirt, she a white beach dress, we stood barefoot in the surf and said homemade vows. I would be her rock, she my butterfly. The metaphor apt for our previous lives and personalities, but presciently malapropos for the reality of the year to come.

Much like our adventitious initial partnering, the rush to formalize such a thing was inescapably the product of circumstance. The spectre of war focuses and realigns priorities, a weird mix of cold rationality blends with overt sentimentality. The military wife is protected, supported, *taken care of* by the government in a way the colloquial partner is not. Conversely, the new spouse back home gives necessary weight to the burden of deployment. To all parties, including the various parents and family members who would in normal scenarios urge caution and patience before such a big life-changing decision, the marriage seems comfortingly inevitable. You see, the life-changing decision has already been made, he is going to war. The gravity of the secondary decision become comparatively negligible. So, just as the primary choice is out of our hands, imposed by the country, the follow-on is likewise determined by reflexive tradition, like so many shotgun weddings.

A decade on, in answering queries of such a young and
(retrospectively) ill-suited pairing, I invariably respond that
I married the day before getting on a plane bound for the
war in Afghanistan. There is a nod, as that is processed,
and then a wave of apparent understanding, and finally
an automatic acceptance, as if something ingrained in our
culture expects that this is of course what would happen.

~

Whether or not the wedding was the high water mark of our
relationship is debatable, though the pictures are quite lovely,
what is certain is that the following year was a steep downward
slide. Inherent psychological bearings aside, one could hardly
be surprised by her subsequent slip into depression.

Our honeymoon was the 12-hour drive back to
Mississippi, so she could watch me get on a plane to go
to war. Leaving her, as a brand new bride, alone.

The weeks to follow, instead of being a fresh beginning for us both,
she spent attempting to set up a new life...essentially alone...a crash
course in a new place that she had followed me to. She probably
should have gone back to New Orleans, but was too proud,
perhaps, to reverse course, despite the shitty hand dealt to her.

The day I landed in Kabul marked eight
months since we had first met.

With geography, moves, and training, we had spent less than
three of those months together. It could be no understatement
to say that we knew essentially nothing about eachother, other
than the belief we were somehow supposed to be together.

In the end, I doubt it matters. By the time I returned,
neither of those two people existed anymore anyway.

~

Afghanistan broke me. Somewhere between the abject poverty, the clash of religions, the ugliness of man's destructive nature, I stopped believing. In anything.

Solitude broke her. Half a globe separated from the man she loved, the man she left her life for, my wife lost her mind. The person I most needed support from, while I was in the shit of war, was completely, utterly unavailable. Incapable of supporting anyone and mired in her own depression.

~

The weekly letters that appear in these pages, she printed out and stacked safely under the bed, but she wouldn't read them. Maybe it was too difficult for her to be confronted with the details of this oppressive thing that separated us. To me, at the time, it just meant she didn't care. Every day I sent a personal note to her alone. These too, went mostly unread, to the best of my knowledge. Every night that it was possible (connectivity was a sketchy thing) I called, skyped, messaged, whatever was available. Some talks were good. Some calls were unbelievable fights. Sometimes I was treated like an inconvenience. Sometimes she didn't bother to wake up, or to be home, when she knew a call was coming. It was frustrating. At times, quite damaging.

Both needed the other to be the support, and leaning desperately in, we fell past each other instead.

We were strangers when I returned. Whatever commonalities we may have originally intended to build on were gone. Even with me back, her bouts with depression did not subsist. I wasn't in the best position to help. I was having post-traumatic nightmares of horrific death. For several months, I swung wildly in my sleep, hitting her more than once.

The war did not end when I left Afghanistan;
it came home with me.

Ingrained with this, presumably, new abandonment
fear, she couldn't handle any level of separation. It was
a fight to leave the house for any reason. It was disbelief
and accusation if I had to work late or had a business
trip. She needed me in her sight at all times.

Arguments were abundant. Many were
peppered with suicide threats.

Alcohol cannot be combined with depression medication.
She didn't want to hear this. She could be alternatively a
zombie, or a raving lunatic, or a perfectly charming person.
There was no rhyme to the song, no predictability. She self-
medicated, unaware of her impaired judgment, worsening bad
situations. I literally never knew which woman I would come
home to. And the winds could shift with little warning.

I have scars on my hands from the countless nights she bit me,
as I restrained her from hurting herself. Nails and teeth have
been dug into my shoulders. There are still marks on my fingers
where she clamped down on them as I dug mashed up sleeping
pills from her mouth. The demon I saw in her eyes that night is
burned into my head, it stared through me as she threw the whole
bottle into her mouth and began chewing. It was an incredible
stalemate, as I wouldn't release the drugs, and she wouldn't release
my fingers, trying her damndest to cleave the knuckles from my
hands. Minutes, hours, I really can't tell you. Many nights I didn't
sleep. Standing vigil, worried what she might do to herself... or
someone else, if she got into her car and drove (this was a popular
hazed desire of hers). I hid keys, hid medicine, hid knives, so that
even if I did doze, the damage would be minimized. She didn't
acknowledge any of this happening, but it haunts me. Still.

Some nights she would simply disappear. Sometimes this
meant driving up and down the streets until I found her
drunkenly pedaling a bicycle. Other times were late night
calls from her friends asking me to come collect her.

Over time, due probably to equal parts settlement, a better doctor, and me having better control over her access to medications, things calmed down. There were still fights—raucous, unbelievable yelling matches—but the suicide attempts and the zombie periods faded away. I started to believe I could live with the state of things, such as they were, however barely.

It was about a year in that place... far from perfect, but somewhat within my patience threshold. Then, in no surprise to anyone, including her, I made my long-awaited break from the Navy, thereby uprooting her dream Hawaiian life.

In many ways the first year in New York was a flashback to the first post-Afghan year. Only now, instead of abusing medication, she refused to take it. The abandonment issues resurfaced with a vengeance.

Divorce became a near daily topic, but thrown at me casually, the way someone might order eggs. Over easy with hashbrowns, and maybe we should just get divorced, then. And a coffee, please.

~

One evening after school I came home to her locked in the closet. I broke down the door. She was attempting to hang herself from the crossbar. Spectacle? Cry for attention? I don't know. I didn't have time to psycho-analyze. It wasn't but a few minutes later I found myself with one finger desperately stuck between her neck and the ribbon she was trying to strangle herself with, the same demon's eyes afire.

Nothing in life prepared me for this.

Surely I was scarred. In many ways I went numb, for a time. I'm not sure there's any other natural response. In that numbness, I lost the patience that had so far kept us afloat, lost the ability to be the stable foundation. In that numbness, I lost the ability to give her the unconditional love she needed. As I lost these only restraining walls, the rest degraded with increasing acceleration.

Failure was not merely an option, it became inevitable.

~

In a number of studies on mental illness, they have articulated how otherwise dormant tendencies towards disorder can be sparked by a traumatic event or an intensely stressful period of their lives. It isn't PTSD, strictly speaking, but an activation of something latent that perhaps would not have occurred were the person to have avoided that trigger event. In the resorting that takes place within my own mind, the deployment and subsequent devolution of her psyche (and our union) are inseparable. They blur together across a unified timeline, a linked event-string set in motion by my departure and impervious to my return.

~

The dissolution was nearly as abrupt as the original pairing. I put her on a plane back to Hawaii, in vain hopes it would help her to regain her sanity. Sitting in our empty home, expecting sadness, I felt only relief. Clarity had arrived. Paperwork and a few months time formalized the cleaving. The numbness began to recede with the winter, quiet depression taking its place.

Our divorce became official on my birthday. It was the first warm day of spring in New York.

I laid on the grass in front of Alma Mater, under the sun, and didn't know what to feel.

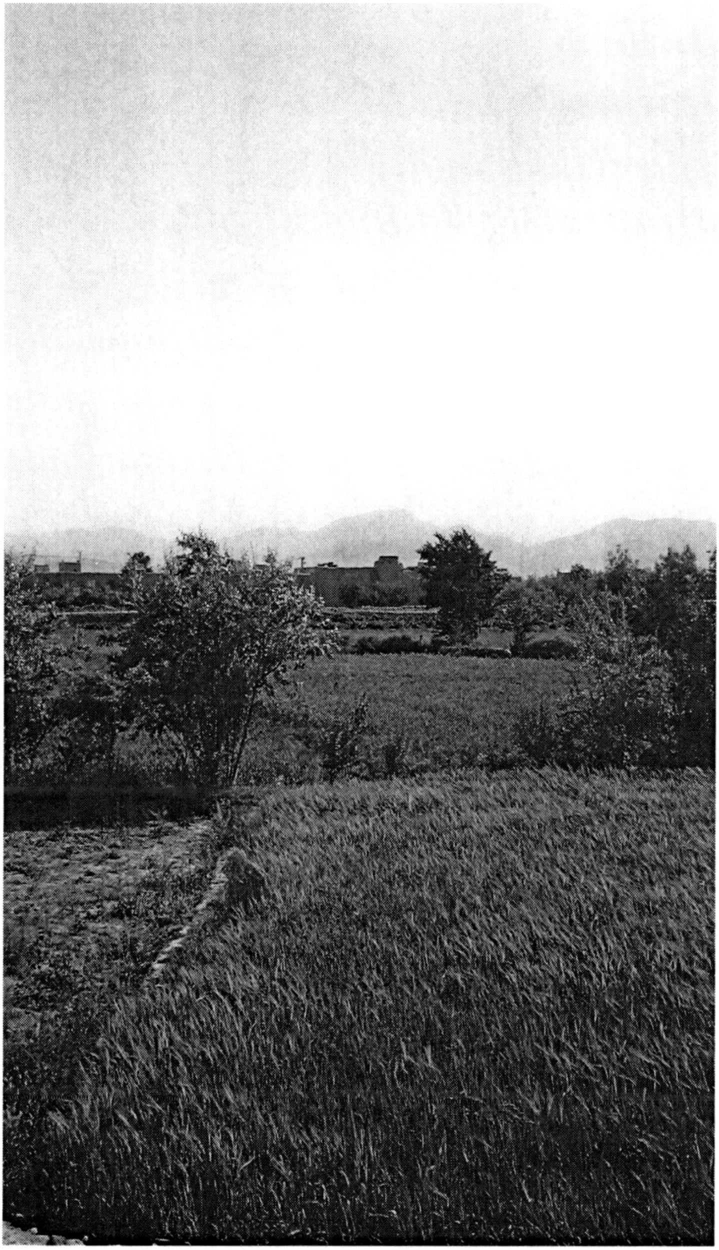

TOUCHDOWN TONER TAKES THE HAND-OFF

PEARL HARBOR, HAWAII, USA — It was a random Tuesday morning, some two years after my return home when I received a call at my desk from a Kansas number. It was my buddy Frank Toner, now in training at some godforsaken Army base in the middle of the corn fields. He was heading to Afghanistan in short order. Not just anywhere, he told me, but to Mazar-i Sharif. To take over the job that had once been mine... in many ways, the job that I had created.

We chatted for no less than an hour. Much about mundane things — what to pack, what to leave behind, what to expect. I gave him every name I knew still in country, every item of any possible importance, and he dug yet deeper into my head to pull out anything that might be of use. The Navy never tells you much, so you rely heavily on old friends. Preemptively, I introduced him to my carpenters, name by name (I can't ever think of them as anything but "mine," however much time has passed). The conversation was punctuated with tell-tale pauses as he seemed to be scribbling down notes, dutifully recording the pertinent information. God bless him, if he was. I never imagined my rusty memories to hold that much weight.

No matter what, I told him, make absolutely sure that Ramin Amiry is your interpreter. Take care of him, and he will take care of you. We broke with well wishes. Good luck, fair winds, and all that rub.

I hung up and called my old interpreter's cell phone. It was approaching midnight in Central Asia. I let him know my dear friend was on the way.

Take care of him Ramin, he is a good man. The best.

Ramin assured me that he would.

Francis Lawrence Toner IV, broad shouldered with a tight blonde crew cut, looked every bit the southern California football star cum homecoming king of Saturday morning television. He was, in fact both, though a touch shorter in real life than the pictures would have you believe.

Recruited to the Merchant Marine Academy on a full football scholarship, he took an extra year to get a degree in engineering, figuring it set him up better for a career in the Navy. Football eligibility exhausted, he walked-on to the school's stellar lacrosse team as a fifth-year senior, and despite having never played the game prior finished out his collegiate athletic career as a solid defensive player for the squad. After graduation, he was commissioned into the Navy's Civil Engineer Corps and stationed in Pearl Harbor, arriving there a few months before I returned from my Afghan adventure.

Appropriately, I first met Frank on an athletic field, where the CEC Wardroom played ultimate frisbee in the wee hours of the morning, in lieu of formal Physical Training. I was called upon to mark the young Ensign. Squat but quick, the former fullback bulled through crowds after the frisbee. It wasn't long before he bulled through me, knocking me to the ground in an attempt to defend. Despite frisbee being intended as a non-contact sport, I was now sprawled in the wet grass and about to have a word with the man about things. What had been an intense, focused glare instantly softened into a sheepish grin, apologetic at having gotten carried away.

It was my first glimpse at his basest trait: simple, infectious joy. Like most people who came into Frankie's arc, we made instant friends.

Our wives too, quickly bonded. The foursome was soon more likely together than not — young, active couples making the best of what Hawaii had to offer.

Always looking for a challenge, about a year after I was back, Frank organized a football team. He downloaded some software from the internet and designed plays for us to run, printing them out on little green cards and laminating them. A hole was punched into the top of the card so we could tie it into our shorts and consult it during the games. As quarterback, Frank would scream out long lines of gibberish containing the number of the play within the muck, trying to confuse the opposing team. One of the plays diagrammed on the card was a trick play where the whole team was to get into an argument about whether or not we were using the correct football. Frank "Touchdown" Toner would walk the offending ball towards the referee on the sideline, and getting there, turn and run for the endzone. There were only four other plays.

~

One night over Mexican food (as ex-Californians we had made a point to find the one decent taco joint on the island and eat there together with the wives on a semi-weekly basis), Frank confided to us that he had been talking to a recruiter for the SEALS — the elite special forces of the Navy. He'd been secretly training with a SEAL unit in Hawaii and had passed all the entry requirements. After his current duty was up, at the end of the year, he was headed to BUD/S, the specialized warfare training school which would prepare him for his new career in spec ops. After the congratulations and the shared excitement, he mentioned offhandedly that, in fact, he'd already be leaving for the session just starting if our current Captain hadn't mandated he finish up his current tour of duty first.

Priorities, Frank, I told him. There's broken toilets in Shipyard. Saving the world can wait.

~

It wasn't too long after that meal that he got called to Kansas instead, as a training pitstop before deploying to Afghanistan, and the best laid plans were torn up and replaced with a new calendar. It was the SEALS who would have to wait out his newly-assigned 15-month tour, before teaching him the proper way of going to war.

A few weeks before he headed off for training, the officers got together for a paint-ball-filled morning at a popular local range. For most of the day, the competitions followed normal split-side arrangements, and played out as colorfully sloppy bastardizations of capture the flag. Our ostensibly professionally-trained officer corps mixed in with teenagers and college-age enthusiasts. Frank adopted the posture of a platoon commander, trying in vain to organize proper movements and strategy, before taking off to get the flag by himself through sheer force of will.

For the last session of the day, the range controllers proposed an alternative exercise. Nobody ever goes for it, they goad, because its impossibly unfair.

"We love impossible," Frank chortles, playing along.

Alright, well, here's the set-up, they continued. Its an endurance test we like to call the "Butch and Sundance." Basically, we take a couple of you strong fellows and put you inside this little shack. Everyone else is outside and tries to capture the house. The game lasts as long as you can take getting pelted.

Frank's hand is up to volunteer before the explanation is done.

"I'm in the house.. with these two," pointing to myself and LT Jake Segalla.

He looks over the hundred or so would-be attackers.

"And we're going to win."

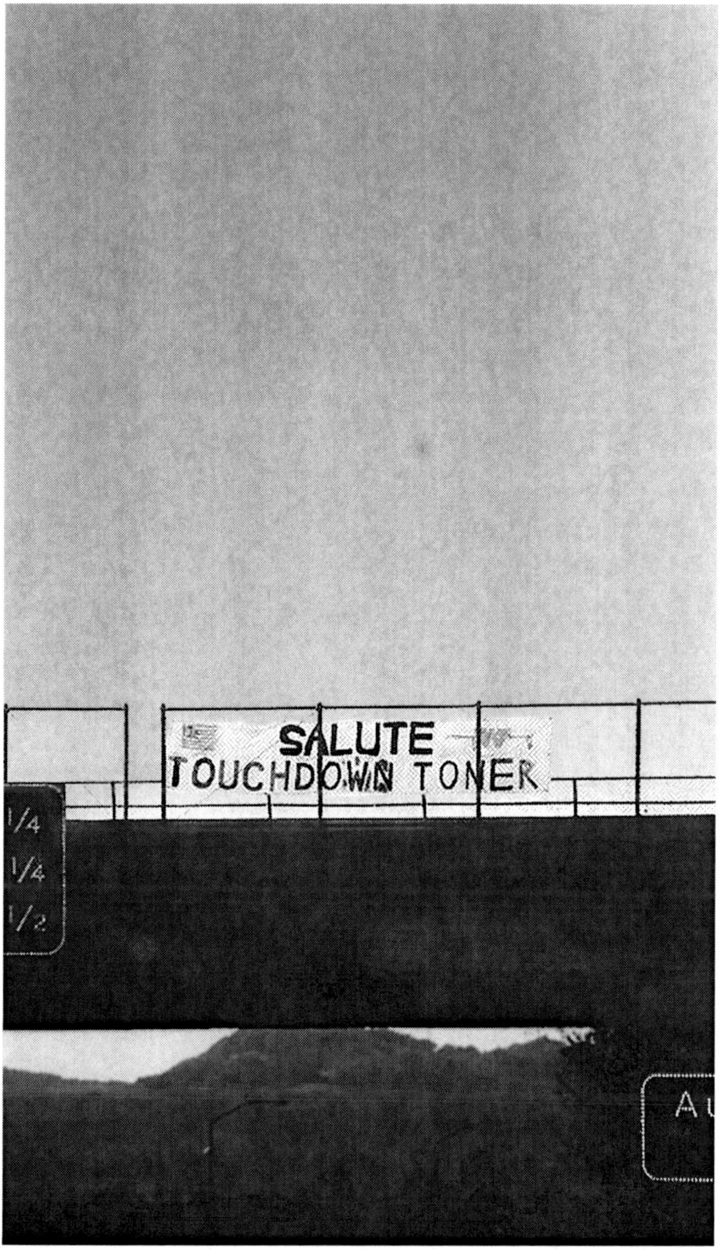
SALUTE
TOUCHDOWN TONER
1/4
1/4
1/2

ALL FALLS DOWN

27 March

It was a sunny Friday morning in Hawaii, as I drove onto the NAVFAC compound, across from the front gates of Pearl Harbor. Uncharacteristically solo today, my neighbor and regular carpool partner, LT Paul McCord,* had been on-call overnight as the duty officer for our command and was already on base.

Pulling into a spot atop the hillcrest in front of our building, I noted Paul's lanky khaki silhouette approaching the car. The roofline blocked his face from view as I dismounted the low-slung Nissan. He met me as I stood, grasping my shoulder with his right hand, the black duty phone pressed in his left. His gaze went from my eyes and out over the campus below the hill, then back as he searched for words. There was no color in his face.

Frank's been hit.

Frank's been hit, man.... We just got a message... Don't know anything else..

Anybody you know still downrange? Can we contact someone?

~

Perhaps as training would have it, action preceded emotion. I ran into my office and dug out numbers, scouring old notebooks and email trails. I started making calls, sending messages, racking my brain for anyone who might know something. I rang Ramin's mobile endlessly, with no answer. Worry began to creep in. I imagined a convoy operation hit with an IED, taking out both of them. Frank wouldn't have gone on any mission without Ramin. Where the fuck was the little fat man to tell me what happened.

Two fruitless hours dripped by, with no word. The vacuum was suffocating. It was a little after midnight in Afghanistan as I walked outside for air. Paul was walking up the hill from headquarters. We met again at the top of the crest, shaded from the late morning sun under a row of kiawe.

He's gone.

Paul bear-hugged me, squeezing my arms hard inside against my chest, an instinctive effort to contain what grief might burst me. None did, I couldn't respond at all.

Frank's gone.

~

An hour passed, I'm told.

Somewhere in that time, Jake also came to find me, and a similar scene replayed... though I don't really remember.

I had gone back to my office, under the weight of information that no one else yet knew. Normal work activity buzzed around me.

Mike James, another battle-tested Seabee, marched slowly to the side of my desk. He put his hand on my shoulder.

"The command is going to make an announcement. All hands meeting in 30."

"I'm going home, Mike."

"I'll tell them."

~

It was three or four in the morning in Mazar, and Ramin wasn't picking up his phone. My worry shifted to the fat man.

I sat in the backyard of our Hawaiian casita, staring through the tropical tapestry of happy reds and greens and yellows, and I tried not to think.

I drank what beer was in the fridge, and when Mike called to check on me, I asked him to bring more. He appeared under the plumeria branches later that afternoon, replenishment in hand, and sat a while. One of us noted the irony of drinking in honor of a Mormon.

The next few days disappeared into a grief-stricken, inebriated haze.

I only remember one moment clearly. We were in some dark, smoky second-floor Irish pub, downtown Honolulu, circle of Navy folks. The kind of place that hides the ashtrays when the cops come. I was off to the side, leaning at the bar, unable to focus on the conversations. Sonny, retired from Spec Ops after a distinguished off-the-record career, put one burly arm around me. His quiet Hawaiian patois belied his hulking frame, softly reassuring, but firm. "I've been there." His black eyes dug into mine, knowing.

"It's ok."

Under his permission, the tears began to flow, emptying out of me. Sonny propped me up as the grief released, and allowed the pain to consume me. The rest of the pub spun around oblivious. He held me there until it was exhausted.

With his free hand, he motioned for two Guinness pints. He toasted Frank, and downed the glass in a single gulp. Then he left me be.

I wasn't the only one who grieved for Frankie, of course. But I was the only one back home who could replay the otherwise amorphous event clearly in my mind. Because Frank's footsteps were my footsteps, his eyes saw what my eyes had seen. We were running the same relay race, baton passing each lap, starting with me and ending up in his hands. The same loops, until the final turn.

~

...It was a sunny Friday morning in Mazar. In deference to Afghan religious schedules, that means that most of the troops at Camp Spann can enjoy a day of rest. Their ANA counterparts aren't reporting to work, instead heading to the mosque for a day of prayer. The inhabitants of Frank's B-Hut gladly take an extra hour's sleep, before putting on the blue and gold Navy-issue sweat suits (authorized only for off-duty use) and stumbling through the gravel over to the chow hall for eggs and hashbrowns. Breakfast will be a bit slower, the lines long for the hot grill, where the head cook dishes it up to order. The crew will take their time and overeat, as there's nothing to rush off to other than maybe a nap or a bootleg DVD movie. As the sun slides across the sky towards late afternoon, someone will take the onus to rouse the lazy troops for a bit of PT. It will probably be Frank. He's scheduled to take off for Kabul tomorrow morning, the first leg of the arduous process of getting home to his wife for two weeks leave. It's his last chance at a proper run for a while.

It will take a half hour or so for the running group to coalesce alongside the road to the front gate. There will be a mishmash of dress, some sticking to their sweats, others switching to PT shorts to go along with their dusty sneakers. Frank dons a kevlar vest, not for protection, but for the challenge of running a few thousand meters with 40 extra pounds strapped to his chest.

Although the run's course will take them outside of Camp Spann, it will stay firmly within the larger area of Camp Shaheen.

Outside of a few speckled days of high-alert, the controlled area has been designated a safe zone for more than six years running. It is where most of these men and women do their day-to-day work, mentoring the officers and sergeants leading the training units for the 209th Corps. Officially, the larger base is considered the same turf as Camp Spann, and weapons and armor are not required to be carried on its grounds.

As the cluster of PT'ers cross out of Spann's gates, the young soldiers at the checkpoint will nod a greeting to the jogging officers — salutes are not appropriate down range. Frank and the others will nod back, and one of the soldiers will log the passage.

From there, the runners will hang a quick succession of right turns, then a left, looping out to the outer walls of Camp Shaheen. *Walls*, being a loose term. These first few sections along the North and West exposures are more properly a high fence, making about half of the perimeter chain link rather than stone. Colonel Ata and I put in a series of requests years before for their fortification, but given the expense and the priorities further down south, the funding, and the project, remains on hold.

In any event, the geometry of Camp Shaheen pleasantly aligns with the Navy standard 1.5 mile run. Minus the corner quadrant cannibalized by Spann, the remainder of the perimeter roughly equates to the test distance.

A half mile or so into the run, along the western edge of the base, the runners will pass the dusty training fields where Frank has been teaching Afghan soldiers to play softball. Years before, the hard parade grounds hosted a series of Dust Bowl football matches between my Navy brethren and the overmatched Air Force scrubs. On another day, there might be a hundred young infantry trainees out here marching, being put through the paces by Afghan NCO's — the drill sergeants themselves having worked through a half dozen years of mentoring and training under the watchful eye of US Navy Chiefs and Army sergeants. Today, the fields are empty. As is the rest of the base.

It will be eerily quiet, then, as the group continues on towards the southwest corner, and the guard tower that marks the run's halfway point. Even on normal days, this stretch is desolate and far from the activity of the base's central operations. It is out of sight as well, from the rest of Shaheen and of the US Army-manned watchtowers of Mike Spann at the opposite, northeastern corner. Far from supervisory eyes, the guards here often visibly slacked off. Hanging out at the bottom of the tower, backs to the fence, rather than in the proper spot above and overlooking the wide expanse of desert outside the wire.

Every man that who rounded that corner feels the chill of exposure, compounded by the long shadows cast from the blank back walls of empty barracks. The prick of awareness comes just as surely on the fiftieth circuit as the first, only beginning to settle as the turn is made back into the sun's glare.

On this holiday Friday, it is of little surprise to the running troop to see one of the ANA tower guards sprawled against the fence, rather than up at his proper post. His uniform blouse is half unbuttoned, disheveled in a manner common to country conscripts not under active supervision. He begins stumbling to his feet, perhaps he's been hiding back here to indulge in some hashish, never expecting an audience.

Frank is the first to realize something is off.
He barks at the group to slow.

The guard raises his issue AK47 semi-automatic rifle and pulls back the trigger, spraying bullets through the air in the general direction of the female runners in the group. LT Florence Choe, the medical officer, is killed in the first volley.

As the rest scatter for cover, Frank yells at the gunman, to draw his fire away from the others. He is the only one of the group with any protective armor. In the guard's momentary distraction, Frank charges towards him to make one last tackle.

The last rounds of the AK47 go through the gunman's own head.

Nurse Choe and Frank lie dead in the Afghan dust, the first and last American military casualties at Mazar-i Sharif.

....

* Paul would himself be blown up in Iraq a couple years later, by a roadside bomb. It was one of two such midnight calls I received that year in Hong Kong about old compatriots. Miraculously, he survived, enduring a coma and long months of rehab, but healing up well enough to welcome his first born into the world in early 2013. Bless'em.

EPILOGUE

Less than two weeks later, Jake and I boarded a plane in Honolulu in our dress blues. We were headed first for New York and the Merchant Marine Academy, then down to Arlington. In stowage we carried some important personal effects, formal honors from the command at NAVFAC Hawaii, and handcrafted memorials made by Frank's enlisted Seabee troops, boys who served under him when he had run the shop at Pearl Harbor.

A few minutes after we took our seats, a stewardess begged our pardon. The captain would like to speak to us.

He was in his fifties, prim and fit in his crisp pilot's uniform. He took a slow knee in the aisle by my shoulder and leaned in.

Is our boy on board? He whispered.

They can't always tell me, so I understand if you can't— "No Sir, we're meeting him at Arlington."

Iraq? "Afghanistan."

God bless him, and god bless you boys. All of you.

He squeezed my arm tight, for a long second, then stepped back to his cockpit.

Jake and I had been assigned the two most-honored roles in the extended pomp and circumstance to follow. He was to be Frank's escort, and I was to be Brooke's, his widow.

The long-held tradition is that neither should travel alone. As the pilot had anticipated, there was a man flying with Frank back from Afghanistan. When he landed in DC, Jake would relieve him, and stay with Frank until the final resting. I was to make sure that his widow was fully taken care of and supported. In truth, Brooke was at least as much support to us as any one was for her, her will and internal strength the only match for Frank's I've known.

It began with a memorial on Long Island, at the Merchant Marine Academy where Frank had been commissioned just a few years prior. Having already been a legend on campus for both football and extracurricular antics (recently enough for the Senior class to remember), he was the school's first casualty in the Afghan War. The ceremony was thick and heartfelt, eventually disassembling into an open-mike session where, one by one, cadets and classmates alike told their most memorable Toner stories... of which, there was no shortage. Laughs far outnumbered tears, as one supposes he'd have preferred.

Afterwards, we drove Brooke down to DC, where we and the family would await Frank's arrival.

~

Arlington National Ceremony is a surreal, rolling green sea perforated with a continuous grid of white teeth, poking up from underneath the surface. To walk among its endless rows of tombstones is to ponder infinity, viscerally.

Or the incalculable human cost of war.

Occasional snatches of drooping oaks punctuate the otherwise uninterrupted vastness. It is under one such stand that our procession slows, and stops. Hundreds of men and women in dress whites circle the gravesite. It is a hero's burial.

Francis Lawrence Toner the Fourth will eventually be recognized with a Silver Star for bravery, in saving the lives of his comrades. A bridge in Rhode Island would come to bear his name. Three thousand people would join a Facebook memorial page to his memory.

But before he became a symbol for the country, Frank was ours—our friend, confidant, and compatriot.

As the winds and rain pick up along the eastern seaboard, blowing the last gusts of winter's chill across the somber scene, I can think only of loss as he is lowered beneath the white stone.

Brooke stands between Jake and I, clutching tightly to my arm, as 21 guns fire, and she sheds bitter tears for the man she loves, who loved her more than anything, the man she's given back to the earth.

She places flowers at his feet, and we tread
slowly away from this sacred place.

It is my last official act in the Navy's uniform.

ACKNOWLEDGEMENTS

Glen Messer, RIP, my first mentor on things navy.. Carlton Boatright, Russ Coolman, and Captain Mike Hassien, who trained and shaped me up right.. Captain Cliff Maurer and Greg Miller who took over the Navy mentorship upon my return.. Jon Uyboco, my partner-in-crime and never-ending source of material.. Frank Dukes, Blake Edwards: endless entertainment..The Mez Goat Locker.. Dave Sweet, the only (Ch)airman worth a damn.. Jake segalla, Paul McCord, Mike James and my beloved CEC brethren not otherwise mentioned (Rob, Geoff, Jake-Mc, Wells, Warren, and so on).. Mike Scorsone, continual cheerleader and confidant both while I was away, and on my return. Ramin, the very, very important man, and my carpenters Monan, Rahim, Zuman, Karim, and Qasim.. Dave Keller, for the foresight to set up the shop in the first place..Orkun Yildiz, my turkish friend with the best tea service in all of Afghanistan.. Col Ata, the baddest m'f'in PWO you could ever imagine.. Major Salim, so long and thanks for all the fish.. Rob T-Bird Talbert who had his mom and all her friends in Australia reading my letters.. Everyone else back home reading my letters and writing back — Maddie, Liam, Alisa, Ken Jones, Douglas D, Don Spec, Bry, Sol, Gaber, Im.. Reid Mizue for taking care of the homefront. the Hernandez clan, who smiled through all the stress and kept sending care packages.. Sonny Makalena for the shoulder and the wisdom.. John Folan, voice of reason.. and God bless Chris Horstman..

My parents, ever supportive, to the point of sending us all rum in mouthwash bottles, and my dear cousins Rob, Jared, and Jon for making sure I was sent off and received home well.. Aunt Nancy who coordinated school supply donations state-side for me..

Qian for patience while I finally finished this book.. H for enthusiastic promotion.. The Immaculate Jesse Keenan and Kristen Bell, gracious volunteer copy-editors.. Brooke Toner, the rock, and of course Frankie — I'll never forget.

LIST OF LETTERS

TRAVIS GOES TO AFGHANISTAN	xxi
TRAVIS GOES TO AFHGAN…ERR..NORFOLK	25
IN THE ARMY NOW	27
DAMN TOURISTS	29
THIS IS MY RIFLE	33
CARNIVAL RIDE, PART I	37
CARNIVAL RIDE, PART II	41
NOTES ON MARKSMANSHIP	45
TODAY WAS A GOOD DAY	49
AND THEN THERE'S THE NOT-SO-GOOD DAYS	55
LAST DAY	57
GAS GAS GAS	61
AN EXERCISE IN CONCLUDING PRELIMINARY COMENCEMENTS	65
THE LOST DAY	73
AT THE SPEED OF MOLASSES	77
WELCOME TO KABUL	83
NOTHING DOING	87
FROM IOWA, WITH LOVE	91
AFGHANI PICTURE SHOW	95
THE USUAL SUSPECTS	101
TURNOVERS	105
CERP IS FOR THE CHILDREN	109
GENERAL DISREGARD	115
ADVENTURES IN INTERPRETATION	119
A LIFE AWAY	125
HAPPY INDEPENDENCE DAY TO YOUR COUNTRY	131
RIVER CITY	135
KELLER'S WOOD SHOP	139
WE HAVE TO HAVE A PLAN	145
PUTTING THE SHOW ON THE ROAD	153
SHOPPING FOR THE SURREAL	159
MISCELLANY, PART I	165
DECOPAGUE	171
GATHER ROUND THE FLAG POLE	177
MICELLANY, PART II	185
THE DUST BOWL	193

THE LION OF PANJSHIR	*199*
TIMELY INTERNATIONAL NEWS BULLETINS	*203*
DIVERSIONARY TACTICS	*209*
THE ROOKIE WALL	*215*
MERRY EID!	*219*
THE SPACEMAN COMETH	*223*
THE REPRIEVE, PART I	*229*
THE REPRIEVE, PART II	*233*
WELCOME HOME (?)	*239*
STATUS CHECK	*243*
SOME IDEAS ARE BETTER THAN OTHERS	*249*
DIA DE LOS MUERTOS	*257*
NAIBI AND THE MAGICAL CHAI BUTTON	*261*
MAHI!	*265*
MORSELS OF UNDERSTANDING	*269*
ASHURA	*279*
CONSIDERING MORTALITY	*283*
ANNIVERSARIES	*287*
ATTACK OF THE 50 FOOT KARZAI	*291*
SNOW DAYS	*297*
TEMPORARY CELEBRITY	*299*
WHO IS TYLER DURDEN / FROM KOREA WITH LOVE	*307*
TOURISTS OF ARABIA, PART I	*315*
TOURISTS OF ARABIA, PART II	*323*
SHORT-TIMERS SYNDROME	*331*
NO WOMEN NO CRY	*335*
EXHALE	*339*
POSTSCRIPT	*341*
STATUES (OF LIMITATIONS)	*353*
LESSONS LEARNED	*361*
ATA ON ATA	*373*
MALIQA NAHID	*379*
SHOTGUN WEDDINGS	*383*
TOUCHDOWN TONER TAKES THE HAND-OFF	*391*
ALL FALLS DOWN	*397*
EPILOGUE	*405*

LIST OF IMAGES

Navy Seabee Logo, created by Frank Iafrate in 1942	p 11-1
Recruitment Poster, circa 1942	17-1
Spent shells on Humvee, Camp Shelby	43-1
1/2-blindfolded author, Camp Shelby	47-1
Shooting range observation tower, Camp Shelby	52-1
"Afghan-Iraqi Village," Camp Shelby	52-2
Morning coffee, Camp Shelby	53-1
Classroom training, Camp Shelby	59-1
Gas chamber, Camp Shelby	63-1
Navy Augmentee Influx, Camp Shelby	68-1
Map of Central Asia	**72-1**
Kabul International Airport	81-1
Hindu Kush mountain range	81-2
Gate-guard tower at Camp Phoenix, Kabul	85-1
Colonel Ata, Facilities Engineer for Northen Afghanistan	89-1
Village girl, northern Afghanistan	93-1
Map of Mazar-i Sharif area and Dehdadi village	**94-1**
Mazar-I Sharif airport security	98-1
Outside the Blue Mosque, center of Mazar-i Sharif	99-1
Village school house, northern Afghanistan	112-1
Jon Uyboco (Johnny U) teaches village boys the Shaka	113-1
Camp Spann, geo-located by the Tennessee National Guard	117-1
Author and his "Terp"	123-1
Inside the office conex, Jon goes native; The Coolman is amused	129-1
"Living room" of author's shared b-hut	129-2
Carlton Boatright hides his eyes from amateur card-sharks	129-3
Ruins outside Camp Shaheen front gate	137-1
Carpenter Zuman & apprentice soldier ride author's ranger	151-1
Zuman and carpentery team build i.t. room at Camp Shaheen	156-1
Author and carpenters put the show on the road	157-1
Colonel Jabar, 2nd from left, inserts himself in group photo	157-2
On the next "This Old B-Hut" the hosts build a deck	169-1
Showing proper respect at the flagpole, Camp Phoenix	183-1
Ramin delivers "take-out" to keep the author from starving	191-1

CROATIAN DREYZDEN HOLDS OFF THE RUSH FOR BIG MINNESOTA	197-1
DWIGHT ATTEMPTS TO REEL IN A PASS AMONG THREE AIRMEN	197-2
SCOTT WOTZKA (BIG MINNESOTA) JUKES CAPT. DAVE SWEET USAF	197-3
IN THE HUDDLE: AUTHOR, WOTZKA, SENIOR DUCHARME, JON, DREYZDEN	197-4
CROATIAN RUNABOUTS	207-1
TOP STUDENTS LINE UP FOR SCHOOL SUPPLIES	227-1
WITH SCHOOL HEADMASTER (R) AND SENIOR TEACHER (L)	227-2
AUTHOR ATTEMPTS TO PRACTICE DARI WITH SCHOOLKIDS	227-3
COLLECT THE WHOLE SET OF NAVY AUGMENTEES IN MEZ	247-1
MERRY-XMAS-HAPPY-EID DINNER	254-1
MARK (THE CAFFEINATED IT GUY) KILLIAN TAKES AIM	254-2
HUSKS OF SOVIET TANKS DOT THE RANGE	255-1
MAJOR SALIM BRINGS A TABLE-FULL OF FISH	267-1
DEHDADI CHILD, JUST OUTSIDE CAMP	277-1
SHRINE ON THE OUTSKIRTS OF MAZAR-I SHARIF	281-1
THE PRESIDENT	295-1
ANA SOLDIER GIVES NEW BOOTS TO A SPIFFILY-DRESSED SCHOOLBOY	303-1
AFGHAN SCHOOLGIRLS IN AWE OF FEMALE SERGEANT	304-1
STUDENTS WITH NEW BACKPACKS AND SUPPLIES	304-2
SCHOOLGIRLS UNPACKING BOXES FROM THE US	305-1
A BOUNTY OF DONATED SCHOOL SUPPLIES AWAITS DISTRIBUTION	305-2
MONAN AND RAHIM UNLOAD A SHIPMENT OF LUMBER	313-1
NEW OFFICE TOWERS IN DOHA, QATAR	321-1
THE "OLD SOUK," SOUQ WAQIF, IN RAS LAFFAN, QATAR	321-2
THE CARPENTER'S SURPRISE THEIR BOSS WITH A NEW OUTFIT	337-1
QASIR, ZUMAN, RAHIM, MONAN, SHOP GUY, RAMIN, KASIM (L-R)	337-2
ZUMAN CHECKS THE FINISH ON NEW BENCHES	346-1
RAMIN TRANSLATING FOR AN AMUSED RAHIM	346-2
MONAN ALMOST SMILES FOR A CAMERA	347-1
THE IMPORTANT MAN UNEASES THE COOLMAN AND JOHNNY U	347-2
ATOP QALA-I-JANGI PRISON	371-1
COLONEL ATA AND THE AUTHOR	377-1
FARMERS' FIELDS OUTSIDE OF DEHDADI VILLAGE	389-1
BANNER ON HWY 101 OVERPASS, NEAR THOUSAND OAKS, CA, 2009	395-1

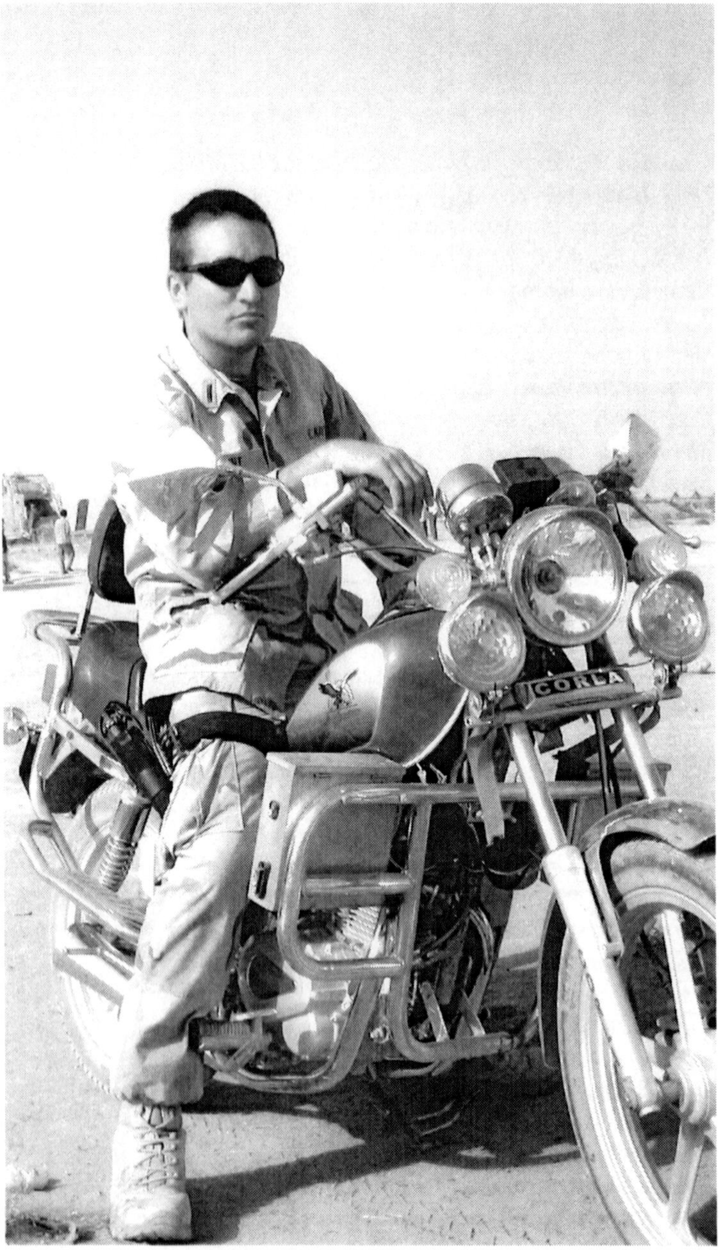
CORLA

ABOUT THE AUTHOR

Travis Jared no longer looks much like the photo on the opposite page, and never actually rode that motorcycle.

The first son of well-meaning gypsies masquerading as medical professionals, he was born in Des Moines, Iowa on the road out of town, spent a few years in the South Carolina woods before trekking out west to Arizona, and eventually settled down for four years of high school in Loma Linda, California.

Enlisting in the Navy while in Architecture school at the University of Arizona, the author was commissioned as a Civil Engineer Corps officer in 2003. He did three tours, in New Orleans, Afghanistan, and Pearl Harbor, before leaving the service for graduate studies at Columbia University in 2009.

Mazar-i Sharif, and the characters within these texts, sparked a fascination for the developing world and the inner workings of its cities. He would return to Asia in 2010 to conduct field research in Mumbai, India for his masters thesis, and again in 2011, to south China for a three year stint as the Director of Urbanus Labs in Hong Kong.

A constant traveler, avid photographer, and sometime writer, Travis was last seen living in Harlem, New York with his partner Jenny and a toothless chihuahua, planning the next adventure.

TL;DR:

It was not entirely unlike being Patrick Stewart in "The Inner Light," only without the interstellar spaceships.